HE IS OUR HOPE

A 366 DAY DEVOTIONAL

FROM THE WRITINGS OF ANNE WATSON

ANNE WATSON

Published by BelieversPress
5525 North Union Blvd, Suite 101
Colorado Springs, CO 80918
1.866.794.8774 | www.believerspress.com

Book design copyright © 2013
Cover and Interior design by Kristi VanDuker
Cover Photo by Janis Rubus

Published in the United States of America
ISBN: 978-0-615-91237-0
1. Religion
2. Family
11.17.13

Always for the King

PREFACE

God said through His servant, Moses:

"So be strong and courageous! Do not be afraid and do not panic before them. For the LORD your God will personally go ahead of you. He will neither fail you nor abandon you" (Deuteronomy 31:6 NLT).

Ever felt like the lone poppy on the front cover? Isolated. Vulnerable. Abandoned. Survivor. What we want is—Interaction. Vigor. Acceptance. Significance. In our world shrouded in a devastating past, uncontrollable present and an insecure future where can we possibly find hope?

Two words—Jesus Christ.

In Christ alone we find forgiveness from past unseemly improprieties. Peace in our out-of-control day to day lives. Security that our future is in heaven with the Father. Jesus shed His blood and died so we might live fully alive.

He Is Our Hope is a compilation of several years of devotions, with the first sent to a coworker in an emotionally tough place. A scripture, few words of encouragement and subject line that read *He Is Our Hope* began the ten-year devotional email ministry.

I've asked God to use this book to break our hearts for what breaks His and to help us love as He loves. God is still in the business of molding our character. Sometimes it's painful. Still, we cling tight to Jesus. After all, *He is our hope.*

A little upfront business for clarification:

»*The Three* is an intimate name given to the Father, Jesus, Holy Spirit
»Jesus, in intimate conversation with the Father, called Him Abba, I often do likewise
»But God . . . two of my favorite words in the Bible
»Beloved . . . another cherished word
»When you see the word Smile all alone, it is me {or possibly God} smiling big
»Webster's Dictionary when used as a reference has been shortened to simply Webster's

God's eternal word. Real. Perfection. True.

For as the rain and snow come down from the heavens, and return not there again, but water the earth and make it bring forth and sprout, that it may give seed to the sower and bread to the eater, so shall My word be that goes forth out of My mouth: it shall not return to Me void [without producing any effect, useless], but it shall accomplish that which I please and purpose, and it shall prosper in the thing for which I sent it (Isaiah 55:10, 11 AMPLIFIED).

 *anuary*

ARISE O LORD

Arise O LORD
go before Your people
Protector. Redeemer. Light.
Holy Spirit cause our hearts, our souls to trust in the
power
of Jehovah—I AM
to protect us from the enemy's lies
his pushing, tugging, prodding us into the depths of
darkness
Jesus, Messiah, You are our Redeemer
our Liberator from sin and self
may we boldly seek *The Three*
our Light in the darkness of this place
may our hearts sing with unparalleled joy and praise
Arise O LORD
reveal Your strength in us
direct us Holy Spirit into our destiny
so that many will see, know, love and spend eternity
with Jesus
Arise O LORD
cause us to seek Your will
allow no one, nothing, to keep us from Your glory
fear is annihilated as we see You
Arise O LORD

_A_ _ll In_

Romans
11:33,36
Oh, the depth of the
riches both of the
wisdom and
knowledge of God!
How unsearchable
are His judgments
and unfathomable
His ways! For from
Him and through
Him and to Him
are all things. To
Him be the glory
forever.

Now is the appointed time. But for what? Turning the page of this new year my spirit senses an urgency. Not of impending doom, rather anticipation that the eyes of the Lord are moving throughout the earth that He may strongly support those whose heart is completely His. *

Perhaps the appointed time is for us to ask if our heart is completely His. Available and ready to believe He has depth of wisdom and knowledge we'll never fully comprehend, yet trust His unfathomable ways. Are we all in for whatever the Holy Spirit directs?

Since Jesus' ascension people propound time as short for His return. Lost souls will perish unless we take up God's banner. Pray. Speak out. Go. There is no need to fear, for from Him and through Him and to Him are all things. To God be the glory.

While reading the Psalms these three words, Arise O Lord, have captivated my attention. The January preface prayer is the result. My sense is, the *Arise O Lord* prayer is for anyone whose heart is completely His.

Anyone who believes—now is the appointed time.

* 2 Chronicles 16:9

JANUARY 1

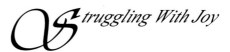

Struggling With Joy

Is the joy worth the struggle and suffering? Many who have gone before us, having experienced God's grace would reply with a resounding yes. Look at Abraham.

> James
> 1:2
> *Consider it all joy, my brethren, when you encounter various trials.*

Several months before we retired God spoke to my spirit, "Remember Abraham." So I looked into Abraham's life. What exactly did God want me to remember?

Abraham moved away from his home not knowing where he would end up. Surely he must have wondered. We moved to Oregon having no family, no church and no home. I definitely wondered. God was with Abraham and promised to bless him. I could see God was with us. The blessing was a bit more difficult to identify.

God showed me Abraham had the hope without seeing the happening. My hope does not lie in the visible or what I think will take place, none of us know what tomorrow holds.

My hope lies in Jesus, my forerunner entering the spiritual realm of heaven, preparing a place for those who know and love Him.

My friend who lost her son in a fatal airplane accident wrote, "The hope doesn't take away the hurt—nor does the hurt take away the hope!"

Is the struggle and suffering worth it? Absolutely. Yes. Not because of the trial, but because of the outcome.

JANUARY 2

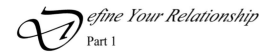

efine Your Relationship
Part 1

> Isaiah
> 43:18, 19
> *"Do not call to mind the former things, or ponder things of the past. Behold, I will do something new, now it will spring forth; will you not be aware of it? I will even make a roadway in the wilderness, rivers in the desert."*

Did you know God watches over His word {Jeremiah 1:12}? An even more astonishing revelation, God desires an intimate relationship with you and me so He can do something new.

God loves. Directs. Counsels. Protects. Provides. Encourages us. His desire is for us to actively pursue Him. God promises we will find Him if we seek Him with all our heart.

I wonder, do you have a *life verse*? A Scripture that defines your relationship with God? I know, there are so many to choose from.

I have two.

> *Psalm 63:1*
> *O God, You are my God; I shall seek You earnestly; my soul thirsts for You, my flesh yearns for You, in a dry and weary land where there is no water.*

> *Psalm 27:4*
> *One thing I have asked from the LORD, that I shall seek: that I may dwell in the house of the LORD all the days of my life, to behold the beauty of the LORD and to meditate in His temple.*

My friend recently shared her Grandmother's life verse, as well as her own heart. With her permission I share it with you:

"1 Corinthians 15:58 is my Grandma's life verse: *Therefore, my beloved brethren, be steadfast, immovable, always abounding in the work of the Lord, knowing that your labor is not in vain in the Lord.*

> Isaiah
> 58:11
> *And the LORD will continually guide you, and satisfy your desire in scorched places, and give strength to your bones; and you will be like a watered garden, and like a spring of water whose waters do not fail.*

Yesterday I was reading that chapter and was struck again with the context – the resurrection chapter. I think Paul is saying that in light of eternity, in light of all that is eternal—be steadfast today, be immovable today, be about the Lord's business today because you'll never regret it and you'll never be wasting your time. I've wasted so much time. It kills me. But He is the Lord of fresh starts, isn't He? I love what Anne Graham Lotz said: 'He's the God of the second chance, last chance, fat chance, and no chance'.

My heart groans this morning to move into a significance of life that I've never known before. I guess I'm feeling (deeply, painfully) that call to go higher up and deeper in again. I believe you know what I'm talking about.

This year: Far more time with Him, far more time in His Word, and obedience (for heaven's sake) to all He's calling me to."

There Is None Like God

Part 1

Isaiah
45:5
I am the LORD,
*and there is
no other;
besides Me
there is no God.*

Do you know the God you worship? Not just know *about* Him, but intimately *know* Him. William Law in *The Power of the Spirit* explains that authentic Christian worship is an attitude of the heart, which is inwardly attentive to God.

Sometimes it's good to go back to the basics, to give some thought to who God is. How can we love, honor, obey, trust, serve, worship God if we don't know who He is? The Bible is loaded with details and facts about God.

Knowing who God is opens our eyes to see His hand in the things around us, helps us to believe our lives hold purpose, gives us confidence there is hope for the future. When we truly know God we want to carry His banner to a lost world so they too can experience and know Him.

I found twenty-five scripture references stating there is only one God. That's always a good place to begin. To know there is only ONE, omniscient, omnipresent, omnipotent Triune God leaves no doubt about His sovereignty.

In Psalm twenty-four David asks:
Who is this King of glory? The LORD *of hosts, He is the King of glory.*

Have you ever asked yourself, "Who is this God I worship?"

Below from God's word a slight snippet of who God is.

I AM	The Lord of hosts
Holy	The Lord my peace
Just	Self existent
Righteous	Good
Strong, faithful, only true God	Savior
Most high God	Redeemer
Eternal God	Teacher
God who sees	Helper
Almighty, all sufficient God	He cannot lie
Lord and Master	Never sinned
Lord who provides	First and Last
Lord who sanctifies	Lord of lords
Lord my banner	King of kings
Lord my shepherd	All in all
Lord who heals	All the earth belongs to Him

Isaiah
45:21

"Declare and set forth your case; indeed, let them consult together. Who has announced this from of old? Who has long since declared it? Is it not I, the LORD? And there is no other God besides Me, a righteous God and a Savior; there is none except Me.

I wonder if we are like those in the Bible who yearn for God? Do we see Him working all around us? Do we see God's hand in our own life? I challenge you to find one, two or all three, of *The Three* on every page of your Bible.

JANUARY 6

God's Naming
Part 1

> **Genesis 32:28**
> NCV
> *Then the man said, "Your name will no longer be Jacob. Your name will now be Israel, because you have wrestled with God and with people, and you have won."*

When reading the Bible I'm always on the lookout for God's names. Found this in Revelation 1:5. In one verse mind you, Jesus is:

- faithful witness
- firstborn of the dead
- ruler of the kings of the earth
- one who loves us
- one who released us from our sins

Come on now. Somebody shout hallelujah. Oh yeah.

Remember the TV sitcom with the theme song, *Where Everybody Knows Your Name*? People visited this place day after day. Some jovial, others depressed, some loud and opinionated, others quiet and reflective. But they all had one thing in common—they were known. We long to be known. Recognized when we walk into a gathering.

I just returned from six days at a lovely secluded cabin in the mountains on the edge of a lake. Sounds perfect, doesn't it? It was. Almost. I had the impression I was there to finish my novel. God had other plans. A wrestling match.

Traversing icy roads in a snowstorm brought back terrifying memories of isolated days shrouded in snow. Not a single human encounter the entire six days. But God unearthed deep trust issues I had stuffed for years.

A.W. Tozer said:
"Begin where we will, God is there first. He is the Alpha and Omega, the beginning and ending." *

Having been a Christian a long time I knew Jesus would never leave me. His promise to *always* be with me rang true in my heart. Still, not until I wrestled with God did I know in the core of my soul no matter what anyone else did or didn't do, God would NEVER abandon me.

Above all, during those six days I realized how deeply God loves me.
> Me—a puff, a breath, a speck in the
>   immense magnitude of the universe
> Me—all alone, on my face, in the arms of my
>   Almighty Abba Father

God released Jacob from the burden of his name, deceiver, giving him a new name, Israel. One who wrestles with God.

God changed and transformed Jacob.

I not only came away from my sequestered time changed and transformed, God gave me a new name.

After six days of seclusion I headed straight to a little place where people talked, laughed, ate great food. I wasn't known, but I sure savored watching them enjoy life.

Signed,
Courageous

*God's Pursuit of Man

> Matthew
> 28:18, 20
> *And Jesus came up and spoke to them, saying, "All authority has been given to Me in heaven and on earth . . . and lo, I am with you always, even to the end of the age."*

*G*ive It Away
Part 1

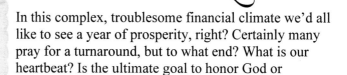

Colossians
1:9, 10
NLT
*So we have not
stopped praying for
you since we first
heard about you.
We ask God to give
you complete
knowledge of his
will and to give you
spiritual wisdom
and understanding.
Then the way you
live will always
honor and please
the Lord, and your
lives will produce
every kind of good
fruit. All the while,
you will grow as
you learn to know
God better and
better.*

In this complex, troublesome financial climate we'd all like to see a year of prosperity, right? Certainly many pray for a turnaround, but to what end? What is our heartbeat? Is the ultimate goal to honor God or accumulate more?

It's been said that prosperity is having all you need with some left over to give away. The operative word here is *need*. Most of us have a long list of *wants*. Look around you. Hasn't God faithfully provided for all your needs?

In the spiritual realm prosperity could be defined as a continual growth in the complete [real] knowledge of God the Father, Jesus Christ and the Holy Spirit, influencing how we live the Christian life, requiring our personal involvement in gaining that knowledge.

Real knowledge calls Christians to a higher standard not haughty superiority. We don't *do* out of a sense of obligation. Rather our love for God motivates and drives us to sacrificially love others as He loved us.

It broke my heart to hear an unbeliever share why he wanted nothing to do with religion. Basically his experience in watching family members who were hurt by 'Christians' brought him to the belief that the institution of the church was all about taking your money and forgetting about you when you're gone.

> Proverbs
> 11:25
> NLT
> *The generous will prosper; those who refresh others will themselves be refreshed.*

And as far as the people who attend church, phonies and hypocrites trying to make themselves look good by doing good deeds, then turn around and stab you in the back to accomplish their own objectives.

Pretty sad commentary on how some unbelievers view Christianity. Devastating commentary on how some Christians display their faith.

In the coming year may we look forward to financial prosperity so we have what we need with some leftover to give away.

May we gain complete knowledge, lovingly giving it away to those who have never stepped foot in a church or understood who Jesus truly is. Those who see Christianity as a religion rather than what it really is—an intimate relationship with God.

May our hearts burst with God's love so it spills out to those who do not know Jesus, their Savior. May the Holy Spirit give us boldness shrouded in love and put an urgency within us to give away real knowledge of *The Three*.

Genesis
1:1
*In the
Beginning
God . . .*

Isn't that what life is all about . . . God? He gives us every breath. He cares for every need. He protects and covers, provides and consoles, comforts and saves. He is our all in all.

God created us for Himself. To love on and to have fellowship with. He cares deeply about the details of our lives. He sees the beginning and the end. He knows the number of hairs on our head and the length of our days. He knew us before we were in our mother's womb. The happenings in our day-to-day lives are no surprise to God.

Lori Eberhardy wrote:
"The touch of your hand comforts me.
The sound of your voice calms me.
My spirit is eager to fly free.
To break away from this fear that has become a burden to me.
At times I feel like a prisoner and this fear is painted thick on the walls that surround me.
So I find an open door and on the other side is you.
I'm not surprised.
It's always you.
You tell me to take your hand.
You rescue me."

God loves us with an everlasting love.

God cares. We are simply called to trust.

God loves us more than our finite brains can imagine. At times we expect that immense love to protect us from all harm, heartache, trouble. Not always.

In the beginning there was no pain. As descendants of Adam and Eve, thanks to their fallen nature and determination to set themselves apart from God and His divine wisdom, we humans are born into trouble.

But God promises to walk with us, to take us through those times when the pain is so fierce we're sure our heart has been ripped in two. Another breath is impossible. God carries us when our hearts lie crumpled on the floor of our souls and we cannot see a way for them to strike another beat. God's heart beats strong for those who can't fathom another moment of excruciating pain.

Is it easy? No. Would we rather not have to live through the pain? Yes.

God promises to comfort the broken hearted.

With sorrow comes a new dependence upon and intimacy with God we never could have had before the suffering. Our faith is tested and stretched. The confidence we once had now grows deep roots, moving out to enliven and comfort the lives of others.

> Isaiah
> 49:13
> *Shout for joy, O heavens! And rejoice, O earth! Break forth into Joyful shouting, O mountains! For the LORD has comforted His people and will have compassion on His afflicted.*

2 Chronicles 20:15,17

For the battle is not yours but God's. You need not fight in this battle; station yourselves, stand and see the salvation of the LORD on your behalf... Do not fear or be dismayed; tomorrow go out to face them, for the LORD is with you.

King Jehoshaphat had a major problem. He and his people were about to be attacked by not one, but three, neighboring nations. Did he align himself with other nations sympathetic to his plight to overcome the enemy by sheer numbers? No. He turned his attention to the Lord in prayer and gathered the people to do likewise.

Imagine how different things would be if we truly believed God is Almighty. Why, we would stand and see the salvation of the Lord.

Consider moments when your children bicker nonstop, those tedious mornings when one refuses to get out of bed for school, or those weekly spats with your spouse. How about an unrelenting tyrant of a boss, an unexpected illness, the loss of a loved one, the enemy's endless whispers that you are incapable, or his shouts proclaiming you deserve better.

How many times do we take matters into our own hands without even realizing it? The Lord God Almighty wants us to trust Him with every battle, moment by infuriatingly fearful moment.

The Lord is with us.

King Jehoshaphat's earnest prayer provides an excellent pattern for us to follow.

In the middle of a hopeless situation Jehoshaphat worships God for who He is, praises Him for His mighty works and proclaims God's power.

"Oh LORD, the God of our fathers, are You not God in the heavens? And are You not ruler over all the kingdoms of the nations? Power and might are in Your hand so that no one can stand against You" (2 Chronicles 20:6).

> 2 Chronicles 20:18
> *Jehoshaphat bowed his head with his face to the ground, and all Judah and the inhabitants of Jerusalem fell down before the LORD, worshiping the LORD.*

What a heart for God.

The king humbles himself before the people revealing his trust in God when he cries out for help, knowing his God will hear and deliver them. Jehoshaphat announces he and the people are powerless and don't know what to do. Oh, but they do know what to do.

"Our eyes are on You [God]" (2 Chronicles 20:12).

Perfect.

Envision what each day might be like if we took everything to God in prayer. Not only would we see God's mighty hand at work, but our intimacy with Him would increase dramatically.

Philippians 3:13, 14

Brethren, I do not regard myself as having laid hold of it yet; but one thing I do: forgetting what lies behind and reaching forward to what lies ahead, I press on toward the goal for the prize of the upward call of God in Christ Jesus.

Regrets, disappointments, unrealized dreams, the past bombards us with 'what if' questions that are likely never to be answered. To harbor what was, leaves little room for God to develop and nurture His plan for the future.

Can we alter mistakes made years ago? Would we do things differently if there were a time machine to transport us back? Personally I would make major changes in how I raised my children. I loved being a Mom. Even with the trials and hardships I enjoyed every day with them.

Our lives would have been much improved, however, had I been wholly devoted to Jesus. Oh, Jesus was my Savior, but not Lord. The absence of surrender revealed itself in every area of my life. In all truth, my children certainly did not see Jesus in me. They saw someone 'playing church.'

There have been many regrets, disappointments, unrealized dreams. Even so, if I choose to live in the past, sorrow and guilt walk through each day with me.

Living Victoriously In The Present
Part 2

God spoke through the apostle Paul to give us hope for today, tomorrow and on into eternity. Paul reminds us of the assurance that God always leads us in victory.

Victorious when there was unrest in his spirit, Paul preferred to live each day glorifying God, not feeling sorry for himself or living in an anxious state over what he had done wrong. Believe me, Paul had a lengthy list of past regrets. However, he chose to concentrate on the prize set before him.

> **2 Corinthians 2:14**
> THE MESSAGE
> *In the Messiah, in Christ, God leads us from place to place in one perpetual victory parade. Through us, he brings knowledge of Christ. Everywhere we go, people breathe in the exquisite fragrance.*

There is much God wants to do in and through us from this moment forward, so that people might breathe in the exquisite fragrance of Christ. There need be no regrets, disappointments, unrealized dreams in your life.

God gives you power to cease dwelling on the past. With excited anticipation you can reach for the adventure that lies ahead. Contentment, delight, incomprehensible fulfillment await.

We have the promise of triumphant victory here on earth, knowing the best is yet to come.

> **Psalm 94:17-19**
>
> *If the LORD had not been my help, my soul would soon have dwelt in the abode of silence. If I should say, "My foot has slipped," Your lovingkindnes O LORD, will hold me up. When my anxious thoughts multiply within me, Your consolations delight my soul.*

How many times have I gone to the Bible downcast and dejected seeking consolation and comfort? Jesus *always* meets me there, no matter my state of mind or heart condition. He helps me through the battle that plagues my soul, the ache that wrenches my heart, the massive lump that threatens to close my windpipe.

Have you ever thought: this situation is hopeless, there is nothing anyone can do. No words from a book will help me out of this. Nothing will ever change?

Wrong!

Jesus *always* meets me there, no matter my state of mind or heart condition. He helps me through the battle that plagues my soul, the ache that wrenches my heart, the massive lump that threatens to close my windpipe.

The Bible is not just a collection of useless words and stories. It is God's living word, able to transform your mind through the power of the Holy Spirit. There is hope there when you feel like giving up, healing when the pain is so horrific you want to die.

Open the Bible. Read it. Know without a doubt God is speaking directly to you. No matter how far your faith has slipped, His word will hold you up.

Psalm
12:6
*The words of
the LORD are
pure words;
as silver
in a furnace
on the earth,
refined seven
times.*

Words fascinate me. Their origin, what they mean, the way they're used. The spoken word has the power to tear down a person's character, cause depression, foster insecurity. Our words can also lift another's spirit, pour forth grace, give encouragement. Negative words kill. Affirming words give life.

I recently viewed the DVD, *Messages from Water* where Dr. Masaru Emoto, a Japanese doctor, explored the healing properties and hidden messages of water. His findings are phenomenal.

Affirming words spoken over the water produced beautiful bright crystals. Negative words yielded disgusting decaying results. Not only the spoken word, but also our thought process can have a tremendous effect on our bodies.

What we put in our mind will saturate the heart. What's in our heart will come out of our mouth.

At one point in the research the doctor tested the results found in water on rice. Cooked rice was separated into two jars. Cheerful, encouraging words were spoken to one and sad, cruel words to the other. After several days the former jar of rice remained white and had a fragrant scent, the latter turned black and gave off a putrid smell.

Imagine the effect the thousands of words we hear every day have on our minds and bodies.

Jewish Tears

Part 1

Thanksgiving and sorrow combine to give light to the truth and reality of God's presence.

With that in mind I offer recent ponderings.

Not long ago I shared how late one night for more than a quarter of an hour the agonizing honk of a lone goose disrupted my thoughts.

Following morning journal entry:
Thank You Lord for helping that poor, lonely, lost, hurting, confused goose last night. Its cry was heart wrenching.

God's later response to me, *that goose is a picture of Israel*, had a compelling impact on my heart. It holds great significance seeing that an increasingly deeper love and angst has been growing in my heart for the Jewish people since visiting Israel several years ago. Specifically, an ever-increasing desire to care for Holocaust survivors.

Jewish Tears
Part 2

What can we give those who have suffered significantly?

After thanking God for His bountiful provisions, my mind turned to what it would be like to have none of those things. To lose it all.

What about the millions of Jews and thousands of non-Jews who suffered during the Holocaust of World War II? They lost it all. Every single thing they had, confiscated. Family. Home. Possessions. Money. Clothing. Food. Health. Legal and moral rights. Personhood. Dignity. Life.

> Psalm
> 115:1, 2
> *Not to us, O LORD not to us, but to Your name give glory because of Your lovingkindness, because of Your truth. Why should the nations say, "Where, now, is their God?"*

Today's Holocaust survivor's story is not all glory-to-glory, laughter and joy. Much of it is lived in insecure torment with deprivation at the forefront.

To truly care for another person we must be willing to give up a part of ourselves to receive their pain. Is it even possible to take on the horrific sins executed against these courageous survivors?

Will they ask us, "Where is your God?"

John
17:3
*"This is eternal life,
that they may
know You,
the only true
God, and
Jesus Christ
whom You
have sent."*

Am I willing to forget my own sorrow—the grief that steals true perspective—and give up that piece of my soul that longs to shoulder the survivor's burden? When I hear their story do I lose the self that would defend, scorn or sneer?

Am I able to give away the love planted by Another—that has grown deep and full? Can I pull this love up—roots and all—knowing the giving will nurture, heal, give new life to another hurting soul?

Am I a sheltered haven for them to abandon their emptiness, fear, anxiety? Can I sit with them without feeling pity, rather sob with regret, guilt and repentance? Will they allow me to touch them with the grace and love of Jesus without speaking a word? Will they sense my desire to listen? To grieve? To smile?

Where is our God? He goes before us. He goes with us. He sings, rejoices and shouts with joy over us. Can we not do likewise for someone? Anyone? God entreats us to give up part of ourselves . . . that they may know.

Can't you just see strong, bold Peter, eyes smiling, mouth grinning, arms waving in the air, encouraging believers throughout the region? Peter's joy effervesces with praises for his Savior. These verses sound like a coach bolstering his team. "You can do it."

If Jesus Christ is my Savior and Lord, then even suffering through the trials we all experience living in this fallen world, should give me reason to shout praises. Right?

Each trial proves the genuineness of my faith. My faith grows because I know I could not have survived the trial had it not been for the assurance that Jesus would carry me.

There is no denying the difficulty of enduring trials, but look at Peter's encouragement.

We are only here for a short stay. And one day we'll see Jesus face to face.

1 Peter
1:6-8

In this you greatly rejoice, even though now for a little while, if necessary, you have been distressed by various trials, so that the proof of your faith, being more precious than gold which is perishable, even though tested by fire, may be found to result in praise and glory and honor at the revelation of Jesus Christ; and though you have not seen Him, you love Him, and though you do not see Him now, but believe in Him, you greatly rejoice with joy inexpressible and full of glory.

-Ticket Ride

Joshua
24:14
*Now, therefore
fear the LORD
and serve Him
in sincerity
and truth.*

God desires a yielded, obedient, trusting servant. Does that describe you?

It described the Israelites—for a time. Joshua challenged the godly men of Israel with God's word. After his admonition the people wholeheartedly agreed to serve the Lord in sincerity and truth. That is, until they found themselves surrounded by nations who worshipped other gods.

Promises of provision, prosperity, pleasure, lured the Israelites from their commitment to the One true God, enticing them to believe carved chunks of wood and silver statues could reverse the effects of an infertile womb and infuse them with profound wisdom.

Don't we do the same? Our initial commitment to God is genuine. We love and trust Him with our whole being. Then we get comfortable, complacent, bored. Whose fault is that? There is *nothing* boring about God. He has one exciting E-ticket waiting for those who take the ride.

But we compromise. Our pledge to faithfully serve God wanes. Other things {idols} capture our devotion with promises of pleasure and prosperity. Our loyalty shifts. Time is spent pursuing other diversions. A jealous God, He will not allow anything to take His place.

Why not choose to stand firm in our commitment to serve God wholeheartedly in the midst of diverse distractions and delights? And resolve as Joshua did:

> *"As for me and my house, we will serve the LORD" (Joshua 24:15).*

Each week the email subject line read, *He is our hope.*
The first email devotion was written to a co-worker
going through a rough time. Watching her from my
desk her countenance seemed heavy and sad. I wrote a
scripture verse with a few encouraging words and
entitled the email *He is our hope*; believing all of life
boils down to that one phrase.

A well-known theologian speaking of Paul's
admonition to believers who are to be separate, once
commented that what sets us apart is the object of our
life.

Hebrews
6:19, 20
GNT
*We have this hope
as an anchor for
our lives. It is
safe and sure, and
goes through the
curtain of the
heavenly temple
into the
inner sanctuary.
On our behalf
Jesus has gone in
there before us.*

Jesus Christ *is* our hope. He ought to be the object of
every action in our life as He was for Paul who addressed the church at
Colossae.

> *When Christ, who is our life, is revealed, then you also will be
> revealed with Him in glory (Colossians 3:4).*

Jesus promised to send the Comforter {Holy Spirit} to help, teach, reveal
spiritual truths, guide. The Holy Spirit speaks words of life to our spirit
revealing Christ to us. All the while working out the Father's perfect will.

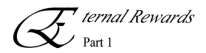

ternal Rewards
Part 1

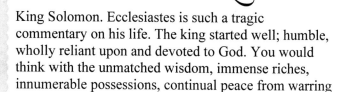

Ecclesiastes 2:10

All that my eyes desired I did not refuse them. I did not withhold my heart from any pleasure, for my heart was pleased because of all my labor and this was my reward for my labor.

King Solomon. Ecclesiastes is such a tragic commentary on his life. The king started well; humble, wholly reliant upon and devoted to God. You would think with the unmatched wisdom, immense riches, innumerable possessions, continual peace from warring peoples that God granted, he would have been more than satisfied.

Unfortunately, Solomon did what so many of us do, he allowed others to influence his life and dictate his destiny. His choice to worship other gods caused spiritual separation between Solomon and the One True God he had promised to serve and honor at the dedication of the temple.

Solomon turned his heart away from God, and, as happens to others who do likewise, he saw life with a distorted view.

Time and again in the book of Ecclesiastes Solomon tells us that life in this world is all vanity and futility. He basically says any reward ever received comes right here, right now. Ouch. That's a pretty dismal treatise especially since Solomon knew the truth, but sadly refused to obey it.

Is it true we receive all our rewards here—now? If so, we better grab all we can.

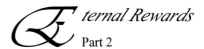

Many things bring happiness. A wedding ceremony, the birth of a child, achieving a personal goal, vacations, family, friends, a safe comfortable home, a stroll, quiet moments. Would these be considered rewards?

Jesus said He came to give abundant life and that our joy is made full in Him. So, would you say abundant life and joy are rewards while here on earth? That depends on how you define rewards.

> Hebrews
> 11:6
> *And without faith it is impossible to please Him, for he who comes to God must believe that He is and that He is a rewarder of those who seek Him.*

A vast majority of the rewards mentioned in the Bible point toward what takes place in the eternal realm. For believers in Jesus Christ, our greatest rewards await in heaven, our eternal home.

It is certainly a great joy to belong to Jesus, have the Holy Spirit dwell inside and be able to come before the throne of God with our praises and petitions.

The commission Jesus gave His followers to bring the lost to Him for salvation, to walk in the Spirit and learn to love as God loves, surely comes under the heading of joyous privilege. Still, more and more I eagerly look to the eternal rewards that lie ahead.

Heart Obedience–The Image Of Authentic Love

Part 1

1 Corinthians
13:11
GNT
When I was a child, my speech, feelings, and thinking were all those of a child; now that I have grown up, I have no more use for childish ways.

As a new believer I had a skewed perception of Christianity. I thought if I tried hard to do all the things God commanded and was very good, God would love me. He would make my life prosperous and happy. My obedience came from a sense of duty.

I even had the whacked-out delusion that God only loved Christians. Wrong.

> *"For God so loved the* world, *that He gave His only begotten Son, that* whoever *believes in Him shall not perish, but have eternal life"(John 3:16).*

The world in this passage pertains to all the inhabitants of earth, the human race. God loves every person. He does not want to see a single one perish.

The Bible is clear, we are either of the world, caught up in the clutches of Satan's lies and deception, or of God, having been received into God's family through the sacrifice of His Son. Jesus died for *everyone*. It's a choice whether we accept His gift of salvation and grow into a mature follower of Jesus.

We have the opportunity to experience and give away His authentic love.

This spiritual growing-up process has taught me that God loved me long before I loved Him. As a follower of Jesus Christ, the Holy Spirit now lives in me, giving direction daily. I'm filled with such intense love for God that I *want* to do the right thing.

The world says, 'what goes around, comes around.' Really? Read the book of Job. God doesn't love us because we are good. He loves us because *He* is good. This longing to receive and give away God's authentic love comes from a heart of gratitude.

Spiritually, I'm growing-up more every day, optimistic that my thoughts and actions are taking on a new direction. Heart obedience to God's word comes not from a sense of duty or what I get out of it, but to express my love and appreciation to Him.

1 Corinthians 13:4-8

Love is patient, love is kind and is not jealous; love does not brag and is not arrogant, does not act unbecomingly; it does not seek its own, is not provoked, does not take into account a wrong suffered, does not rejoice in unrighteousness, but rejoices with the truth; bears all things, believes all things, hopes all things, endures all things. Love never fails.

Romans 12:1

Therefore I urge you, brethren, by the mercies of God, to present your bodies a living and holy sacrifice, well pleasing to God, which is your spiritual service of worship.

Lilias Trotter writes in her journal dated November 1908, in her book *A Passion for the Impossible*, of visiting Sister Eva of Friedenshort in Miechovitz Germany:

"Outwardly, the place we have landed in is the ugliest & bleakest & barrenest one has ever seen . . . Inwardly it is all aglow, as I never knew a place to be in all my life—on fire with a spirit of sacrifice that does not even know itself to be sacrifice, it is so the natural expression of love."

Can you envision living in such a way that when you express your love through a sacrificial deed it flows so naturally the thought doesn't even cross your mind that it might be a sacrifice?

Imagine magnanimous giving because it's your normal customary response to the Holy Spirit's love dwelling inside you. If that were the case, our moment by moment, day-to-day life would indeed be a spiritual service of worship pleasing to God.

That's impossible, you say. How can anyone live like that in today's fast paced world? The Father has not changed. Jesus has not changed. The Holy Spirit has not changed. God's word has not changed. If it was true in the first century and in Lilias Trotter's day, it is still true, relevant and possible today.

In the twelfth chapter of the book of Romans Paul tells us how to live this naturally sacrificial life, clearly stating believers cannot live this way without the help of the Holy Spirit.

Romans
12:9, 10
THE MESSAGE
Love from the center of who you are; don't fake it. Run for dear life from evil; hold on for dear life to good. Be good friends who love deeply; practice playing second fiddle.

That being said, is it possible for our lives to be like those Lilias Trotter describes in her journal? "On fire with a spirit of sacrifice that does not even know itself to be sacrifice, it is so the natural expression of love"

Absolutely.

Philippians 4:12

I know how to get along with humble means, and I also know how to live in prosperity; in any and every circumstance I have learned the secret of being filled and going hungry, both of having abundance and suffering need.

Quite a bold statement. What is this remarkable secret that gives Paul the assurance he can live through anything?

> *I can do all things through Him [Christ] who strengthens me (Philippians 4:13).*

Paul made this valiant declaration with confidence, secure in knowing he had strength and authority through the power of Jesus Christ. This extraordinary power, God's pure power, resides in every believer through the Holy Spirit.

Believers in Jesus possess the resources to encourage growth, stamina to cope with impossible situations, courage to stand firm in the face of the enemy, ability to defeat our sinful desires and denounce the self-doubt the world provokes.

Paul is an impressive example of trust and perseverance in tough times. We too can trust the Holy Spirit's indwelling power to overcome our own tough experiences.

We have the means to be content in any and every circumstance. Like Paul, we know the secret—Jesus Christ. He is with us in prosperity and in suffering. He promises to sustain, encourage, defend and love us. What more could we ask?

February

Aloneness begs another chance

Grief Trumps Trust

Isaiah
61:3
DARBY
*To appoint unto
them that mourn
in Zion, that
beauty should
be given unto
them instead
of ashes,
the oil of joy
instead of
mourning, the
garment of praise
instead of the spirit
of heaviness:
that they might be
called terebinths
of righteousness,
the planting of
Jehovah, that he
may be glorified.*

I have to agree with Kermit the Frog, "It's not easy being green."

In my case, it's not easy being human. The human race strives for happiness almost at all cost. As Christians we tend to feel guilt or a sense of weakness when dark clouds of hopelessness or depression loom. After all, we have the joy of the Lord. Many would say we ought to respond to bitter sorrow and desperate aloneness with a smile and positive response.

Hardly.

There are times when our emotions transcend logic and take us places we desperately try to avoid. Insecure feelings often elicit doubt. Faith evokes trust. Grief, on the other hand, trumps trust.

That is until we choose to believe God, even when our emotions don't match what we know to be truth. Faith in the unseen brings victory. God shapes a heap of smoldering ashes into a beautiful soul that offers praise in the midst of tough experiences, entering into deeper intimacy with Him—that He may be glorified.

Harsh day. Aloneness hinders, haunts, hurts. Tears flow unrestrained by time or shame or reason. The ache never ending. Familiar surroundings caressed by strong hands with a tender touch . . . so long ago.

John
14:18
NCV
"I will not leave you all alone like orphans; I will come back to you."

Words, numbers scripted, months before unearthed by mere chance. Really?

Voiceless void. Alone on top of a peaceful hill longing for more. Breathe in the cool morning. Close my eyes and face the warm glow.
Deep sighs. Unbound tears.
No geese today. Why?

Reason eludes time. Purpose lost. Reality fresh once again, evoking more pain. Through sobs, halting whispers, choking cries for answers. Spoiled plans, shattered dreams.

Where are the geese?! *

Unexpected waves of heavy grief. Permanent loss permeates my soul. Damp earth clumps and clings to roots. No people roots. Belonging no where, to no one.

Quiet emptiness invades my mind. Silence—everywhere—silence.
Forgotten. Aloneness.

* For me, the presence of geese is God's way of saying He hears me.

*U*ncompromising Judgement

Psalm
105:4-5
*Seek the LORD
and His strength;
seek His face
continually.
Remember His
wonders which
He has done, His
marvels, and the
judgments uttered
by His mouth,*

She sits by the window, a torrent of tears fall to the floor. "Why me Lord? I thought you loved me. Why doesn't this nightmare end? Help me."

When life was good, her health fine, she had little time for God. No time to thank Him or seek His will. As her stomach threatens to erupt, her head throbs, she cries out to God. "Why have you allowed this infestation of cancer in my body?"

We cannot know the mind of God. Yet one thing is certain, where once she spent little time with Him, now due to circumstances beyond her control, she calls out to Him hourly. Once an afterthought, she desperately longs for more of Him. The truth that God is faithful to fulfill every promise now replaces her fear and anger.

How can we live with such adversity? We do what this passage suggests, seek the Lord continually and reserve a place in our memories for the wonders He has already done.

Search the Scriptures. God's faithfulness brought people to their knees, praising Him for His miraculous works. And believe it or not, through adversity we learn to be grateful for His uncompromising judgments.

Suffering. Not a very pleasant topic. Yet suffering is part of everyday life. Some gloss over afflictions with a smiling face and happy demeanor pretending they don't exist. Others stuff suffering deep inside where it festers, hoping it will go away.

> **1 Peter 5:10**
> *After you have suffered for a little while, the God of all grace, who called you to His eternal glory in Christ, will Himself perfect, confirm, strengthen and establish you.*

Having been born into a sinful world, suffering, trials, temptations are common to every human being. The question is, how do we handle the suffering we encounter, especially for the sake of the gospel? Are we facing it head on, or head stuck in the sand?

Sometimes it feels like we are in a barren place.

In all reality, a barren place is the best place to be. For there alone, quietly sitting in God's presence, we can see His hand of encouragement and provision to make it through the suffering.

God's Masterpiece
Part 1

Ephesians
2:10
ISV
For we are his masterpiece, created in Christ Jesus for good works that God prepared long ago to be our way of life.

Everyone suffers loss. We struggle hoping to catch a glimpse of joy and hope, found only in one place.

My deep appreciation to those who expressed concern after reading the Aloneness poem. My loss may appear more prevalent and raw due to the life events I now experience and share with you. Yet in the midst of it all God's hand, His design, is in every detail.

We are God's masterpiece, His workmanship. God planted His unique vision in each of us. Something He alone can accomplish when we are willing to seek His direction and supervision in this exciting adventure called life. Life in Christ.

Funny, but this aloneness is actually a writer's world. Well, not complete aloneness. Human beings were created for community, for relationship. Writers however, often take time away at a quiet, safe haven similar to my home. Tranquil, secluded spots far from city busyness, with beautiful views to stimulate creativity to meet a deadline.

Even in the aloneness this is exactly where God would have me.

God's creativity has no bounds.

Our lives are a bare canvas, a blank sheet of paper.
How many of us encourage Him to paint His
picture, to write His story? Our own sketches offer
little depth or detail. His layers reveal fullness
of lines, shadows, texture, shading.

A writer's outline is flat, no emotion, dynamic dialogue
or character growth. God adds foreshadowing,
development, backstory, intrigue. His art, His story,
creates new life.

When we trust God's hand, our lives move forward
increasing life-giving depth with each brush stroke,
every movement of the pen.

Hebrews
13:20, 21
*Now the God of peace,
who brought up from
the dead the great
Shepherd of the sheep
through the blood of
the eternal covenant,
even Jesus our Lord,
equip you in every
good thing to do His
will, working in us
that which is pleasing
in His sight, through
Jesus Christ, to whom
be the glory
forever and ever.
Amen.*

It is not a matter of *if* we will suffer loss, but rather *when*. The question is,
will we go through the struggle encouraging God's design and equipping,
all the while praising Him for the spiritual growth of the experience?

John 13:1
NCV
It was almost time for the Passover Feast. Jesus knew that it was time for him to leave this world and go back to the Father. He had always loved those who were his own in the world, and he loved them all the way to the end.

If I do not love, I am nothing.

Love—accepting the fact that others are accountable to God, not me and my judgments. Can I know someone living a sinful life, look past the sin, see the hurting soul and just love them?

Can I speak genuine words of encouragement to the hardened one abused since childhood who only sees a future filled with more? Is there room in my heart for the drunken cries or hopeless obscenities? Would I wash the feet of an unrepentant liar?

Jesus did.

There are times I encapsulate myself in a cocoon of safe people not wanting to be tainted by 'them' who live in the world. In that cocoon I lose sight of why I am here. To give away every ounce of love Jesus pours into me.

To care. To serve. To love.

So set on my agenda, rushing from this errand to that appointment, I look right past those Jesus stopped to touch. To love.

I am in such a hurry to accomplish, achieve, finish, that I miss opportunities to spend time with those who need to know Jesus. To care with a smile, kind word, gentle touch, the holding of a door for an infirmed old man, a silent prayer in line at the market, a humble response. To love.

John
13:34, 35
"A new commandment I give to you, that you love one another, even as I have loved you, that you also love one another. By this all men will know that you are My disciples, if you have love for one another."

The clock on my wall ticks the seconds away, never to be lived again. My mind runs to the minutes, hours and days I've failed to make the decision. To love.

If I do not love, I am nothing.

Two Steps Forward
Three Steps Back
Part 1

Life. Two steps forward, three steps back.

"But I don't want to do that."

† Have I not called you to this?

"Yes, but . . ."

† Did you not say you would go anywhere, do anything I commanded?

"Yes. But I can't. I don't know how. I'm not trained for this."

† Precisely!

Ouch. Ever have a conversation like that with God? I recently did. And like Moses I conjured up every kind of excuse for why He had the wrong woman for the job. Seems a battle was about to ensue.

Fear enters the very core of our being when God asks us to step into the murky storm-tossed waters. It's difficult to see beyond the ten-foot waves of doubt and insecurity. When God takes us to the next level of trust and intimacy we can't imagine why He would have us do something we have absolutely no talent or desire for.

Exactly. Precisely.

FEBRUARY 9

Alrighty then.

Self-absorption, inhibition, a vicious nasty mood; nothing more than Adam and Eve's original sin—I want what I want and I want it now. More often than not we allow God very little say in the matter because in all honesty, what God wants is not what our stubborn will or failing flesh wants.

Obedience without conditions. God desires simple unabashed T-R-U-S-T in His direction, discernment, decisions. His will.

In the proud roaming of our manor we are unwilling to grant the Holy Spirit access to securely locked doors or to throw back luxurious runners to reveal hidden catacombs beneath.

We have buried our secret places so well that even we have forgotten the code to gain entry into secluded memories of deception and heartache. We are unwilling to release the wretched pain that destroys any possibility of joy.

> Romans
> 12:3
> PHILLIPS
> *As your spiritual teacher I give this piece of advice to each one of you. Don't cherish exaggerated ideas of yourself or your importance, but try to have a sane estimate of your capabilities by the light of the faith that God has given to you all.*

FEBRUARY 10

Romans 12:1
THE MESSAGE
So here's what I want you to do, God helping you: Take your everyday, ordinary life— your sleeping, eating going-to-work, and walking-around life— and place it before God as an offering. Embracing what God does for you is the best thing you can do for him.

But how?

We cannot ever hope to reside in God's joy, sing for Him, dance before Him, if we do not encourage the Holy Spirit to enter, examine and extricate the sin that dwells amongst the pious and orderly relics of Me, Myself and I.

The very foundation of our manor is at risk if the Holy Spirit does not shore up our faith against the disintegrating lies that threaten to erode the resolve we once had to keep redemption, forgiveness, grace, mercy as the cornerstones. The determination to protect and defend our stately castle at all costs has replaced surrender and trust.

Somewhere in the midst of wrestling with God, He reminded me of the myriad things He accomplished in the past when *I couldn't*. He brought me back to the reality that the ultimate goal of my life is—Him.

The battle cry shifted.

FEBRUARY 11

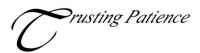

Ever heard someone say, "He has the patience of Job?" When I look at Job I don't see patience as much as I see faith and trust in his Sovereign Redeemer. Job lost everything dear to him. His body was wracked with pain and his 'friends' relentlessly harangued his character. Yet in one brief statement Job unveiled his heart:

> Job
> 19:25
> *"And as for me,*
> *I know that my*
> *Redeemer lives, and*
> *at the last He will*
> *take His stand on*
> *the earth."*

> *"Though He [God] slay me, I will hope in Him"*
> *(Job 13:15).*

There was no light at the end of the tunnel or pot of gold waiting on the other side of Job's tragedy. He could see no good thing in his life. Still, Job knew even if life here did not improve, in death he would see God's deliverance.

Perhaps you live in chronic pain, have been diagnosed with a terminal illness, lost someone dear to you or are under heavy persecution. Maybe you've lost your job and are forced to claim bankruptcy. When trials ensue, it's difficult to nurture the same mindset as Job, isn't it?

As Christ followers we receive power to overcome through His Spirit. When circumstances seem darkest He carries us. Even when we cannot see what tomorrow holds, believing God is faithful we can proclaim as Job did:

> *"As for me, I know that my Redeemer lives."*

 # rink This Cup

John
18:11
Jesus therefore said to Peter. "Put the sword into the sheath; the cup which the Father has given Me, shall I not drink it?"

What is the cup God has given you? Perhaps you are in physical pain, mental misery, emotionally empty or spiritually separated. Jesus drank from each of these cups in just a matter of hours.

Knowing the severe pain He would suffer even before it took place, Jesus chose to bear the brutality. We can withstand trials, overcome temptation, bear heartache, by the very fact that Jesus Christ suffered on the cross to take our agony upon Himself.

God, in His divine wisdom, has a purpose for each cup He gives. Often one we do not understand. We see only the challenge of hanging by our fingertips struggling to endure.

Jesus was well acquainted with pain and heartache. Even though excruciating, Jesus knew His purpose, to reconcile mankind to the Father. He determined to drink the cup even to the point of death.

When you've lost all hope and can't take another hour of suffering, remember God has a purpose. You may not understand what it is until long after the suffering has ended. Be assured God knows your pain. He promises to be your strength.

Don't give up. Jesus trusted His Father with His very life. Can we do any less?

FEBRUARY 13

Here I sit alone in this beautiful park. Bible, notebook, pen in hand. Listening. Watching. Inhaling.

Dogs trot, shepherded. One jumps to catch a frisbee. People talk. Children laugh. Park machinery grinds. Geese squawk demanding breadcrumbs.

> **Psalm 68:6**
> *God makes a home for the lonely; He leads out the prisoners into prosperity, only the rebellious dwell in a parched land.*

Old man lumbers along, small yippee dog pulls him faster. Solitary man's metal detector scours the ground. Young man in secluded clump of trees sits on a hidden bench, smoking. Lonely people.

Geese walk single file behind white leader. Middle-age couple hold hands, strolling. Little boy chases geese. Elderly woman struggles behind walker, artificial legs stiff. Encouraging friends follow. Hunkered man sits alone in motorized wheelchair, hands move slowly.

Strong coffee. Fresh cut grass. Pine clippings. Cigarette smoke.

Precious smiles, warm hugs. 'I love you' whispers. Unspoken words, hidden secrets, lost touches.

Aloneness begs another chance.

FEBRUARY 14

Help Lord!
Part 1

> **Psalm 121:2**
> *My help comes from the LORD, who made heaven and earth.*

Thumb through my journals and you'll find the most repeated word is *help*. It seems I am continually asking God for help with one thing or another. Help me love, help me give grace, help me extend kindness and compassion. Help me accomplish this task or begin another, help me do my job well. Help me see others through Your eyes. Boy, do I need help.

The word help implies coming alongside or working together in a joint effort. If I'm asking God for help, then I've got to do my part. Sometimes my part is to trust or obey. Sometimes it's to wait for His answer.

It could mean stepping out to follow His direction. The assistance and support {help} of the indwelling Holy Spirit grants me the privilege of becoming an instrument for God's use to accomplish His purpose.

Ever heard someone say, "Well, you know the Bible says God helps those who help themselves?" That's not what my Bible says. I wonder what version they have.

Rather God encourages His people to call upon Him, seek Him, allow His power to work through them. Jesus said:
   "Apart from Me you can nothing" (John 15:5).

FEBRUARY 15

This is exactly the cry for help that dominates my journals. I'm sinking here Lord. I'm overwhelmed with my circumstances. This help screams for salvation.

When I'm at a loss for what to do and only God's divine intervention will redeem the situation, I remind myself of life-giving verses that promise nothing is impossible for God who made the entire universe. Did you know there are some one hundred billion galaxies? That's right, billion with a 'B'. Incredible. We serve a BIG God.

When we feel all is lost and there's no way to fix what's broken, it's critical to remember God's numerous past interventions. If we believe He hears us, then we can trust Him to answer. And we can watch expectantly for the miraculous outcome.

Do I believe God will help me? You betcha.

Psalm
61:1-4
THE MESSAGE
God, listen to me shout, bend an ear to my prayer. When I'm far from anywhere, down to my last gasp, I call out, "Guide me up High Rock Mountain!" You've always given me breathing room, a place to get away from it all, a lifetime pass to your safe-house, an open invitation as your guest.

Go–Take The Land

Part 1

The Lord has placed your inheritance before you. Go— take possession. Do not fear.

A plethora of riches await Christ followers when we follow His lead. Unfortunately we reject the opportunity to go and take possession of them. We are satisfied to experience an infinitesimal fraction of the extraordinary life God offers.

Many of us bear the earmarks of the two and a half tribes of Israel who chose to remain on the 'safe side' of the Jordan. They were unwilling to venture beyond the good land to take ownership of the abundant territory God promised them. We too, tend to be content with a place that is comfortable.

Our refusal to put forth effort to move forward and possess God's *best* thwarts a deeper more profound knowledge of and relationship with Him. Why do we remain where we are when clearly God's best waits for us?

The status quo suffices. Besides, there are giants in the land.

Be strong and courageous. Are we ready to receive that command and run with it?

Complacency has become the enemy that stands between us and the promise land. We don't even make the effort to go, let alone take possession. We squander the deeper advantages of God's numerous promises when we choose to loiter where we are.

Promises like:

- •greater intimacy with Jesus
- • deeper knowledge of God
- • power to live a victorious life moment by moment
- • freedom from fear and anxiety
- • strength and peace in the midst of battle
- • perseverance, proven character, profound security
- • continual transformation of our minds
- • assurance that in Christ we can do all things

Don't ever remain content where you are. Go. Know God intimately. Do not fear or be dismayed, do not become complacent. Go. Take possession of all God has for you.

The Christian life is an adventure. Live it!

Joshua
1:9
"Have I not commanded you? Be strong and courageous! Do not tremble or be dismayed, for the LORD your God is with you wherever you go."

Laziness

Part 1

Ecclesiastes
5:3
*For the dream
comes through
much effort and
the voice of a
fool through
many words.*

This verse is framed and sits on my desk where it continually reminds me that this is *so* me. For years I voiced my dream to write, but did precious little of it. So when I address laziness here, each word-arrow is poised to hit the bullseye of this writer's heart.

Laziness is an unmoved spirit content to slip deeper and farther into the world of self; self-pity and self-reliance. This self is unmotivated because it thinks only of ME—I want what I want, not what God wants.

Laziness shows up in our jobs, relationships, spiritual growth, even in recreation. It takes more energy to care about someone and interact with them then it does to just do nothing or what pleases me. With modern technology and caller ID we pick and choose when and with whom we talk. When in all probability God put that person in our path to listen to, counsel, laugh with or encourage.

Laziness is unproductive. Not that we need to be *doing* all the time. Productivity is not necessarily doing something. It can be a time of concentrated inner questioning and listening to the Holy Spirit's responses. Productivity can simply be walking and talking with God, amazed by His creation, thankful for His presence, awed by His majesty.

Philippians
3:8
*More than that,
I count all things to
be loss in view of the
surpassing value of
knowing
Christ Jesus my Lord,
for whom I have
suffered the loss of all
things, and count
them but
rubbish so that I may
gain Christ.*

Laziness is knowing the thing God called us to and choosing to do something else instead. There's that *doing* again—my way. God is not a sentinel who passively stands watch over our lives. He is constantly working to accomplish His master plan that humanity would know Him for who He is. He has invited us to join Him in this vast salvation mission.

Laziness is not in God's vocabulary. He would have us stop the busyness that our laziness demands, and put aside all else, but *Him*. To take what He has placed in us, from the moment of our conception; the creativity, talent, drive, desire, passion, and listen when He says, "This is the way, walk in it."

Not with fear or anxiety or clouded vision. No. With the clarity and certainty that God has chosen this path for our life. He promises to equip us. He will go with us. We have the humble privilege of going forth to serve our King this very day.

Right now, this moment, I am going after the dream with effort, vigor, enthusiasm and excitement.

 The Next Breath
Part 1

Psalm 62:5-8

My soul, wait in silence for God only, for my hope is from Him. He only is my rock and my salvation, my stronghold; I shall not be shaken. On God my salvation and my glory rest; the rock of my strength, my refuge is in God. Trust in Him at all times, O people; pour out your heart before Him; God is a refuge for us.

"Do you trust Me? Do you *really* trust Me?" That question God asked some time ago has resonated in my mind and heart for months.

Trust is an elusive thing. It's difficult to grab hold of and not let it slip away.

Yet we are instructed to trust God for provision, strength, faithfulness, protection. To believe He is sovereign, all-knowing, all-powerful, everywhere present. We can trust the promises in His living word.

To trust God is to have bold, secure confidence and assured reliance on His character, ability, strength and truth. To seize God's promises, to hold on for dear life, especially when you know them in your mind but can't quite move them to your heart, is to believe God's divine plan supersedes everything that *appears* contradictory to His loving character.

FEBRUARY 21

Does trusting God mean we don't question Him? No.

King David often questioned God during difficult times. Still David came to the conclusion that he would praise God no matter what was going on around him.

Job questioned God regarding his demoralizing situation, yet he said, *"Though He slay me, I will hope in Him."*

> Job
> 13:15, 16
> *"Though He slay me, I will hope in Him. Nevertheless I will argue my ways before Him. This also will be my salvation, for a godless man may not come before His presence.*

Trusting God takes on a whole new meaning when you have absolutely no control over your situation. It means even when the ache is so excruciatingly painful you want to scream, "I can't bear this another minute, take it away," somewhere deep inside you believe Abba will walk with you through all the unbearable moments.

Trusting God is believing the impossible even when you can only see the probable. It means you have confidence that your darkest hour will cease with your next breath. And when the darkness closes in again, you are convinced God will be there to infuse you with another breath.

As the old hymn says, there really is no other way to be happy in Jesus, but to *trust* and *obey.*

earch Rigorously
Part 1

2 Peter
1:2, 3
*Grace and peace
be multiplied to
you in the
knowledge of
God and of Jesus
our Lord;
seeing that His
divine power has
granted to us
everything
pertaining to life
and godliness,
through the true
knowledge of
Him who called
us by His own
glory and
excellence.*

Peter, a rough, rugged fisherman, uses the endearing term 'beloved' in his letters to fellow believers in Jesus Christ, to express his genuine love for them and to encourage them to receive the benefits of a *true* knowledge of Jesus Christ.

What exactly is a *true* knowledge of Jesus Christ? It's revelation of who Jesus is and of humbly receiving salvation because of His sacrifice. It is the realization of His position as Lord. As grateful bond-servants {those who voluntarily serve the Master they deeply love} we choose to surrender our whole life to Him.

Believers have the privilege as partakers of the divine nature to receive divine insight and *true* knowledge through the power of the Holy Spirit.

True knowledge of Jesus grants us everything pertaining to life and godliness. Now, that's one huge promise. I wonder how many of us take that promise to heart? We have power to escape the corruption in the world and our own self-centered human nature.

Everything we need to live a God-honoring life is there for us to seize.

Peter would have us gain this personal and intimate *true* knowledge and thereby grow in faith. In so doing we ardently join in God's plan to spread the gospel, the good news about Jesus, our Master.

Our faith gives rise to moral excellence, through moral excellence an understanding of what it means to control the flesh and lust that clearly want their way. Self-control encourages perseverance, a determination to push through when we want to give up.

This life of pleasing God produces a new awareness for those around us. Our judgmental attitude shifts to a passionate desire for them to know Jesus.

How then, do we live this life of purity, holiness, moral excellence? We, beloved, are to diligently mature in this *true* knowledge of Jesus Christ. To learn from His example.

Someone has said that Jesus is on every page of the Bible. If so, why aren't we rigorously searching? I want that *true* knowledge. Don't you?

2 Peter
1:2, 3
THE MESSAGE
Grace and peace to you many times over as you deepen in your experience with God and Jesus, our Master. Everything that goes into a life of pleasing God has been miraculously given to us by getting to know, personally and intimately, the One who invited us to God. The best invitation we ever received!

Ecclesiastes 5:15, 16

As he had come naked from his mother's womb, so will he return as he came. He will take nothing from the fruit of his labor that he can carry in his hand. And this also is a grievous evil-exactly as a man is born, thus will he die. So, what is the advantage to him who toils for the wind?

Great question. God expects us to work as illustrated by His example. Still, since we come into this world naked with nothing and leave with nothing why do we work so hard to accumulate things?

Why go to all the trouble and stress of a job if none of what we work for goes with us into eternity? King Solomon gave one explanation. We labor bringing attention to our achievements to reveal our superiority over others. It's called rivalry.

Why work so hard when nothing goes with us when we die? Our labor has one goal—to show the love of Christ to a desperately needy world. There *is* something we take with us when we leave this earth . . . souls.

I wonder how many souls there will be in heaven who ecstatically commend us with this statement, "I am here because of you."

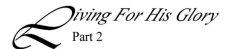

At one time I was impressed by intelligent professors, beautiful models, artists who paint intricate pictures of the sea or even more impressive, the likeness of another person. The list of imposing impressions went on and on. Today however, others impact my life.

Like the single mom who day after day earnestly raises two active, wiry preschoolers. Take the boss who manages with compassion and fairness. The bed-ridden elderly woman who writes encouraging notes to men and women in prison.

Ecclesiastes
2:11
Thus I considered all my activities which my hands had done and the labor which I had exerted, and behold all was vanity and striving after wind and there was no profit under the sun.

Look at the police officer, just and upright with each offender, the doctor who prays for his patients. Or how about the salesman who encourages a client whose wife has just left him?

What do all these people have in common? They perform their duties as unto the Lord. They don't work to accumulate, they work to emulate the One they love.

Praising The Victor
Part 1

Ephesians
6:10, 12
*Finally, be strong
in the Lord and in
the strength of His
might . . . For our
struggle is not
against flesh and
blood, but against
the rulers, against
the powers,
against the world
forces of this
darkness, against
the spiritual forces
of wickedness in
the heavenly
places.*

From the first day of seventh grade I noticed a change in my son, a shift in behavior. Each day grew worse. We had a close relationship and it broke my heart to see him withdrawing from our family. We talked. Rather I talked. He responded that nothing was wrong. Well, of course he did. After all, he was a teenager.

In a matter of two weeks his rebellion exposed itself repeatedly in disrespectful words and actions. Clearly an alien from the nether world had taken over my son's mind and body.

It came to a head one day when I asked him to do some little chore. He spouted off something about not being a slave. Ah, yeah. You guessed it. I lost it. Don't remember much of the lecture that ensued, but I do remember the first words out of my mouth.

"What is going on with you? We are *not* the enemy here. This is your home. We love you."

Come to find out he had started hanging with a new *friend* at school. I use that word with extreme mother-bear animosity.

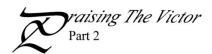

After twenty-one days Daniel received an angelic visitation giving him a glorious revelation that reminds us where the battle is fought.

So many times when we are in the middle of a heated argument or frustrating situation we tend to forget just *who* the enemy is. It's not the person spewing forth hurtful words or the one with the, 'you've got the problem not me' attitude.

Trust me, Satan's scheming influence with the full support of his host of cohorts is all around us wreaking havoc in every kind of subtle and overt way possible. He especially hates Christians. The enemy uses every avenue of deception to attack, subvert, conquer and divide.

We are temporal beings. The battle is supernatural taking place in the spiritual realm. Praise the Living God the enemy has no power when we proclaim the victorious name of Jesus Christ.

Daniel
10:12, 13
"Do not be afraid, Daniel, from the first day that you set your heart on understanding this and on humbling yourself before your God, your words were heard, and I have come in response to your words. But the prince of the kingdom of Persia was withstanding me for twenty-one days; then behold, Michael, one of the chief princes, came to help me, for I had been left there with the kings of Persia."

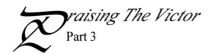
raising The Victor
Part 3

Daniel spent weeks mourning over the things happening around him. He humbled himself before God, fasting and praying fervently. Although the Bible doesn't say it, I personally suspect Daniel did not set a time frame on his praying and fasting. His spirit was in such turmoil, it's my guess he simply made up his mind to pray and fast until he heard from God. No matter how long it took.

Since our struggle is not against flesh and blood, we must first recognize who the enemy is and define his attack strategies. Satan uses many deceitful tactics to draw us from the truth that we are victorious in Jesus Christ. The enemy will try to use:

Fear	Discouragement
Disillusionment	Anxiety
The Unknown	Bitterness
Guilt	Pride
Abilities	Rebellion
Greed	Insecurity
Denial	Grief
Depression	Death
Loneliness	Prestige
Control	Criticism
Illness	Confusion
Achievements	Uncertainty
Money	Appearance

Notice I said the enemy will *try* to use deceitful tactics.

As with Daniel, our spiritual battle is fought with prayer. Proclaiming Jesus the victor and remaining strong in the Lord gives us power to stand firm against the schemes of the devil.

FEBRUARY 29

 March

We humans search for
significance every day
not knowing the
One who gives it

our Greatest Need
Part 1

Mark
3:10
*For He [Jesus]
had healed many,
with the result
that all those who
had afflictions
pressed around
Him in order
to touch Him.*

Touch has a significant affect on we humans, especially when that touch comes from the Messiah. Jesus' touch transforms the lives of all who experience it.

Studies have shown human touch can bring about emotional stability, heightened mental awareness and physical healing. It has been said we need twelve good hugs every day.

Imagine those who have no contact with people day in and day out, shut-ins who either cannot physically leave their residence or those who choose to live an isolated lifestyle. Their hug quota increases dramatically in just one week. Eighty-four times they failed to experience the therapeutic touch of another human being.

Research has also shown when domestic animals are taken into areas where people are ill, say an oncology, chemo clinic, holding or just touching the animals brings encouragement, smiles and a sense of well-being to those who are undergoing treatment.

Touch has an amazing impact.

MARCH 1

When people heard of Jesus' healing power they sought Him out. No doubt some felt it was impossible for them to have an audience with Him after seeing the thousands pressing in around Him. Still, for many their faith that Jesus was who He said He was, led them to believe if they simply touched Him or the hem of His garment they would be healed.

> Mark
> 8:22
> *And they came to Bethsaida. And they brought a blind man to Jesus and implored Him to touch him.*

Whether it's physical, emotional, mental or spiritual affliction, why not expand your faith? Touch Jesus. He knows you better than you know yourself.

You might seek physical healing, but Jesus may heal your heart of the anger, bitterness, unforgiveness, that lingers there. You could be struggling with an emotional affliction, He might heal the spiritual distance that has come between you and Him.

To touch Jesus in faith means to believe He will heal that part; mind, attitude, character, body, soul, spirit, that has the greater need.

True, Jesus is not standing before you in the physical sense, but He promises to be with His followers always. Let me encourage those who are hurting to reach out and touch Jesus. Trust Him to heal your greatest need.

Significance
Part 1

2 Peter
3:3, 4, 9
Know this first of all, that in the last days mockers will come with their mocking, following after their own lusts, and saying, "Where is the promise of His coming?" The Lord is not slow about His promise, as some count slowness, but is patient toward you, not wishing for any to perish but for all to come to repentance.

Every life has unique significance to God.

We humans long for significance. We want our lives to have meaning. Yet most never realize that significance, that 'calling' on their lives. Not because it doesn't exist. It does.

Some know their calling, but are too frightened of the unknown to step out and pursue it. Others have not reached the point where they are willing to ask God what their significant role might be. And regrettably, many, dare I say the greater number of people in this world, won't even take the first step to acknowledge that God exists or to accept His gift of salvation.

I recently watched a movie that had absolutely no redeeming value. Yet God used that film to reveal a sad commentary on what happens every day in the *real* world where the vast majority live in emotional poverty as the movie characters did.

We humans search for significance every day, not knowing the One who gives it.

Sadly many of us Christians keep our lives so under wraps with other like-minded people we are seldom thrust into a world of bars, drugs, prostitution, demon possession. The world of the unsaved, those who are perishing.

I'm not saying we need to hang in that world, but if we strive to follow Jesus' example to seek and save that which is lost, why do we orchestrate our lives so the unseemly side of life is never encountered and kept where it belongs?

Matthew
9:12, 13
But when Jesus heard this, He said, "It is not those who are healthy who need a physician, but those who are sick. But go and learn what this means: 'I desire compassion, and not sacrifice,' for I did not come to call the righteous, but sinners.

After watching that unsavory movie I came away so saddened for the actors and the characters they portrayed who struggled with loneliness and strived for significance, that I prayed for every person involved in making the movie.

God showed me the utter futility and hopelessness of those who do not know Jesus Christ as Savior. They go through each day looking for something, anything, to fill the empty longing in their souls, to give their hearts peace, only to try one more thing that does not satisfy.

> Revelation
> 22:20
> *He who testifies to these things says, "Yes, I am coming quickly." Amen. Come, Lord Jesus.*

Please hear my heart. I am not saying Christians have it all together. But one thing we do have is hope in the person of Jesus Christ. I remember thinking on my drive home from the movie theatre, *why am I so disgusted with those people? Jesus, these are exactly the people You would have hung out with. The ones You came to save.*

Would we really want Jesus to return today, this very moment? Of course that's the heart-cry of everyone who knows Him as Savior, but what of our loved ones who do not? What of the millions of lost people around the world living a futile existence with no hope?

A pastor once said that church is not just for Christians. Church is a place to bring the lost to meet Jesus. Are we willing to ask God to use us in the *real* world, to show compassion to the lost and hurting around us, to tell them they can have a life of significance thanks to God's unconditional love?

True, our battle cry must be, "Come, Lord Jesus." Perhaps not to take His church home quite yet. Rather to infuse us with a passion to do what He has called us to do.

God does not want *any* to perish.

MARCH 5

He [Jesus] breaks the power of canceled sin. *

That line from Charles Wesley's hymn has captured my mind for months. Why is it that many who have received God's gift of salvation through His Son, Jesus Christ, cannot break free of the sin that ensnares them?

Choices. I suspect we all regret choices made in the past, often carried into the present. Choices we'd like to redesign or repent of.

> Hebrews
> 12:1
> *Therefore, since we have so great a cloud of witnesses surrounding us, let us also lay aside every encumbrance and the sin which so easily entangles us, and let us run with endurance the race that is set before us . . . .*

There is a sharp distinction between regret and repentance. Noah Webster's 1828 dictionary defines regret:
To be sorry for. Repentance is the relinquishment of any practice, from conviction that it has offended God.

True repentance requires heart change. All too often we live in the slavery of regret failing to choose the freedom of repentance.

Wesley's hymn goes on to say:
He sets the prisoner free.
His blood can make the foulest clean—
His blood availed for me.

> *. . . . fixing our eyes on Jesus, the author and perfecter of faith, who for the joy set before Him endured the cross (Hebrews 12:1).*

* *O For a Thousand Tongues to Sing* – Charles Wesley

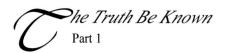

> John
> 18:38
> *Pilate said to Him*
> *[Jesus], "What is*
> *truth?"*

An extremely profound question.

There are those who do not believe absolute truth exists. Really? Just because one doesn't believe truth exists does not make nonexistence a reality.

People say, especially in a heated argument, that you have your truth and I have mine. Actually in this particular situation aren't we dealing with perspective or what some might call point of view?

Truth is based on fact. Frequently exemplified through actions. Jesus often revealed the truth of His words through His actions.

Have Jesus' claims been proven to be true? Are the prophecies in the Bible true? A resounding yes. Time and again proof has been found, through archeological, scientific and historical facts. Just ask author, Lee Strobel, who set out to prove them wrong.

God cannot lie. Since all Scripture is inspired by God—ergo all Scripture is truth. That's not to say there aren't people in the Bible who lie, after all, the angelic Satan, the father of lies, does it continually.

When I say all Scripture is truth it means everything God breathed into the individual writers to record; every subject, every detail, is true.

"What is truth?" Pilate asked.

Truth stood before him.

It always makes me smile when Jesus says something like:

> *"Now I have told you before it happens, so that when it happens, you may believe" (John 14:29).*

When He says, "I tell you the truth," He means, in reality, in fact, believe it.

I've sat in courtrooms numerous times listening to arguments wondering how the judge distinguishes the truth? Questions are asked, information presented, witnesses brought forth. Sometimes a witness fumbles with a response, perhaps trying to recall an original lie, or would that be perspective? They attempt to speak with confidence, but seem more confused than confident.

Just this week a family member was involved in a court proceeding where lie upon lie was presented with the outcome looking pretty hopeless for my loved one. But God miraculously intervened. Truth was revealed.

An honorable judge, who did not take that which had been written as fact, asked relevant probing questions of the person intent upon deceit.

Oh how we need to know the One who is Truth to set us free.

> John
> 18:37
> *Therefore Pilate said to Him, "So You are a king?" Jesus answered, "You say correctly that I am a king. For this I have been born, and for this I have come into the world, to testify to the truth. Everyone who is of the truth hears My voice."*

MARCH 8

 *orgiveness*

Part 1

Luke
23:34
*But Jesus was
saying, "Father,
forgive them; for
they do not know
what they
are doing."*

Forgiveness brings peace to a troubled soul.

Imagine yourself standing in a shower beneath the water's gentle flow. You tip your head back and let the soothing warmth cascade over your body. Inhaling a deep breath you release a sigh of pure unencumbered tranquility. God lavishes us with His abundant love in much the same way when He showers us with the sweet balm of redemptive forgiveness.

To know our sins are forgiven through the blood of Jesus Christ is pure peace and with indisputable confidence we can bring closure to those unsettling questions we've all asked; where did I come from, what is my purpose here, where am I going when I die? These questions scream for answers the unbeliever does not have.

Once we accept God's gift of forgiveness we are saved from the outer darkness {the place where there is no Light because God is not there}. The Holy Spirit quickens our hearts and minds to understand God's word where the answer to every important question is found.

There are those who would argue forgiveness is gauged by how virtuous or respectable we are or how many good deeds we do for others. Some say we must remain diligent to keep every commandment.

No. We are saved and forgiven through Jesus Christ *alone*.

What if on the cross Jesus was not only asking the
Father to forgive sinners, but what if He was
also saying to us, "Forgive *them*, for they do not know
what they are doing?" Could it be Jesus
exhibited the standard of forgiveness we are to show
one another?

> **Colossians
> 3:13
> NCV**
> *Bear with each other,
> and forgive
> each other. If
> someone does wrong
> to you, forgive that
> person because the
> Lord forgave you.*

Webster's defines forgiveness as:
To give up resentment of or claim requital for; to cease
to feel resentment against; to pardon or to allow (an
offense) to pass without punishment.

Forgiveness begins the healing process in you, not in a relationship, not in
the other person, but in *you*. "But I don't want to forgive them," you say.
"They knew exactly what they were doing when they abused, criticized,
harassed, assaulted me." Did they?

I've been reading various passages in the book of First John. The major
premises are:
  • God's love
  • to know and have fellowship with the Father, Jesus and the Holy
    Spirit
  • to overcome sin

When you see God's forgiveness, you see God's love. From creation to the
new heaven and new earth, God is always about love.

orgiveness
Part 3

1 John
4:9

*By this the love
of God was
manifested in us,
that God has sent
His only begotten
Son into the
world so that we
might live
through Him.*

Love always love—Fortunately for us God does not say, "Okay then, stay miserable, stew in your own juices. Come back and we'll talk when you're ready to forgive."

God offers encouragement and helpful ways to forgive others. He might use His word or the Holy Spirit. He could employ certain circumstances, prayer, counsel, confrontation or the loving reprimand of a friend. He speaks to us through nature, songs, the writings of others. God uses whatever it takes to help us understand what true forgiveness looks like.

Love always love—Some say the life of a Christian includes godly guilt. I'd have to disagree. Loving conviction by the Holy Spirit is not guilt. His work is not meant to cause shame and disgrace. It's meant to lovingly reveal the present condition of our hearts so we can confess, repent, live victoriously.

Love always love—When Jesus asked from the cross for His Father to forgive, He not only petitioned God's forgiveness for those who did not accept the gift of salvation or believe Him to be the Messiah or those who had no idea who they mocked, brutally abused and crucified. Jesus also set the ultimate example for us to follow.

MARCH 11

Think about what Jesus said, "Forgive them, for they do not know what they are doing." Now think about the person{s} you hold a grudge against, the one you've sworn never to forgive.

Colossians
1:13, 14
*For He [the Father]
rescued us from the
domain of darkness,
and transferred us to
the kingdom of His
beloved Son [Jesus],
in whom we have
redemption, the
forgiveness of sins.*

What if, just maybe, they really don't have a clue how much their words have crushed your spirit or their actions have thrust a dagger through your heart? Could it be they are ignorant of the dramatic affect they've had on you? It could happen.

Whether they are ignorant of the affects or not, the point is, for your gaping, festering wounds to heal, *you* must forgive. Fill in the blanks. "I forgive _____ for _____."

Speak the words out, write them down, shout them to God. Whatever it takes, just do it. And every time a negative thought arises, speak those words again. Ask the Holy Spirit for help. Jesus sent Him to be our Helper.

Freedom from bitterness and anger probably won't happen overnight. Although nothing is impossible with God. The desired results may take some time. However, one day you'll think of that person you've chosen to forgive and the resentment will be gone.

1 Peter
5:10
THE MESSAGE
The suffering won't last forever. It won't be long before this generous God who has great plans for us in Christ—eternal and glorious plans they are!—will have you put together and on your feet for good.

Imagine the sheer joy of waking up to realize you are precisely in the middle of God's will. Oh, it may not seem like it when the trials and disappointments come. You may ask, as I have, "Where are You God?"

Our struggles are no surprise to God. He really does use all things for His glory. Yes, even the suffering.

This morning my heart overflows with thankfulness for the privilege and opportunity to serve God in what He has called me to do. Write.

For months my eyes have not seen His purpose or my significance. My thoughts have focused on the aloneness and what has felt like the ripping apart of my heart.

Longing to be taken out of my misery many times I've cried out, "Come Lord Jesus. Come." Frankly, I can see how people turn to alcohol, drugs or even suicide to stop the excruciating pain of loss.

But God—made us for better things.

With renewed excitement and determination and a sense of urgency, I am moving forward with the goal of finishing the work He has begun.

This promise of God's equipping grants me conviction, confidence, courage, to step out with zeal for what He has called me to do in serving Him.

God's equipping for my destiny has become clear. Not only has he given me this incredible mountaintop retreat, He has also given me time and solitude. Most important, He has given me the power and presence of the Holy Spirit to use the gifting and talents within.

British Canon, George Body, born in 1840 writes:
"Cannot He change trembling efforts to help into deeds of strength? Cannot He still, as of old, enable you in all your personal poverty 'to make many rich?' God has need of thee for the service of thy fellow men. He has a work for thee to do. To find out what it is, and then to do it, is at once thy supremist duty and thy highest wisdom. 'Whatsoever He saith unto you,' do it."

Hebrews
13:20, 21
Now the God of peace . . equip you in every good thing to do His will, working in us that which is pleasing in His sight, through Jesus Christ, to whom be the glory forever and ever.

Moving Forward
Part 3

> Joshua
> 1:9
> *"Have I not commanded you? Be strong and courageous! Do not tremble or be dismayed, for the LORD your God is with you wherever you go."*

Reading through old journals, I noticed within a two-week span, God had spoken to my spirit twice, "Time is short, make the most of it."

Did He want me to make the most of every day as a surrendered vessel? Was His message that I need to believe my significance comes from Him?

Whether it's the loss of a beloved's life, a home, business, job or anything that takes away our sense of security or identity, loss is agonizing.

Holly Ruddock writes in her excellent and revealing book, *Life in Your Losses, Transformation Through Trials:*
"Our ashes may be used to rebuild a life in a barren land. They may be used to build roads to take the gospel to those who need our story of hope. They might even be used to be a doorway for your ministry or destiny. One thing I know for certain is that they will not be wasted in the hands of our Savior."

We need search no further for significance, God has it waiting for us. There is little doubt God's eternal, glorious plan includes using every loss and victory, every heartache and delight, every experience and emotion, to bring a lost, dying world to Himself.

MARCH 15

Is there joy in suffering? You bet. Not only does God draw us nearer to Himself, He teaches us humility, perseverance, trust, hopefulness. Which in turn grows our character, our faith and intimacy with Him. Suffering is profitable, don't you think?

Reflect on a time when you felt especially close to God. What were the circumstances? I would venture to say most of us would recount complex times of sorrow, anxiety, pain or hopelessness.

Looking through the annals of biblical history we see people who had their own place of suffering. Most suffered for the sake of God's name or the gospel of Jesus Christ.

> 1 Peter
> 1:6, 7
> *In this you greatly rejoice, even though now for a little while, if necessary, you have been distressed by various trials, so that the proof of your faith, being more precious than gold which is perishable, even though tested by fire, may be found to result in praise and glory and honor at the revelation of Jesus Christ.*

Some say those of us who live in the United States don't know what real suffering for the gospel is. Sometimes I wonder if that isn't true when I think of the millions of martyrs in foreign countries who have gladly suffered and died for the gospel of Jesus Christ.

The joy is not the suffering, it is the end result.

Forgiveness Is Saying I'm Sorry
Part 1

Words. Written words, spoken words, a plethora of words float around in my head throughout the day. As a writer I like to examine the possibilities, to explore how words transport us into countless adventures. As a student, definitions and original language intrigue and invite me into deeper meaning when doing project research.

Hurtful words make you cry. Hilarious words make you laugh until you cry. Romantic love letters fill you with assurance of being desirable and cherished. The word that holds the most significance for me is the word of God.

For the word of God is living and active, sharper than any two-edged sword, piercing to the division of soul and of spirit, of joints and of marrow, and discerning the thoughts and intentions of the heart (Hebrews 4:12).

Did you know this living word, every letter, sentence, paragraph, chapter and book, completely inspired by God, could discern the intentions of your heart? Not sure we want that goin' on.

Still, through the guidance and conviction of the Holy Spirit the word of God speaks directly to the core of every dilemma, difficulty, delight, revealing who God is and who we are.

MARCH 17

Words are used to criticize, condemn, revere, respect, confound, stupefy, amaze, astonish, engage, engross. Whew.

Take the word *release*. Webster's says:
To give up in favor of another—discharge from obligation or responsibility.

> Acts
> 13:38
> *"Therefore let it be known to you, brethren, that through Him [Jesus Christ] forgiveness of sins is proclaimed to you."*

Does it remind you of another word? Forgiveness maybe?

As I walked through the Bible asking question after question about this word, forgiveness, the reality of what true forgiveness is caused me to catch my breath and shed tears. I realized forgiveness is giving up what rightly belongs to me, anger, bitterness, resentment, retaliation, in favor of another.

How many times have we pulled away, flashed a disgusted glare or responded with silence without realizing what we were doing? Or maybe we did. I wonder if we grasp the internal torment and pain *we* inflict on others?

We have all the ammunition to fight the charge to forgive and win. Even when it hurts. Rather than pushing someone away with spite and retribution, wanting punishment, we are to receive them with an approachable heart. When we let go, release *all*, and choose not to recall the offense we are extending grace not just from our lips, but from our heart.

Forgiveness Is Saying I'm Sorry

Part 3

1 Peter
2:21

For you have been called for this purpose, since Christ also suffered for you, leaving you an example for you to follow in His steps.

Can we truly forgive if we haven't dealt with our own subtle revenge, spoken or internalized, stuffed or given to rage?

Forgiveness is not letting the other person off the hook. Forgiveness is recognizing what our own wicked heart looks like, dark and sinful when grace is not poured out in the form of love.

Forgiveness is realizing our ungodly responses whether revealed, kept locked inside or unspoken are as horrendous as the original offense and in desperate need of redemption. We cannot truly forgive unless we *release* our 'right' to hold on. Many would take that as caving or weakness, when in reality the one who forgives like this is the strong one.

Jesus, our example, whose heart unlike ours, is, and always has been absolutely pure, forgives completely, thoroughly, unconditionally. When He says you are forgiven—believe it. When He tells you He loves you—receive it. When He says forgive—do it.

Forgiveness is saying I'm sorry. First to God. Then to the person who offended you.

or God So Loved
The World

Since Adam and Eve's sin in the Garden of Eden we humans have longed for reconciliation with God.

Full redemption, complete forgiveness, reconciliation, are all found at the Cross of Jesus Christ.

Guilt need not retain its tight grip. Pride no longer puffs its chest with superiority and arrogance in the service of self. Lies lose their power to bite the tongue or sear the conscious. Greed for money, time, possessions, dwindle as we selflessly give them away.

> 1 John
> 4:16
> *We have come to know and have believed the love which God has for us. God is love, and the one who abides in love abides in God, and God abides in him.*

Look at the Cross. If your heart does not ache for the One hanging there, you may wonder if you truly grasp the immense love poured out through the blood of an innocent man.

Do you recognize yourself there? Bowed down, eyes tear stained, whispering humble words of gratitude. Now turn around. Glimpse the empty grave. Fall to your knees again and surrender your will. Determine to devote your life wholly to the One who is risen—Jesus Christ, the Lord.

MARCH 20

Move Forward in Fear And Trepidation

Part 1

Hebrews 11:32-34

And what more shall I say? For time will fail me If I tell of Gideon, Barak, Samson, Jephthah, of David and Samuel and the prophets, who by faith conquered kingdoms, performed acts of righteousness, obtained promises, shut the mouths of lions, quenched the power of fire, escaped the edge of the sword, from weakness were made strong, became mighty in war, put foreign armies to flight.

Whew. Imagine.

We believers in Jesus Christ are part of a rather large, often infamous, family. Many wait even now, for transition to heaven. While here however, we are charged to follow the example of those who have shown uncompromising faith.

The writer of Hebrews reminds us of the faithful acts and often turbulent results of those who trusted God. In the written index describing those tortured, mocked, scourged, imprisoned, stoned, sawn in two, tempted, put to death, five words stand out; 'from weakness were made strong'.

Noah certainly had little understanding of what God was up to when he went forward and pounded the first peg. Abraham traveled without a map, destination or heir.

Moses, with all the schooling and riches the known world could offer, knew there had to be more. Drawn to his own from the beginning of his faith journey, Moses had a fierce desire to protect, defend, lead. Yet forty years later he was more than hesitant.

Many of us are scared out of our wits to go forward with God's calling without seeing the end result. And we have nothing like what these saints experienced. Their faith grew stronger with their obedience to do what they had absolutely no ability to do on their own.

Contrary to our way of thinking, it is our weakness God wants to use so others see His strength.

Let us not lose sight of our fore families' examples. Even without receiving the fulfillment of the promise, their faith and trust in God ultimately carried them to something far better beyond all imagination—heaven.

I wonder how many of us will obey and step forward with nothing to encourage us but trust in Almighty God?

Keep moving forward *especially* in fear and trepidation.

Hebrews 11:13, 39, 40 PHILLIPS

All these whom we have mentioned maintained their faith but died without actually receiving God's promises, though they had seen them in the distance, had hailed them as true and were quite convinced of their reality . . . . All these won a glowing testimony to their faith, but they did not then and there receive the fulfillment of the promise. God had something better planned for our day, and it was not his plan that they should reach perfection without us.

Psalm 107:23-28

Those who go down to the sea in ships, who do business on great waters; they have seen the works of the LORD, and His wonders in the deep. For He spoke and raised up a stormy wind, which lifted up the waves of the sea. They rose up to the heavens, they went down to the depths; their soul melted away in their misery. They reeled and staggered like a drunken man, and were at their wits' end. Then they cried to the LORD in their trouble, and He brought them out of their distresses.

Can't you just visualize the psalmist's scene? These men were fishermen, this was their profession. Day after day they encountered every kind of threat the deep could throw at them. Although lifethreatening they knew God had authority over all creation.

God's power came upon them in a mighty storm causing gigantic waves; 'they rose up to the heavens, they went down to the depths'. These waves were humungous.

Unable to keep their balance as the ship tossed violently, the seamen were scared out of their wits. Yet they knew what to do. They cried out to God.

I heard a story about Larry Ellison, Co-founder and CEO of the Oracle Corporation. As a participant in the Sydney-to-Hobart yacht race, his boat was one of few to finish the race.

> Psalm
> 107:29
> *He [God] caused the storm to be still, so that the waves of the sea were hushed. Then they were glad because they were quiet.*

Not long into the race, one hundred fifteen boats sailed into a full-fledge hurricane. Each crew had weathered storms before, but this was unlike any they had ever encountered, with up to one hundred foot swells dwarfing their vessels.

What began as an exhilarating competition of brawn and brains ended as a cataclysmic encounter with the sea. The men did not know from one minute to the next if they would inhale another breath.

Beginning the race with high hopes each crew thought only of controlling the course of their ship with precision and skill. They were determined to run the race and win the prize.

As the storm grew in intensity, the waves rapidly expanded into violent deadly swells, threatening to capsize their miniature crafts and crush them into tiny pieces of driftwood. When they lost control of their vessels they simply held on, hoping for a reprieve.

The Lord Speaks
Part 3

Psalm
107:30, 31
Then they were glad because they were quiet, so He guided them to their desired haven. Let them give thanks to the LORD for His lovingkindness, and for His wonders to the sons of men!

Yesterday we left a flotilla of yachts fighting a turbulent sea.

You have to believe some must have prayed to God for help. After all, He caused the ferocious tidal waves, who better to ask for relief?

For some reason, God spared the lives of the crews of forty-two of the original one hundred fifteen luxury cruisers, including the life of Larry Ellison, a famous, highly visible personality. Perhaps God delivered these so they could tell of His mighty power.

Even though Larry Ellison did not give God glory for their miraculous rescue, his well-publicized story recalling the entire event certainly revealed the hand of Almighty God.

When we are stuck in a raging storm, money problems, family trials, loss of employment, illness, God would have us cry out to Him. He may choose to calm the storm or be the strong arm that ushers us through it. Either way He deserves our humble praise for the wonders He performs.

MARCH 25

We don't have to be highly educated or trained at a seminary for people to recognize that we have been with Jesus. The only requirement is that we take time out of our busy schedule to be with Him.

When we set aside time to listen to and learn from Jesus, amazing things happen. His character invades our senses. We realize we love Him even more then the last time we spent one-on-one time with Him. Having been infused with the joy of His presence we experience a longing for more of Him.

> Acts
> 4:13
> *Now as they observed the confidence of Peter and John, and understood that they were uneducated and untrained men, they marveled, and began to recognize them as having been with Jesus.*

Being with Jesus gives us greater confidence that He is who He says He is. We want to emulate His compassion, kindness, humility, honesty. His character. It's only natural that others see the transformation in us and marvel.

Why then is it so easy to lose sight of how precious it is to be with Jesus?

Simply put . . . other things are more important.

**1 John
2:25**
*This is the
promise which
He Himself made
to us: eternal life.*

A promise gives a person reason for expectation.

I've been thinking about Adam and Eve and how Satan duped them into believing his lies. God created man and woman to live forever in communion with Himself. God never intended for us to die either physically or spiritually.

But die we must thanks to the hatred of the enemy of our souls and lack of trust Adam and Eve had in God's promises. God promised life without death if they would only honor Him as God Almighty and obey His command.

For some reason we humans believe we know more than the One who created the universe and all it contains. Sad. In more ways then one.

We try hard to keep our promises. Unfortunately, we often fail. Not because we aren't sincere when we make the promise, more likely because we start to think about how that promise will affect us personally. Outside influences or voices cause us to renege on the promise thinking it's unrealistic or impossible.

God's promises however, are real and true. They never fail to come to fruition. God cannot lie. It is completely contrary to His character and nature. What God says, He does.

MARCH 27

If God makes a promise in His word you'd better trust He *will* follow through. When God uses the word *will* that's a promise that He is going to bring about what He said.

I've always had a distaste for Satan, but in recent months I've learned to hate him for his deceitful, disgusting, devious design and continual attempts to thwart God's perfect plan for humanity.

I know, I know, many of you are saying, "Whoa, hate that's a pretty strong word." Yep. And here are a few more that fit; detest, abhor, abominate, loathe.

Throughout the Bible you'll find the enemy's feeble attempts to prove how unfaithful God is, not to mention reminding God how disobedient and fickle we humans are. You may also notice that God is not threatened by Satan's sabotage and subterfuge. God, being all-powerful, all-knowing, omnipresent is loving, just, trustworthy.

When God promised Adam he would die if he ate from the tree of knowledge of good and evil, the warning was not to squelch Adam's freedom, but to protect him. This same God also promised deliverance from our sin and eternal life through Jesus Christ.

Joy–What Joy
Part 1

Nehemiah
8:10
*Do not be grieved,
for the joy of the
LORD is your
strength.*

Grief or joy?

There are days I wake up and pull the covers over my head. The thought of tackling the trials that await are enough to make me tell God in no uncertain terms. "It's too hard here."

So much pain and discouragement, heartache and evil. What benefit could I possibly be to this world? I'm just one lowly imperfect person.

Woe is me. Woe is me.

Then like cool water to a withered flower I sense God's Spirit within me. My mind is revived with a sweet thought; *the joy of the Lord is my strength.*

Joy is not measured by what lies ahead, what I have or don't have, nor is the measuring rod how I feel.

Pure unadulterated joy is . . . God.

Morning songs.

Psalm
28:7
NLT
The LORD is my strength and shield. I trust him with all my heart. He helps me, and my heart is filled with joy. I burst out in songs of thanksgiving.

Slowly moving the covers from over my head down to my chin, I am in awe of another magnificent sunrise.

My heart bursts out in songs of thanksgiving when I compare my life to others. Like the cancer victim frail and gaunt who struggles to walk or the woman with chronic back pain who smiles in spite of the throbbing ache.

Or the homeless family with no food to eat, hot water to shower or safe place to lay their heads. The parent who suffers with the loss of a child. Consider the drug addict who cannot kick the habit or the quadriplegic unable to move a single muscle.

Why, I ought to be living a joy-filled life every second of every day. Each morning I have a choice. Will this day be miserable or will I acknowledge no matter what happens the Lord is my strength?

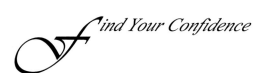

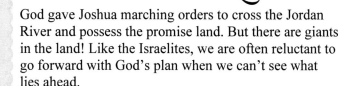

Joshua 1:8
"This book of the law shall not depart from your mouth, but you shall meditate on it day and night, so that you may be careful to do according to all that is written in it; for then you will make your way prosperous, and then you will have success."

God gave Joshua marching orders to cross the Jordan River and possess the promise land. But there are giants in the land! Like the Israelites, we are often reluctant to go forward with God's plan when we can't see what lies ahead.

God assured Joshua He would go before him and defeat anyone who came against him {including the giants}, commanding Joshua *four* times to be strong and courageous. Do you think God was trying to make a point here? Ah, yeah.

Why is it so difficult to live through uncertain times as God's strong and courageous warriors? Lack of confidence maybe? Confidence in ourselves—or God?

Joshua was to put his confidence in God alone and to meditate on His word continually. The results? Prosperity and success.

Victorious living amidst trials, frustrations, emotional ups and downs is to *know* God's word and *live* it. That's where most of us fall short. Even when we know what the Bible says we don't necessarily cling to it as if it were our lifeline while *living* it out.

Take the Joshua challenge. Be strong and courageous. Go forward.

April

Hope is the spark that ignites lost dreams
into flames of possibility

 *Light Of The Risen Lamb*

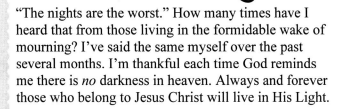

John
8:12
NCV
Later, Jesus talked to the people again, saying, "I am the light of the world. The person who follows me will never live in darkness but will have the light that gives life."

"The nights are the worst." How many times have I heard that from those living in the formidable wake of mourning? I've said the same myself over the past several months. I'm thankful each time God reminds me there is *no* darkness in heaven. Always and forever those who belong to Jesus Christ will live in His Light.

Darkness equates to dismal hours of unanswered questions, loneliness, bitter cold, evil happenings and death. Light, on the other hand, releases life, a sense of hope, new growth, warmth, revelation.

Tears flow freely when I hear David Phelps sing *No More Night*. The lyrics shift my thoughts from the darkness that pervades to the reality of heaven, causing me to shout praises for my Savior. The chorus goes:

No more night, no more pain
No more tears, never crying again
And praises to the great, "I AM"
We will live in the light of the risen Lamb

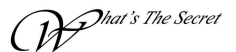

What's The Secret

Webster's defines prisoner:
A person deprived of liberty and kept under involuntary restraint, confinement.

Haven't we all been held captive in some kind of prison? People are shackled to guilt, bitterness, anger. Others wallow in self-pity, never seeking freedom. Then there are those who have learned the secret to being set free.

> Psalm
> 142:7
> *"Bring my soul out of prison, so that I may give thanks to Your name; the righteous will surround me, for You will deal bountifully with me."*

The prophet Isaiah proclaimed it long before the actual event.

> *The Spirit of the LORD God is upon me, because the LORD has anointed me to bring good news to the afflicted; He has sent me to bind up the brokenhearted, to proclaim liberty to captives and freedom to prisoners—To grant those who mourn in Zion, giving them a garland instead of ashes, the oil of gladness instead of mourning, the mantle of praise instead of a spirit of fainting. So they will be called oaks of righteousness, the planting of the Lord, that He may be glorified (Isaiah 61:1, 3).*

The fulfillment of this prophecy came in the person of Jesus Christ.

Isn't it time to throw off the heavy chains of despair? Liberation is ours. Grab it. Live victoriously. Every day. Jesus came to set the captives free. Believe it.

APRIL 2

$\mathcal{A}$lways God's Glory
Part 1

Ephesians
3:20, 21
NKJV
*Now to Him who
is able to do
exceedingly
abundantly above
all that we ask or
think, according
to the power that
works in us, to
Him be glory in
the church by
Christ Jesus to
all generations,
forever and ever.
Amen.*

I wonder how many of us really believe God is able to do exceedingly abundantly above all that we ask or think?

No way. Can't be. Never happen. Not in this lifetime.

Webster's defines:
Impossible - incapable of being or of occurring
Challenge - to arouse or stimulate especially by
            presenting with difficulties

Facing an impossible challenge? Insurmountable obstacles you can never overcome? Worn out, worn down, ready to give up, give in?

Really?

There have certainly been many impossible challenges and seemingly insurmountable obstacles in my life. Foremost in my mind is October 30, 2009, my Beloved's graduation to heaven.

When I laid down to sleep that night I told God, "Don't let me wake up." But wake up I did and thus began the arduous journey of breaking. Deepening my faith. Believing.

As true followers of Jesus Christ we have been granted power beyond anything we've ever known before. Believe it.

All for God's glory.

The apostle Paul prays that we might be filled up to all the fullness of God. This fullness is the glory of God dwelling within us. I can't even wrap my mind around that. Still I know it to be true. God's word reiterates it time and again.

Paul prayed we would be strengthened with the Holy Spirit's power and rooted and grounded in Christ's love. Yet we suppress the Holy Spirit's power. Why?

Are we ready to believe God is able? Even though our finite brains cannot conceive of that much power and love? Even more, do we fervently ask Him to fill our entire being so that He can unleash His power in and through us?

> Ephesians
> 3:18, 19
> *[That you] may be able to comprehend with all the saints what is the breadth and length and height and depth, and to know the love of Christ which surpasses knowledge, that you may be filled up to all the fullness of God.*

The purpose of all this breaking. Deepening. Believing. Asking. Unleashing the Holy Spirit's power.

God's glory. Always God's glory.

Jehovah-Shammah Is There
Part 1

Psalm
68:5, 6
NCV
*God is in his holy
Temple. He is a
father to orphans,
and he defends
the widows. God
gives the lonely a
home. He leads
prisoners out
with joy.*

In the realm of longing for God, the hunger is not for more knowledge. It's not even a need for His promises. This yearning is for more of *Him*. And when we lose sight of that we fall headlong into the domain of loneliness.

Some say loneliness is a state of mind. They tell us to snap out of it. Think positive. Get out around people. Many have confessed to feeling lonely even in a crowd.

Loneliness is not a state of mind. It is a state of heart. Hannah knew it, as did Naomi, Peter and the apostles. Even Jesus experienced separation and an aching loneliness while on the cross.

Gloria Gaither in her book, *We Have This Moment*, describes an early morning visit to a little deli in downtown New York:
"I've come . . . to this place . . . to escape the loneliness for a while and hear other human voices talking—friendly voices who sound comfortable with each other . . . Together the city and I start this day: Lord, are you there? In the streets? In the faces? In me?"

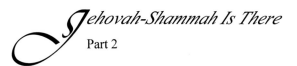

God is there when everyone is around and when no one is around. He fills the empty places of the heart, keeping us according to His word. But how many of us believe that when we cannot see it?

> Jeremiah
> 29:13
> *'You will seek Me and find Me when you search for Me with all your heart.'*

Haven't we all, at one time or another, experienced that harsh hopelessness only the love of God relieves? His agape love that sees something considerably precious in us, is an all encompassing love that pierces the dark loneliness of the heart reminding us that *nothing* can separate us from His love.

God's love does indeed lead prisoners out with joy. The empty chasm of the heart, consumed with this love, learns to humbly forgive others and ourselves.

John Newton, converted slave trader said:
"I am persuaded that love and humility are the highest attainments in the school of Christ and the brightest evidences that He is indeed our Master."

God, our ever-present victorious warrior, understands loneliness. His love binds up the brokenhearted. He fills the emptiness with Himself.

> **Psalm 42:1, 2**
> *As the deer pants for the water brooks, so my soul pants for You, O God. My soul thirsts for God, for the living God; when shall I come and appear before God?*

Jesus said:

> *"Come to Me, all who are weary and heavy-laden, and I will give you rest" (Matthew 11:28).*

I enter God's rest when I am in His presence. There is profound peace and fullness of joy found there.

Deep inside there is an insatiable thirst for more of God that has yet to be quenched and like the psalmist, I continually yearn for more of Him.

Just where is God's presence to be found? The Lord told the prophet, Jeremiah:

> *'You will seek Me and find Me when you search for Me with all your heart. 'I will be found by you' (Jeremiah 29:13).*

God is there when we pray {talk to Him}. The Holy Spirit graciously intercedes for us with groanings too deep for words.

God's presence is found throughout the Bible. He longs to meet us there. We need go no further than Genesis 1:1 for His presence to impact our senses. God is omnipresent, He is everywhere at all times. Yet just comprehending that fact does not make for the intimacy I crave.

When I set aside every matter that detracts from God, seeking Him with all my heart, something incredible happens. My senses come alive.

I sense God's presence in the graceful geese flying in formation overhead, majestic mountains in the distance, thundering rain clouds, azure blue sky.

I hear God in a whispering breeze. I catch His scent in fragrant flowers, the leaves of a tomato plant, aromatic needles from a massive fir. I taste Him in nourishing morsels of the harvest, His word, His kindness. I feel His presence in the sun's penetrating warmth and cool gentle snowdrifts.

> Psalm
> 27:4
> *One thing I have asked from the LORD, that I shall seek: that I may dwell in the house of the LORD [in His presence] all the days of my life, to behold the beauty of the LORD and to meditate in His temple.*

Those who love God with every fiber of their being know when they're resting in His presence and when they're not. In today's world, with more work to conquer, activities to experience, exhaustion to overcome, we take little time to bask in God's presence. When myriad distractions take priority we miss out on the most exciting, stimulating encounter of our lives.

I love a good challenge. Every day for one week, let's cut out something—anything—in our busy schedule and meet with God during that time. Ask for nothing except His presence.

Philippians
1:20
THE MESSAGE
I can hardly wait to continue on my course. I don't expect to be embarrassed in the least. On the contrary, everything happening to me in this jail only serves to make Christ more accurately known, regardless of whether I live or die. They didn't shut me up; they gave me a pulpit!

After reading this verse you can see why Paul of Tarsus is one of my heroes. No matter what situation he found himself in, he proclaimed Jesus as the Christ.

Picture this; Paul is among unbelievers preaching the good news of Jesus Christ. Menacing men use every weapon to stop him. They chastise, beat, stone, put him in jail. No matter the obstacle Paul unremittingly shares the truth. He is determined for everyone to know his Savior.

You know that popular saying; when life gives you lemons, make lemonade? I wonder if whoever coined that phrase was thinking of Paul?

This astonishing apostle says, *they didn't shut me up; they gave me a pulpit!* I don't know about you, but for me the slightest sign of embarrassment, ridicule or scorn and my proclamation of Jesus is squelched.

I mean, I don't want to shove my faith down anyone's throat or be offensive or politically incorrect. Right?

Wrong response.

Paul makes it clear he doesn't care who does it, or how it's done. The bottom line is Christ proclaimed. Every trial is an opportunity to share Christ, whether in the way we respond, or even in the things we choose *not* to do while in the midst of it.

Though difficult at times, it is possible to see obstacles as opportunities. If we can get our minds off ourselves long enough to humbly ask the Holy Spirit to fill us with power, courage and boldness we can turn impossible situations into prospects to share the hope of the gospel.

Philippians
1:18
THE MESSAGE
So how am I to respond? I've decided that I really don't care about their motives, whether mixed, bad, or indifferent. Every time one of them opens his mouth, Christ is proclaimed, so I just cheer them on!

When we start to think life has dealt us a miserable hand, we need to remember Paul and take the unpleasant, unhappy, seemingly unbearable situations and bring glory to Jesus the Messiah.

Part 3

Philippians 3:8

More than that, I count all things to be loss in view of the surpassing value of knowing Christ Jesus my Lord, for whom I have suffered the loss of all things, and count them but rubbish so that I may gain Christ.

Come on now. Let's get excited about this Christian adventure we're on.

Can't you just picture Paul announcing to the Philippians that the Christian life is an exciting adventure not tedious boredom? Paul's exuberance to share Jesus Christ is an inspiring illustration of a life completely sold out to the Savior. A life each of us might want to emulate.

Paul lives what he believes, attracting various people by his actions and responses. Some condemn and mock him, others physically harm him, but he is so devoted to Jesus Christ the abuse doesn't faze him. Paul shares Jesus with everyone, everywhere.

I'm so caught up with poor me or consumed with the fact that I'm experiencing mental misery, physical pain or a spiritual wasteland my devotion to Jesus is easily swayed. When I read a passage like this exposing my self-centeredness, it breaks my heart.

When am I going to get it? It's not about me. Everything, absolutely everything, is about Jesus.

Jesus is the One we're living for.

APRIL 11

Pride takes on many forms doesn't it? God will not be mocked. He is holy.

The failure to recognize and grasp God's holiness can cause us to take His instruction and exhortation lightly or disregard His commands altogether. Better known as sin.

We are often tested to see if we hold God up as holy. If we believe Him and go forth as He commands. There are consequences to disobedience. Sometimes we blame those consequences on others or worse yet . . . on God.

Some time later in his desert experience, Moses blamed the people for his disobedience to God's command. True, their whining and complaining aggravated Moses, but it was his anger that gave way to rebellion and sin. He did not believe God.

Moses' pride got in the way. He took matters into his own hands. Bad choice.

Numbers 20:10-12

Moses and Aaron gathered the assembly before the rock. And he said to them, "Listen now, you rebels; shall we bring forth water for you out of this rock?" Then Moses lifted up his hand and struck the rock twice with his rod . . . But the LORD said to Moses and Aaron, "Because you have not believed Me, to treat Me as holy in the sight of the sons of Israel, therefore you shall not bring this assembly into the land which I have given them."

A uthenticity
Part 1

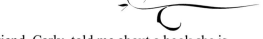

My new friend, Carly, told me about a book she is reading, *Authentic Beauty*. A thoughtful look into God's definition of real beauty.

Carly is an extremely beautiful young woman. Her infectious smile lights up a room and without even realizing it she captures the rapt attention of admiring young men. Her beauty however, is most certainly not confined to her outer appearance.

My friend's unmatched beauty goes deep into her soul and spirit. Her sincere desire is to delight herself in the Lord and become a godly woman ready to wholly serve and honor Him.

Carly's example of a surrendered heart is a source of inspiration and encouragement to live a life devoted to Jesus Christ. Her sweet friendship is indelibly etched upon my heart.

APRIL 13

Authentic is another one of those words you gotta love.

Webster's defines authentic:
Not false or imitation: real, actual. Authentic implies being fully trustworthy as according with fact; genuine. Genuine implies actual character not counterfeited, imitated, or adulterated.

Both authentic and genuine, if referring to a person with authentic beauty, would mean the person is exactly what's claimed.

But how does God define authentic beauty? One who loves Him above all else, with a desire and determination to obey and surrender to His will, for His glory. God looks at the unseen domain of the heart.

> Matthew
> 23:27, 28
> THE MESSAGE
> *"You're hopeless, you religion scholars and Pharisees! Frauds! You're like manicured grave plots, grass clipped and the flowers bright, but six feet down it's all rotting bones and worm-eaten flesh. People look at you and think you're saints, but beneath the skin you're total frauds."*

Jesus made it clear no matter how beautiful the outer appearance, godly character rests within the inner man {woman}:
> *"Woe to you, scribes and Pharisees, hypocrites! For you are like whitewashed tombs which on the outside appear beautiful, but inside they are full of dead men's bones and all uncleanness. So you, too, outwardly appear righteous to men, but inwardly you are full of hypocrisy and lawlessness."*

No authenticity there.

Proverbs
31:30, 31
*Charm is
deceitful and
beauty is vain, but
a woman who
fears the LORD,
she shall be
praised. Give her
the product of her
hands, and let her
works praise her
in the gates.*

The apostle Paul prayed on behalf of all believers for the power of the Holy Spirit to strengthen us inside, knowing if we are established in Christ's boundless love we will be filled up with God's fullness. Certainly not by anything we might try to bring about, but totally by the Holy Spirit's power.

To develop godly character, God would have us set our minds on things above, on Christ, who is our life. We are to bring our minds back to those things that are true, and honorable. Looking to do what is right, keeping our souls pure and lovely.

Our character, shaped by Christ's example, ought to excel, allowing us to gain a good reputation. When we look to Christ we see that which is excellent and worthy of praise. We are to think about these things and live according to Christ's example.

My friend, Carly—exemplifies genuine, authentic beauty with a heart fully devoted to God. Her example inspires and encourages me to gain real, authentic inner beauty.

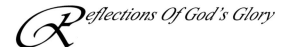

Notes From Morning Reflections

Psalm
19:1
ESV
The heavens declare the glory of God, and the sky above proclaims his handiwork.

Thank You Lord for profound simplicity. Intricacies of a spider web. The soothing song of the wind chime dancing with my Beloved's gift—fishing lures.

Raindrops balance atop blades of grass. The tenuous sway of delicate daffodils. Color. Slivers of sun shifting across the valley.

Scenes from a hilltop. Feast for the eyes. Budding trees. Rain soaked fields embrace the warmth of the sun. Green. Drifting clouds stirred by a whispering breeze. Spring. Pink buds. Whistling birds. Moss. Horses laughter. Colts dancing. New life.

Holding friends. Hearing friends. Loving friends. Family friends.

Time. Evasive. Quick. Precious. Forever. Given over to Another. Elusive. Short. Rare. Quiet. Busy. Consuming. Careful. Fleeting. Lovely. Filled.

Breath. One day, a thousand years—A thousand years, one day. Stop. Wait. Listen. Ears to hear.

Words. Grow the mind. Purify. Cause to gasp. Splinter reality. Carry heavy burdens. Open wide the spirit. Forgive. Embrace. Console. Reveal. Entice. Soothe. Relieve. Release. Give life.

Lips speak. Uplifting. Good. Encouraging. Life-giving truth encased in grace from a love-filled heart.

Praise. Desire. Purpose. Destiny. All that surrounds me, from God. His creation. His hand. His universe. His eternity.

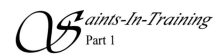
Philippians 2:3, 4

Do nothing from selfishness or empty conceit, but with humility of mind regard one another as more important than yourselves; do not merely look out for your own personal interests, but also for the interests of others.

We don't have to wonder about God's power in a person's life, it's seen in the way they treat others, especially in how they respond to those who don't know Jesus Christ. These Christians do not consider what might benefit them. But rather live out Paul's exhortation to the Philippians.

It's God's power working through these saints that identifies them as sold out to Jesus. The reality of what Jesus did on the cross so changes them that humble servanthood becomes a way of life.

These disciples live according to the example set by their Savior. Under the direction of the Holy Spirit they aspire to fill the needs of others. Humility and love become their standard. They aren't identified by their words, but by their actions.

Do these people really exist anywhere on the planet? Oh yeah. They're everywhere. Each one progressing in the learning process. Committed to God's purpose.

Saints-in-training, they begin every day determined to glorify and honor God no matter how demanding or difficult the circumstances.

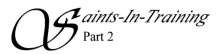

Saints-in-training are first and foremost servants of Jesus Christ, giving up the right to themselves, dedicating their lives to His will. There is an inner beauty and joy that rest within their spirit. Though far from flawless, their character is Christ-like taking on His attributes in the life long process of sanctification.

> 1 Corinthians
> 4:19, 20
> _But I will come to you soon, if the Lord wills, and I shall find out, not the words of those who are arrogant but their power. For the kingdom of God does not consist in words but in power._

Paul gives an apt description:

> _More than that, I count all things to be loss in view of the surpassing value of knowing Christ Jesus my Lord, for whom I have suffered the loss of all things, and count them but rubbish so that I may gain Christ (Philippians 3:8)._

Perfect? No. They falter and stumble, make mistakes, fall short. Yet they are unafraid to step out when the task seems impossible, unashamed to confess their sins, receive forgiveness, learn from their mistakes. They walk in the Spirit and humbly submit to His leading.

These people are definitely out there. Quietly serving in nursing homes, hospitals, schools, soup kitchens, pre-schools, at work, at home. They tenaciously live out this adventure called Christianity to the fullest.

Seeking His Treasure
Part 1

**Proverbs
23:4, 5
THE MESSAGE**
*Don't wear
yourself out trying
to get rich;
restrain yourself!
Riches disappear in
the blink
of an eye; wealth
sprouts wings and
flies off into the
wild blue yonder.*

What is it about money that causes temptation, dishonesty, loss of integrity? In today's culture money is an indispensable commodity and since the barter system is no longer in play throughout most of the world, money is the medium by which necessary things like food, clothing and shelter are purchased. So often we hoard our wealth because we're afraid we won't have enough.

Enough for what?

We go from contentment with our met needs, to craving our wants and making sure we get them at all costs. Money brings with it the promise of security, power, prominence, honor, respect, happiness; as well as envy, anxiety, bitterness, anger, deceit, greed. Greed is an interesting word.

Webster's describes greed:
A selfish and excessive desire for more of something (as money) than is needed.

The more money some acquire, the more their insatiable craving grows. Will they ever have enough?

APRIL 19

I know a man who claims he can't retire until he has a million dollars in assets. Really? Will he be content with the one million or will he monitor the stock market wondering if he ought to accumulate more?

This man's perspective reminds me of Jesus' parable about the rich man who built a larger barn to house his crops. The man sat back and believed he had it made. God tells him he's a fool and that very night he will die. Who will get his barn full of crops now?

> Ecclesiastes
> 5:15
> GNT
> *We leave this world just as we entered it—with nothing. In spite of all our work there is nothing we can take with us.*

Would you say money is the root of all evil as many are quick to quote from the Bible? Not really. It is the *love* of money. That insatiable desire for more that brings about any number of evils.

We can't just give money up like a bad habit. It's a necessity. True, but ask yourself how you view money. Is it wanted to meet your needs or is it needed to meet your wants? The love of money is a heart issue.

Stop hoarding. Give generously to others as God leads.

Choose Wisely
Part 1

Matthew 27:15-17

Now at the feast the governor was accustomed to release for the people any one prisoner whom they wanted. At that time they were holding a notorious prisoner, called Barabbas. So when the people gathered together, Pilate said to them, "Whom do you want me to release for you? Barabbas, or Jesus who is called Christ?"

Have you ever wondered why Barabbas was chosen as the prisoner for the multitude to consider for release over Jesus? Could it be Pilate chose Barabbas because he was one of the most dangerous, treacherous prisoners they had under lock and key? One who deserved and needed confinement.

Pilate knew in his heart Jesus was innocent. He wisely perceived the Jewish leaders had delivered Him for trial because of envy.

Perhaps Pilate thought, *surely if I put the name of this loathsome criminal before the crowd alongside this innocent man, they will choose Jesus*. Sadly, they did not. Fearful of the increasingly hostile crowd, Pilate chose to release Barabbas and hand Jesus over for crucifixion.

In the Old Testament the Lord laid out a plan for the Israelites to live a holy, God-honoring life. They could either choose life, the blessing—a life of obedience and victory. Or death, the curse—a life of defiance and bondage.

APRIL 21

Joshua challenged the Hebrews to choose wisely. To choose life.

God does likewise with us. We make hundreds of choices everyday. Some good, some not so good.

God does not force anyone to obey. He graciously gives us a free will to make choices. He wants those choices to stem from our love for Him. Have you ever obeyed someone because you were threatened, coerced or intimidated?

That's not God.

Joshua
24:15
"If it is disagreeable in your sight to serve the LORD, choose for yourselves today whom you will serve: whether the gods which your fathers served which were beyond the River, or the gods of the Amorites in whose land you are living; but as for me and my house, we will serve the LORD."

Some are saying, but what about God's wrath? God is just. He directs us in His word for our good, not from cruelty or callousness or to take away our fun. Think about it. Do you tell your children they can't ride their bikes in the street or wade in a raging river or they have to go to school because you're a tyrant? Of course not.

God challenges us to choose wisely. He sent the Holy Spirit to help believers with the untold daily choices we must make.

Why not take the challenge? Choose wisely this week.

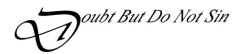

Doubt But Do Not Sin

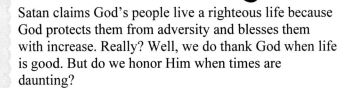

Job
1:9, 10
*Then Satan
answered the
LORD, "Does Job
fear God for
nothing? Have
you not made a
hedge about him
and his house
and all that he
has, on every
side? You have
blessed the
work of his hands,
and his
possessions have
increased in the
land."*

Satan claims God's people live a righteous life because God protects them from adversity and blesses them with increase. Really? Well, we do thank God when life is good. But do we honor Him when times are daunting?

There are those who scream in anger, "There is no God. He would not make me go through this torment if He were real." Some simply give up, bawling, "I've had enough. How can a loving God allow this?"

Did Job cave? No. He questioned. And thanks to his so-called friend's advice he doubted the God who had blessed him abundantly. Still Job praised his God.

We tend to forget the good God has done when Satan attacks, when we're in the middle of affliction or suffering. And if you are questioning the authenticity of evil beings in the spiritual realm, think again. *

Our God is all-powerful, all-knowing. He may not restore our health, job or possessions as He did Job, but when we trust His faithfulness our faith increases a hundredfold.

* Ephesians 6:12

Pity parties. Mine come on slow. One thing tweaks me then another makes me sad. In the end woe-is-me becomes my heart's cry. The focus on God grows narrow. The emphasis on me, myself and I grows broader.

The once productive life of glorifying God turns into slovenly days of nothingness. Hours are spent feeling sorry for myself because I am not the person I long to be. Ratknuckles.

Psalm 139:14 says:
"I will give thanks to You, for I am fearfully and wonderfully made; wonderful are Your works, and my soul knows it well."

Psalm 139:15, 16
My frame was not hidden from You, when I was made in secret, and skillfully wrought in the depths of the earth. Your eyes have seen my unformed substance; and in Your book they were all written, the days that were ordained for me, when as yet there was not one of them.

When did we lose sight of that truth? How did we allow ourselves to sink so deep into the miry pit? We waste precious time looking to the world for acceptance when we already have it abundantly from God.

We have God's pleasure because we are. Not because we do. We were created in His image for His glory. That alone ought to puncture every saggy balloon at the party.

The next time we're tempted to throw a pity party, remember God created us with a purpose in mind.

Exodus
33:15, 18
*Then he said to
Him, "If Your
presence does
not go with us,
do not lead us up
from here." Then
Moses said, "I
pray You, show
me Your glory!"*

A pastor once said, "Pain is inevitable, misery is optional."

It has been more than a year of sorrow and awakening. Not a day has gone by that God hasn't shown me something of His glory. In the process graciously exposing my failures and potential.

At times I've been like a frightened mouse scurrying from one place to another, stopping only long enough to frantically search for a way out of this maze {funny I would use that analogy, I'm terrified of mice}. Other times God uncovered a courageous warrior from somewhere so deep inside I honestly did not know she existed.

I had no idea a body could hold and shed so many tears, yet at the same time experience the complete assurance God loves me and that *all* His promises *and* heaven are real.

Jesus has lifted, carried, covered and held me, revealing Himself in a whole new dimension I may not have experienced had it not been for my husband's death. It has been a severe mercy just as Sheldon Vanauken shares in his book by the same name.

APRIL 25

Dreams have a strange way of vanishing when brutal reality strikes. Nevertheless, God's unknown future beckons me.

Mark Batterson in his insightful book, *In a Pit with a Lion on a Snowy Day*, challenges Christians to take a risk. He reminds us that obedience to God is a willingness to do whatever, whenever, wherever God calls us, and that faith is risky business. Batterson says we can't experience success without risking failure.

I am grateful for the privilege, yet a little frightened of the challenge to step out and fulfill God's destiny for my life. Excitement for joining God in whatever that adventure looks like, wherever it takes me, overrides the fear.

2 Corinthians
4:7-10
NCV
We have this treasure from God, but we are like clay jars that hold the treasure. This shows that the great power is from God, not from us. We have troubles all around us, but we are not defeated. We do not know what to do, but we do not give up the hope of living. We are persecuted, but God does not leave us. We are hurt sometimes, but we are not destroyed. We carry the death of Jesus in our own bodies so that the life of Jesus can also be seen in our bodies.

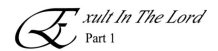
Psalm
150:6
*Let everything
that has breath
praise the LORD.
Praise the LORD!*

Smile.

Thank You Lord for the gift of hearing.

Life abounds. Praise the Lord.

Beautiful sounds.

Quail warble to one another. "Come beloved, sit beside me in the cool of the oak tree."
"No, come to this bush where we can hide."
"No, the oak is sturdy and this limb secluded—leaves surround. Come beloved, sing with me, exultation for life."

Anxious mother bawls, summoning her calf, offering life-giving nourishment. Bright green finches, chirp, chirp, chirp, chirp—laughter; bathing one another, encouraging flight.

Red, purple, pink, orange. Yellow, lavender, green, white blossoms stretch and shout thankful praises for the sun's restorative touch.

Squirrels skitter amongst dry leaves squealing the call—hurry, hurry, hurry. Deer prance, glide, leap buck brush and manzanita bushes; up over the mountain to sheltered rest, confident of tomorrow's provision.

APRIL 27

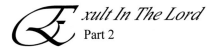

Life abounds. Bless the Lord.

Psalm
103:22
*Bless the LORD, all
you works of His, in
all places of His
dominion; bless the
LORD, O
my soul!*

A wasp wails distress signals to those in the empty nest.
"Come out, come out! Live." But none come, none
buzz or fly as if floating. "Lost, all are lost."

How can we miss the urgency to call the lost to Jesus?

Whirring wings. Tiny funnel beak drinks in revitalizing nectar in seconds. A
smile in the humming. Applause for purpose.

Colts whinny, gallop, buck, meander. Strutting strength and glory.

Papa, Mama, Younger glide. Brawny wings of red tail hawks skim and
swoop, clutching prey— survival. Peacock screeches from core of a hundred
pines—making a joyful noise? Jittery caw.

Black, redheaded woodpecker peeks over the edge of a limb seeking, calling
her—ending aloneness.

Solitary paraglider catches the wind. Silence. What must it feel like to soar
above the mountains through white fluff, ever closer to heaven?

**Romans
5:3, 4**
*And not only this,
but we also exult
in our tribulations,
knowing that
tribulation brings
about perseverance;
and perseverance,
proven character;
and proven
character, hope.*

To hope is to expect with confidence. We know that we know. Thank God for the hope of heaven through the sacrifice of Jesus, our Messiah. Where would we be without hope?

I sincerely believe we could not possibly survive in this world without hope. We would eventually shrivel up and die, whether physically, emotionally or spiritually.

Take my friend whose world is crumbling around her. This Christian life is nothing like what she expected. Insecure from betrayal and fearful from abuse, the pain in her soul extending throughout her body causes my friend to withdraw and withhold.

We Christians deal with a vile enemy who would have us throw-off all hope and believe we are destined for adversity and failure. When we lose hope, we wake up miserable believing our situation is never going to change. We muddle through the day shuffling our feet, our mind runs amuck with 'what ifs'.

Who hasn't wondered at some time, why go through the motions when the brutal pain of loss, abuse, betrayal, threatens to clutch a tight fist around their aching heart and rip it out?

Personally, I've told God, "It's too hard here."

APRIL 29

My friend believes she is destined to exist in the darkest depths of a confining pit gazing at distant light, knowing she can never live there. Darkness encases her soul, pushing in, squeezing the life out. Why try again only to receive the same results, maybe worse?

Why try again? Because my friend belongs to Jesus Christ. And *He* is her hope.

> **Romans 5:5**
> *And hope does not disappoint, because the love of God has been poured out within our hearts through the Holy Spirit who was given to us.*

The truth of God's love and the comfort and strength the Holy Spirit provides, encourages us to look into the face of the One who gave His life so we could experience victory. Jesus not only wants to pull our desolate hearts from the isolation of a murky pit, but His living example instills even more profound hope.

Jesus' determination did not come from His circumstances. It came from knowing the Truth-Giver intimately and believing His promises are real. His hope, even in the most heinous circumstance—crucifixion—was *in* Him. Somewhere *in* every Christian, no matter how appalling the situation, an infinitesimal spark smolders under the weight of dark ash.

Hope is the spark that ignites lost dreams into flames of possibility.

May

Come Holy Spirit
Come
throw open every door
every secret place
cause my heart to
release its burden
remove the mask of
insecurity
give me a new identity
Beloved . . .
bought with His very blood
Forgiven . . .
despite my humanness
Released . . .
JOY

God Can–And Does
Part 1

Isaiah
58:11
"And the LORD will continually guide you, and satisfy your desire in scorched places, and give strength to your bones; and you will be like a watered garden, and like a spring of water whose waters do not fail."

Such an encouraging verse with, five, count them, five 'ands' linking together God's promises.
The LORD {Jehovah – I AM} will . . .

God alone has intimate knowledge of the uncertainties and difficulties that lie ahead. He will satisfy our desires even when we dwell in those empty, uncomfortable places.

God strengthens us and through His power we endure when we want to give up. Resting in the One who never fails, we thrive, succeed, prosper. God can and does accomplish His purpose.

Still, those lonely, daunting places can take a tremendous toll. How do we make it through when discouragement, doubt, disappointment lurk in the shadows? There are times when we station ourselves deep in the center of those barren places only to waste away from lack of sustenance. We dwell in spiritually parched lands hungering and thirsting for God, but can't seem to find Him through the mirage of uncertainty.

God is faithful to comfort, console, calm. The question is, will we allow Him to guide and strengthen us so we can flourish in our day-to-day lives?

I don't know where you are in your scorched, desert place. Perhaps you have endured the loss of a job, years of accumulated savings, health, a loved one, your confidence and self-worth. Trust me, you can believe God remains faithful and trustworthy.

There have been many times I've dwelt in the sweltering heat and blistering solitude of a spiritual and emotional desert. Right now I'm about to embark upon a new endeavor where I anticipate parched, challenging periods of insecurity and uncertainty.

Isaiah
40:28, 29
Do you not know?
Have you not heard?
The Everlasting God,
the LORD, the
Creator of
the ends of the earth
does not become
weary or tired. His
understanding is
inscrutable. He
gives strength to the
weary, and to him
who lacks might He
increases power.

The Christian Writers Guild offers a one-year course where the basic premise is to finish writing and seek publication of my novel. Included is an intense five-day residency with published authors and other professionals in the writing field, as well as the owner of the Christian Writers Guild, Jerry B. Jenkins. Just a tad intimidating.

Even though in the days ahead I will most definitely find myself in those scorched places, I see this as a thrilling adventure. Allow me to encourage you and myself, to believe God can and does.

Jonah Days
Part 1

James
1:23, 24
GNT
Whoever listens to the word but does not put it into practice is like a man who looks in a mirror and sees himself as he is. He takes a good look at himself and then goes away and at once forgets what he looks like.

Be careful what you pray for. I've been yearning for a deeper intimacy with God for a long time. And I don't mean simply increased cerebral knowledge. My parched soul pants for His satisfying living water.

In this process of seeking Him, the study of His word and my time of solitude have somehow become shallow, unfulfilling. Like I have to get past something to get to the other side.

While praying for understanding God put a mirror to my soul illuminating the heart of the prideful woman who really lives there.

Ever had a Jonah day, as *Anne of Green Gables* puts it? A day when just about everything you say or do is wrong? I've been having a lot of them lately.

No two ways about it, pride is flat-out ugly. Exposing itself in sly subtle ways others may or may not observe. The bottom line is God hates pride and arrogance. Why? Because it turns our hearts from His loving care and perfect plan to seek fulfillment from other sources.

I don't much like God's mirror. Or Jonah days for that matter.

Truth be known, until I seek God in *everything* and accept the fact that apart from Jesus I can do *nothing* I will continue to stick that proverbial foot in my mouth, hurt others with my words {whether intentional or not} and thereby declare what truly fills my heart.

Praise God the Holy Spirit seizes this beast of pride and changes my heart. With the veil of self discipline and 'I've got it covered' removed, freedom reigns. The Holy Spirit is continually transforming me into the image of Christ from glory to glory. Hallelujah.

Thank You Lord that You never give up on me. And that at the end of each Jonah day You still love me.

2 Corinthians
3:17, 18
Now the Lord is the Spirit, and where the Spirit of the Lord is, there is liberty. But we all, with unveiled face, beholding as in a mirror the glory of the Lord, are being transformed into the same image from glory to glory, just as from the Lord, the Spirit.

MAY 4

1 Corinthians 2:9

But just as it is written, "Things which eye has not seen and ear has not heard, and which have not entered the heart of man, all that God has prepared for those who love Him."

While putting hard copies of previous devotions into a binder I took some time to read a few.

Tough months.

Having thought of myself as a proponent of speaking those things which encourage and edify, it was pretty obvious the past several devotions had not shown proficiency in practicing that.

I asked you to share in my struggles, but had little to say about the joys, visions, revelations, transitions, breakthroughs, God had revealed. Perhaps we can begin this month on a better note.

One of thanksgiving.

One of questioning.

How can I whimper about the things I don't have when God has given me so much?

Is there a tinge of kingdom value in this moment and what does that mean?

Where do I see God's glory? What does it look like? What does it sound like?

Just how much do I love God? How do I show it?

MAY 5

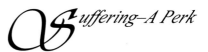

I'd much rather share in Christ's joy then His sufferings. Joy is fun, light-hearted. It's how Christians live. Right? Wrong.

Joy is certainly part of the bounty. Suffering too is a bonus. How can I say suffering is a perk? Suffering unites us to Christ in ways nothing else can.

> 2 Corinthians
> 1:5
> *For just as the sufferings of Christ are ours in abundance, so also our comfort is abundant through Christ.*

To undergo grievous sorrow, unwarranted betrayal or the anguish of affliction gives us the tiniest taste of what Jesus suffered. We will never undergo the intense agony He endured on our behalf. When pain comes, and it will, as sure as desolate winter follows a vibrant fall pallet, we can be certain Jesus experienced the same heart wrenching tribulations and more.

To share in the sufferings of Christ can mean persecution for our faith. In foreign countries entire families are massacred for not renouncing their faith in Jesus Christ. First century believers were put in prison, brutalized, whipped, burned at the stake, torn apart by starving lions and crazed dogs. That's suffering.

Why go through this torture when all they need do is disavow their relationship to Jesus Christ? A sincere depth of love and appreciation for Jesus' sacrifice rides on the tails of the reality that eternity lay ahead and to deny Jesus would result in denial of them before His Father.

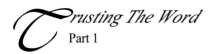

Trusting The Word
Part 1

What is it about God's word that draws us? Sometimes I get so excited to open the Bible and see what God has to say that I'm like a little child tugging on her mother's skirt, begging her to read a favorite book.

God's word provides merciful comfort in the aloneness. Soothing consolation in the never-ending waves of grief. Gracious conviction when losing sight of who I am. Trustworthy counsel in the path I am to follow.

God's word quenches my parched thirst with His living water and satisfies my craving soul with nourishing spiritual food.

God's Word

• bears abundant fruit	• cleanses and sanctifies
• redeems from death	• is our sword
• is truth	• is life
• is prophetic	• brings joy
• gives boldness	• performs its work in those who believe
• saves	• humbles
• grows and multiplies	• convicts
• builds up	• encourages
• produces faith	• transforms
• is powerful	• invites

And the Word (Christ) became flesh (human, incarnate) and tabernacled (fixed His tent of flesh, lived awhile) among us; and we [actually] saw His glory (His honor, His majesty), such glory as an only begotten son receives from his father, full of grace (favor, loving-kindness) and truth (John 1:14 AMPLIFIED).

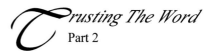

The Christian life is meant to be exciting. Like the varied examples of believers in the Bible who were not passive about their faith, but vibrant, continually moving forward, we too can eagerly watch and anticipate what God will do next.

Matthew
4:4
But He answered and said, "It is written, 'Man shall not live on bread alone, but on every word that proceeds out of the mouth of God.'"

However we cannot look forward to what God will do if we can't see past our passive, ordinary, everyday existence.

God's word is living and active. We can stand still in the 'what we already know' about His word or move forward with new revelations God wants to reveal. A major part of growing in our knowledge of God and being part of His plan is active participation.

Reading and contemplating God's word is essential for believers if we don't want to remain trapped in the dormant life of the humdrum. We read it to know Him. After all, how can we trust His character if we don't know Him? We read expecting to meet with Him, anticipating a deeper intimately.

Leading us into to a life of adventure.

Mark
4:18, 19
NCV
*Others are like
the seed planted
among the thorny
weeds. They hear
the teaching, but
the worries of
this life, the
temptation of
wealth, and
many other evil
desires keep the
teaching from
growing and
producing fruit in
their lives.*

I am a root digger. You see, *real* gardeners pull their weeds out, roots intact, even when the gangly underground tuber stretches from one side of the yard to the other.

But then what do I know? I've only been engaged in this seasonal sport {some lightheartedly call a hobby} for a relatively short time.

Gardening is definitely a contact sport, with strategic challenges lurking behind every bush, under every leaf. You must be in shape to tackle the deadly pathogenic fungi and the dreadful twolined spittlebug. Good conditioning is imperative to ward off the curious yellow jacket and industrious honeybee.

Many own the ever-popular weed whacker. Those two words have been forbidden to enter my gardening vocabulary. That is until we purchased twenty acres of prime mountain property. Whew.

Still, whacking weeds does not render them lifeless, simply stunted with the intent to multiply and loom ever larger next year. Unlike my well maintained *rooted* area—Yeah right.

MAY 9

Gardening includes skirmishes with those ever-leering critters that gather at the top of the hill overlooking your well-tilled garden plot to devise their game plan. You know that's what they're doing when they stand up on their hind haunches, pat their greedy little paws together, salivate, clack their chops, awaiting the abundant feast that is sure to materialize in a matter of weeks.

Weeds, an education in themselves, come in a number of varieties. Like the, pull them and the roots come up as easily as plucking the petals of a poppy, variety.

> Romans
> 12:2
> *And do not be conformed to this world, but be transformed by the renewing of your mind, so that you may prove what the will of God is, that which is good and acceptable and perfect.*

How about the secret hiders? They snuggle up in the crevices of rocks hoping to remain unseen. It's infuriating when you grapple to rescue one of your wheezing plants from the weed's stranglehold and the ungrateful shrub attacks with inch and a half spiked thorns.

Then there is the stubborn type that take the not-so-gentle prodding of a long handled, two-pronged weeder or if that's unavailable, a sturdy old fashioned screw driver {don't tell my husband}. There's the weed that entwines itself amongst the roots of other plants holding onto life with everything it's got.

So like us, isn't it?

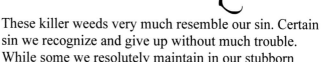

Romans
12:1

Therefore I urge you, brethren, by the mercies of God, to present your bodies a living and holy sacrifice, acceptable to God, which is your spiritual service of worship.

These killer weeds very much resemble our sin. Certain sin we recognize and give up without much trouble. While some we resolutely maintain in our stubborn rebellion. How about the sins we are determined to grip tightly because we don't think of them as sin? They aren't that bad, they're just . . . habits.

Really? Why then is the Holy Spirit gently prodding us to relinquish them because of the destruction they cause us or someone else? And how about the sin we think we've hidden from everyone, including God? Not.

How many times has God exposed my sin only to have me strike back with excuses, justifications, defensive explanations, rationalized reasoning?

God lovingly shows me He has a better way, His best, if only I'll relinquish my hold and allow Him to transform my soul by renewing my mind.

There is such peace and freedom when we present our bodies acceptable to God by pulling those weeds {sins} out, roots and all.

Philippians 4:6-7
Be anxious for nothing but in everything by prayer and supplication with thanksgiving let your requests be made known to God. And the peace of God, which surpasses all comprehension, shall guard your hearts and your minds in Christ Jesus.

Ever have days you wish never would have happened? There is a difficult period of time I experience every month. I call it the 'dark days'. It's hard to explain just what happens, but it's a miserable time I would rather do without.

From my journal:
Oh Lord the dark days engulf every part of me. There is no energy, no excitement, nothing to accomplish. Jesus please take me through these days and help me get my mind off of 'poor me'. You are Lord of even the dark days. Thank You that You hear, You care about me even now. Thank You that I can come to You with everything in prayer and supplication with thanksgiving and Your peace will guard my heart and mind especially now when I'm so vulnerable. I give You praise Lord because You are the one true God who always fulfills His promises.

I may not *feel* good, but God's promises are real. I believe He is the God of *all* my days.

God is perfectly capable to overcome—even the 'dark days'.

Palpable Faith
Part 1

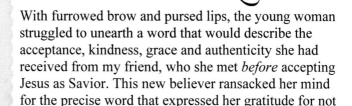

Acts
4:13
NLT
The members of the council were amazed when they saw the boldness of Peter and John, for they could see that they were ordinary men with no special training in the Scriptures. They also recognized them as men who had been with Jesus.

With furrowed brow and pursed lips, the young woman struggled to unearth a word that would describe the acceptance, kindness, grace and authenticity she had received from my friend, who she met *before* accepting Jesus as Savior. This new believer ransacked her mind for the precise word that expressed her gratitude for not being judged, one that capsulized my friend's captivating faith.

"Her faith is so . . . so . . . palpable."

I smiled and nodded in agreement knowing what she had articulated with facial and hand expressions did indeed describe my friend. But palpable? That word ricocheted around my brain throughout the day into the night. Exploring Webster's revealed eloquently more than my anticipated definition.

Palpable - capable of being touched or felt: TANGIBLE
Easily perceptible by the mind: MANIFEST [readily perceived by the senses and especially by the sight - easily understood or recognized by the mind: OBVIOUS]

MAY 13

Palpable. A word I am growing fond of.

You see, my friend, whose faith was described as palpable, had been with Jesus. She has no idea her faith is tangible and obvious. All she knows is she loves Jesus and wants to boldly give that love to others.

How I long for my faith to be palpable. Faith that accepts and loves as Jesus did. Leper. Prostitute. Lame. Weak. Depressed. Blind. Liar. Proud. Poor. Homeless. Rich. Ignorant. Religious. Beggar. Intellectual.

> Luke
> 6:38
> *"Give, and it will be given to you. They will pour into your lap a good measure—pressed down, shaken together, and running over. For by your standard of measure it will be measured to you in return."*

Oh, for eyes to see the hollow emptiness and hopelessness in those who have yet to know. To pour out God's indescribable love upon them. That judgmental attitudes would be annihilated and we would see others as those Jesus loves immensely and wants with Him in heaven. After all, He gave His life.

God's love. Forgiveness of sin. What was. What is. What will be. We will probably never know the full extent while here.

Palpable faith boldly gives His love away.

> **Psalm 142:5**
> *I cried out to You, O LORD; I said, You are my refuge, my portion in the land of the living.*

Having revisited this passage it struck me, God has been my refuge in more circumstances then I can count. Whether drowning in a sea of depression or mentally removing myself from an unbearable situation, God has always been my refuge.

Then there was the time He became my portion.

If you will indulge me, I'd like to go back in time.

May 2006 is etched in my memory forever. For an entire month my body strenuously battled a severe reaction to the notorious Southern Oregon poison oak. Having never been exposed to the deadly toxin, I helped clear, stack and burn dead vines {or so I thought}, buck brush and blackberry bushes from the lower part of our twenty acres.

Picture me 'protected' from head to toe. Large brim hat. Protective glasses. Kerchief over my mouth. Long-sleeve shirt, overalls, socks to my knees, boots, gloves. Yep I was ready for battle.

Rake plants into pile. Hug pile. Stack to burn. Again and again. Hour after hour.

The poisonous oil touched every piece of clothing and at certain private intervals during the day—need I say more—much of the exterior of my body. Applying the appropriate soap guaranteed to rid me of any trace of the venomous plant was simply precautionary.

At that time we lived in a small fifth-wheel awaiting the county's approval of an application to build on the property. Little did we know our clothing and boots had deposited the noxious oil everywhere in our temporary burrow.

Psalm
73:26
*My flesh and my
heart may fail, but
God is the strength
of my heart and
my portion
forever.*

The dispersion began slowly. A few red splotches on my face, wrists, behind the knees. Itching a bit. Within a couple of days it had spread to most of my body. One of the four doctors I saw during that endless month told me I kept getting re-infected. He said the invisible oil was probably on everything in our fifth-wheel.

As I lay on the couch sobbing, terrified to move or touch anything, blisters all over my body, intolerable itching I could not scratch, agonizing pain that extended into the nerve endings under my skin, a dear friend called and told us to pack up and come stay at her house. She and her husband were lifesavers.

Over the counter meds kept the pain and itching at bay for short three hour stints. Sleeping continuously for days, the blisters grew larger, the pain more intense. Lying in that bed hour after hour, slipping in and out of drug induced sleep, I remember praying three simple words over and over, "God help me."

> **Lamentations 3:24**
> *"The LORD is my portion," says my soul, "therefore I have hope in Him."*

My body went into shock. The poison oak was winning the battle.

After almost two weeks of progressive deterioration, I think my husband and friends were fearful my vital organs could not take much more. The ER doctor, third in a succession of four doctors, wanted to inject a drug that would remain in my system for twelve hours. The same drug another doctor said had helped cause the subsequent outbreaks.

Looking back it's almost funny—almost. I jumped off that ER examining table like it had scorching rocks under the sheets and screamed, "No!"

With his less than eloquent bedside manner the ER doc shrugged his shoulders, said there was nothing more he could do for me and walked out.

Hope was waning. Still in and out of drug induced sleep, my body shivered for extended periods waiting for the nonprescription meds to take effect. Even though incoherent, I sensed God's presence. At one point I remember whispering, "God You are all I have."

One last doctor.

In the examining room the cool air entering from the back of my patient's gown soothed the oozing blisters and burning skin. When the doctor walked in and saw me standing with arms open wide so as not to rupture the blisters, tears streaming down my face, her eyes filled with sympathy. She slowly shook her head. If I could have gone to my knees I would have. I begged her, "Please help me."

Psalm
119:57, 58
The LORD is my portion; I have promised to keep Your words. I sought Your favor with all my heart; be gracious to me according to Your word.

Fortunately God had heard my plea as well. The doctor talked me through the previous two weeks explaining the situation in terms I could understand. Her prescribed medication worked almost immediately. My body began the twenty-one day process of healing.

In the midst of the painful struggle, comprehension of and appreciation for many things took place. Two kept coming to mind.

God is my portion. He will walk with me. Even if He takes me home He will never leave me.

The other revelation came while experiencing the loving, compassionate care three precious people gave me day after day. I finally grasped the essence of Jesus' life, ours as well.

Love God and love people. Nothing else really matters.

Awestruck and Undone
Part 1

Isaiah
40:25, 26
THE MESSAGE
"So—who is like
me? Who holds a
candle to me?"
says The Holy.
Look at the night
skies: Who do you
think made all
this? Who marches
this army of stars
out each night,
counts them off,
calls each by name—
so magnificent! so
powerful!—and
never overlooks a
single one?

The question arose, what is God's glory?

Pastor Dan Haakenson's quote comes to mind; "God's highest purpose is the display of His glory."

Some would say God's glory is the wow factor when something takes place that should never have happened. Miracle?

Others might point to Moses whose relationship with God was enviable. The Lord spoke with Moses face to face. Surely he must have seen God's glory. Yet even with their intimate relationship Moses still asked God to show him His glory.

God's glory. How does one describe utter awe and the sense of being absolutely undone? Everything else ceases to matter.

The prophet Isaiah said it well when he had a vision of the LORD:
"Woe is me, for I am ruined!" (Isaiah 6:5)

God's glory surrounds us. We simply need eyes to see, ears to hear.

Praising God through music can give us a wondrous glimpse of His glory. Not to mention the wind's whisper through rustling leaves. Spring's colorful splendor. The unleashed power of a mighty steed. Bountiful food from a single grain. An encouraging smile. A heartfelt tear. Wise counsel.

> Isaiah
> 6:5
> *Then I said, "Woe is me, for I am ruined! Because I am a man of unclean lips, and I live among a people of unclean lips; for my eyes have seen the King, the LORD of hosts."*

We humans originally reflected God's perfect image.
Until sin entered in. We were created to reveal God's glory. But how can this be? We are talking about God Almighty who spoke the stars into existence, named each one and keeps them right where they belong.

Through the sacrifice of Jesus Christ, whosoever will, has the advantage of adoption into God's family and through that adoption the privilege to draw near to God's throne of grace.

We reveal God's glory in numerous ways.

$\mathcal{A}$westruck And Undone
Part 3

John
14:10
THE MESSAGE
Don't you believe
that I am in the
Father and the
Father is in me?
The words that I
speak to you aren't
mere words. I don't
just make them up
on my own. The
Father who resides
in me crafts each
word into a
divine act.

God's glory is revealed in those who are wholly devoted to Him through the fruit of the Spirit; love, joy, peace, patience, kindness, goodness, faithfulness, gentleness and self-control.

Jesus displayed God's glory by doing and speaking only as His Father directed. He lived out His Father's will perfectly. Impossible for us you say? Maybe. Still, as believers we can learn from Jesus' example and through the power of the Holy Spirit give it our best shot.

But how?

Selfless servanthood. Laugh more. Judge less. Risk. Rebuke evil. Stand firm. Speak truth. Shed tears of compassion. Pray continually. Listen more. Forgive. Humbly obey. Exhibit courageous faith. Live in unwavering trust. Look to the unseen set before us. Censure old names. Embrace new names.

Just a glimpse of what it looks like to stand awestruck and undone at God's glory.

MAY 21

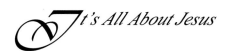

It's not about you.

How often has the Holy Spirit whispered that into my spirit? How many times have I seen my selfishness in the desolate faces of homeless children, hollow eyes of lonely elders, defiant anger of those in bondage to drugs or alcohol?

> Deuteronomy 8:3
> *Man does not live by bread alone, but man lives by everything that proceeds out of the mouth of the LORD.*

Someone asked why Christians are so judgmental and prejudice. Could it be some live according to their own rules rather than God's word? Jesus said the greatest commandment is to love the Lord with all your heart, soul and mind. We are also to love others as Jesus did. Frustration after frustration, trial after trial.

We begin well, loving God and others. Slowly the focus shifts to hurtful words spoken to us in haste or our own thoughtless actions toward another. True, we are to deal with the effects of life, to forgive and ask for forgiveness. But once settled, it is imperative to shift the focus back to God and stop dwelling on what was.

A new believer asked a profound question. "Why do Christians keep Jesus a secret?"

We ought to be sharing this good news wherever we go and live as if life is all about *Jesus*.

Because really . . .

It's not about you.

Fully Alive

1 Chronicles
29:11
"Yours, O LORD,
is the greatness
and the power
and the glory
and the victory
and the
majesty, indeed
everything that is
in the heavens
and the earth;
Yours is the
dominion, O
LORD, and You
exalt Yourself as
head over all."

King David knew what it meant to truly worship God. The day they brought the ark of the covenant up to Jerusalem, the king became so unbridled in his worship he danced with abandon before the Lord and all the people.

Someone wrote they want to live life *fully alive*. King David understood that.

What does living fully alive look like?

- a heart of thanksgiving
- awaken the senses
- understand God's mercy
- give away grace
- smile more—frown less
- love expecting nothing in return
- find something encouraging to say
- realize your God-given talents, gifts–use them
- find someone who has less than you—give them something precious
- laugh out loud
- give doubt away
- receive forgiveness
- praise God for joy even if you don't *feel* it
- ask God for an adventure
- give hugs
- speak truth
- stroll with someone you love
- eat your favorite food—once a week
- tell someone you are thankful for

That is a tiny offering of what it looks like for me. What does living *fully alive* look like for you?

MAY 23

Oh how frail and feeble our flesh becomes. Thankful for salvation, yet still groveling in sin. We justify our inadequacies and quickly judge the sins of others. What manner of person this one— the Christian? Forgiven, yet fallible, determined yet indecisive, grateful for mercy yet unable to offer grace.

Romans
6:1-2
GNT
What shall we say, then? Should we continue to live in sin so that God's grace will increase? Certainly not! We have died to sin—how then can we go on living in it?

For years I lived with the misconception that God only loved Christians because we had become a part of His family by the blood of Jesus. In the course of reading the gospel of John, I came across John 3:16:
"For God so loved the world."

Those words struck me like a lightning bolt. God *loves all* people whether they believe in Jesus or not.

God loves every thief, liar, murderer, drug addict, adulterer, embezzler, every single human being. God has always loved the sinner, but hated their sin.

How then do we as believers find deliverance from the power of sin? Paul encourages us to walk by the Spirit. Led by the Spirit we are no longer held captive by the deeds of the flesh.

reative Power
Part 1

Genesis 1:1

In the beginning God created the heavens and the earth.

Ah, the creativity of God. Always new, never repeated exactly the same way twice. The One who created all things continually exhibits His clever creativity through nature, people, animals, life.

Go outside into the center of a snowstorm and carefully observe the snowflakes drift to earth. Each one is unlike any other ever formed. Look at humans. Every person God created from Adam and Eve throughout history is unique. No two are the same. Even identical twins have distinctive differences. Amazing.

God certainly had a sense of humor when He created animals. I watched a nature program that showcased a peculiar bird performing a mating dance. This guy looked perfectly normal until the dance began. The feathers on his head fanned out to form a corrugated sphere around his face and beak. His body blew up to three times its normal size to take on the look of a huge black balloon, while he danced a backward slide across the ground to impress the fortunate female who watched in fascination and bewilderment with her head cocked to one side.

Each animal, insect, plant is extraordinary, having their own special purpose. Even so, I cannot understand why God created the pesky, destructive ground squirrel, {better known as diggers here in the Northwest} irksome mosquito, common housefly or dreadfully noxious poison oak.

Go figure.

I so admire the creativity God ingrained in people. To be sure there are many who do not acknowledge the fact that God put the talent, ability, thought process, within them to produce great art, writings, teaching, scientific theories, music, etc. Those who know God, have little doubt where every creative thought and bone originated.

Revelation 4:11
"Worthy are You, our Lord and our God, to receive glory and honor and power; for You created all things, and because of Your will they existed, and were created."

One of the amazing things about God is He does not duplicate or reproduce what has already been fashioned. His creations are repeatedly new and different. Look at the flowers and plants in your garden. I'll bet they don't look the same as they did last year or even the year before.

The same is true for people. Some fret and wonder how they will come up with a new story or distinctive art piece or imaginative way to teach. God would not have us go to our 'already done that' file and pull out something that formerly proved successful, tweak it and expect it to bring about revelation or wide-eyed amazement.

No. God wants to pour into us *His* new idea, ingenious musical score, innovative theory, insightful story, vibrant painting, thought-provoking sculpture.

MAY 26

Creative Power
Part 3

God wants to pour into us His new thing.

Think about the best vacation you've ever had. Did you go back to the same spot and try to recreate the fun and adventure of the original trip? Didn't happen, did it?

We are such creatures of habit. We believe if something went well once it will work just as well the second time. If it isn't broke, don't fix it. That's not how God works. The Holy Spirit's power is within us to create something fresh and exciting each day.

God promises to make all things new one day. Even now, He has much to accomplish and wants to use His Beloved to do it through the gifting and talents He created in us.

So don't fret about how you can surpass the last successful project. Simply ask God to accomplish *His* new thing. He loves to work in us so we stand back in awestruck wonder and praise Him for the astonishing things *He* has done.

When I pray do I *believe* God will answer or do I *hope* He will answer? The centurion believed, the woman with the hemorrhage believed, Jairus believed, the people of Sychar believed, the disciples believed. Do I really believe?

Jesus challenged us with that question. Jesus told His disciples:

> *"Truly I say to you, if you have faith and do not doubt, you will not only do what was done to the fig tree, but even if you say to this mountain, 'Be taken up and cast into the sea,' it will happen. And all things you ask in prayer, believing, you will receive" (Matthew 21:21).*

Philippians 3:8
More than that, I count all things to be loss in view of the surpassing value of knowing Christ Jesus my Lord, for whom I have suffered the loss of all things, and count them but rubbish {dung KJV} so that I may gain Christ.

Many take that to mean we will receive anything we ask for. Look a little closer. See the tiny word 'if'? *If* you have faith. Faith comes from believing, believing from trust, trust from experience. When Christ is my all in all, everything else is superfluous. I love that word.

Imagine believing your conversations with God have real meaning. To know as a follower of Jesus Christ He actually hears your prayers and responds to them.

Absolutely.

Hebrews
3:19-4:1
AMPLIFIED
*So we see that
they were not able
to enter [into His
rest], because
of their
unwillingness
to adhere to and
trust in and rely
on God [unbelief
had shut them out].
Therefore, while
the promise of
entering His rest
still holds and is
offered [today],
let us be afraid
[to distrust it], lest
any of you should
think he has come
too late and has
come short of
[reaching] it.*

It's only been a few months since my husband's home-going. Yet I've asked God time and again during those agonizing, seemingly endless days, "What do You want me to do? Surely I need to be *doing* something; volunteer, help, give—something."

My sense is that for now I am to rest in God. This resting however is not to be confused with doing nothing. This is a time to grow my knowledge of and intimacy with Him. To immerse myself in His word {even if my brain is still unable to fully concentrate} and allow the Holy Spirit to heal, teach, comfort, direct.

During this time of resting that niggling question from God, "Do you *really* trust Me?" continues to surface. Last week while at my kitchen window observing a particularly gray, dismal, dreary day, missing the love of my life, deep-seated questions arose bringing doubt and fear.

Persistent questions bounced from my husband to God.

Is there really a heaven? Are you there enjoying all God promised? Will I see you again? Is there joy and wonder where you are?

God, is Your word true? Will I someday be transported into the presence of Your Son, see Him face to face? Are Your promises real?

It wasn't three minutes later God set a vivid, dramatic rainbow in the sky. Within seconds another arched above the first. God's promises *are* real.

Immersing myself in God's word while resting reinforces the certainty that His promises are real. He does what He says.

God never has to prove Himself to His creation. But oh how it makes me smile when He does.

> Hebrews
> 4:2, 3
> AMPLIFIED
> *For indeed we have
> had the glad tidings
> [Gospel of God]
> proclaimed to us just
> as truly as
> they [the Israelites of
> old did when the
> good news of
> deliverance from
> bondage came to
> them]; but the
> message they heard
> did not benefit them,
> because it was not
> mixed with
> faith (with the
> leaning of the entire
> personality on God in
> absolute trust and
> confidence in
> His power, wisdom,
> and goodness) by
> those who heard it . . .
> For we who have
> believed (adhered to
> and trusted in and
> relied on God) do
> enter that rest.*

MAY 30

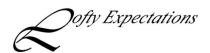
Lofty Expectations

Micah
7:7

But as for me, I will watch expectantly for the LORD; I will wait for the God of my salvation. My God will hear me.

I recently told someone I could never live up to their lofty expectations. Their response? "We all have expectations of everyone." Is that true?

I suppose we expect food for our hungry bodies, water to quench our thirst, payment for a hard day's work. Spouses expect fidelity. Most would like to think their lives have purpose. We desire respect and understanding from others. Still . . .

The more years that pass, the less I expect of anyone. Perhaps it's because of former disappointments when my expectations were shattered. Maybe it's a hope that if I don't put expectations on others they, in turn, will let me be.

I wonder, do we have expectations of God? I do. I expect He will keep His promises and provide for my basic needs. I expect four seasons, a sunrise in the morning, the moon and stars in the sky at night. I expect God hears my prayers *and* answers them.

Does God have expectations of us? Indeed. He wants us to love Him with all our heart, soul, mind and strength.

Do we all have expectations of everyone as this person implied? Maybe. But wouldn't it be great if we chose not to put our skewed expectations on anyone? Instead if, like Micah, we watched expectantly for the Lord.

June

Expectation smothers grace

God Is Enough
Part 1

Psalm
42:11
Why are you in despair, O my soul? And why have you become disturbed within me?
Hope in God, for I shall yet praise Him, the help of my countenance and my God.

Is God enough?

My friends and I have discussed that question at length. When stripped of everything we care about, everyone we love, is God really our all in all, our very breath?

• when you are wedged in the center of your losses
• when the bank attaches an eviction notice on the front door of your foreclosed home
• when your boss calls you into his office to say with the economy so bad the company is downsizing— your position has been eliminated
• when the doctor enters the room with doleful eyes extending frightening test results
• when the sheriff or armed services knock on your door to say your son or daughter will not be coming home
• when you are living in the dregs of sin, the very pit of hopelessness
• when the reality that years of illegal drug use has taken every good thing from your family
• when the love of your life is taken home to heaven

Is God enough?

Psalm
22:1, 2
*My God, my God,
why have You
forsaken me? Far
from my deliverance
are the words of
my groaning. O my
God, I cry by day,
but You do not
answer; and by night,
but I have no
rest.*

David knew how it felt to be afflicted, stalked, hunted, closed in on all sides by the enemy; to be innocent and guilty, honored and deprived, in despair. Yet David knew God was his rock, his redeemer, his shield, a very present help in tight places.

Years ago as a new believer in Southern California growing in my knowledge of God, I was living in a deep place of intimacy with Him like nothing I'd ever experienced before. Surely it could only get better. Right?

For three tortuous years after moving to the Bay Area, I did not sense, feel or hear from God. The words in the Bible no longer jumped off the page with clear understanding, wisdom, direction. In extreme inner torment I could not figure out what I had done wrong. I cried out to God over and over.

No response.

Nothing.

Oswald Chambers says that when God is silent He is building our character. Boy, did I need a lot of character development.

David's determination to trust God whether He delivered him, sensed His presence, heard His voice or not, impressed me.

God Is Enough
Part 3

Psalm
59:17
*O my strength, I
will sing praises
to You; for God is
my stronghold,
the God who
Shows me
lovingkindness.*

The psalmist had a love so deep, a trust so strong, he would not let go of his God.

Three long, dry years does not an excited soul make. Still, confident this Christian life was worth fighting for, I determined not to let go of my faith, to trust God's faithfulness as His word had promised.

Indeed, my character did grow. God tested my faith and certainly by no means of my own, rather by the indwelling strength and power of the Holy Spirit, I persevered.

That time of solitude caused me to rethink struggles, to see with new eyes and a more sensitive heart for others around me who were hurting. It's been said we cannot empathize with others until we have experienced the same kind of pain, grief or suffering.

God carried me through. He brought me out on the other side with a greater understanding of who He is and a profound gratitude for how much He loves me.

Even today, in the midst of a time when *my life will never be the same again*, in this moment by moment crying out to God, I can say more confidently than ever before—God is enough.

The love of God, a vital part of a Christ follower's being, becomes essential like food, water, oxygen, permeating every cell.

So I ask you, why do we, who are indelibly ingrained with this love, allow fear to immobilize us? If we are consumed with God's love, there ought not be any possibility of embracing a single morsel of fear. Why do we permit fear to cripple us when God's love casts out all fear?

Fear paralyzes. Derived from the one through whom it originated, the deceiver himself. We know fear does not come from God, yet we allow its sneaky presence to creep into our minds and hearts.

Recognizing and nurturing God's love for what it is, perfect, holy, all-powerful, all-knowing, fear loses its grip.

> 1 John
> 4:16, 18
> PHILLIPS
> *So we have come to know and trust the love God has for us. God is love and the man whose life is lived in love does, in fact, live in God, and God does, in fact, live in him . . .*
> *Love contains no fear—indeed fully developed love expels every particle of fear, for fear always contains some of the torture of feeling guilty. This means the man who lives in fear has not yet had his love perfected.*

We have the power to overcome fear. It's a choice. The dominance of fear or the peace of God's perfect love.

**Titus
1:15, 16
PHILLIPS**
Everything is wholesome to those who are themselves wholesome. But nothing is wholesome to those who are themselves unwholesome and who have no faith in God— their very minds and consciences are diseased. They profess to know God, but their actual behavior denies their profession, for they are obviously vile and rebellious and when it comes to doing any real good they are palpable frauds.

There's that word palpable again.

Listening to words.

Compliments. Complaints. Respect. Whining. Coercion. Encouragement.

"Lovely dress, beautiful shoes . . .
"I can't remember the last time . . .
"How can you love someone who does something like . . .
"I'm a Martha, you know . . .
"Did you see that guy begging by the freeway . . .
"Get a job . . .
"Why do they stay together . . .
"I crawled up in God's lap and felt His heart . . .
"Sing your best song on your worst day . . .
"Love God more than . . .

We talk a good tale. Lip service.

We say we know God, but do our actions show it? Jesus said:

> *"Not everyone who says to Me, 'Lord, Lord,' will enter the kingdom of heaven"*
> *(Matthew 7:21).*

One day He will declare to them:

> *"I never knew you; depart from Me, you who practice lawlessness"*
> *(Matthew 7:23).*

They called Him Lord, but refused to do what He commanded.

Actions, not words, reveal the heart.

How do we truly *know* someone? *Know* God? Spend one-on-one time together. Communicate. That would include listening.

When was the last time you turned off every electronic gizmo; computer, cell phone, IPOD, TV, radio, and sat still long enough to have a conversation with God? Yes that requires discipline, but it is *so* worth it.

How can we tell if someone *knows* God? The apostle John makes it palpably clear.

> *If we say that we have fellowship with Him and yet walk in the darkness, we lie and do not practice the truth; but if we walk in the Light as He Himself is in the Light, we have fellowship with one another, and the blood of Jesus His Son cleanses us from all sin. If we say that we have no sin, we are deceiving ourselves and the truth is not in us (1 John 1:6-8).*

1 John
2:4-6
THE MESSAGE
If someone claims, "I know him well!" but doesn't keep his commandments, he's obviously a liar. His life doesn't match his words. But the one who keeps God's word is the person in whom we see God's mature love. This is the only way to be sure we're in God. Anyone who claims to be intimate with God ought to live the same kind of life Jesus lived.

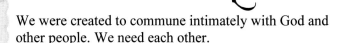

John 13:14-17

"If I then, the Lord and the Teacher, washed your feet, you also ought to wash one another's feet. For I gave you an example that you also should do as I did to you. Truly, truly, I say to you, a slave is not greater than his master, nor is one who is sent greater than the one who sent him. If you know these things, you are blessed if you do them."

We were created to commune intimately with God and other people. We need each other.

In the Garden of Eden, Adam encountered loneliness when he realized all the animals had partners, but he did not. God had compassion for Adam's plight and created Eve to compliment Adam as a companion and to have another human to fellowship with.

God's word repeatedly shows us we are to interact with, serve, give to, comfort, console, others. We are not an island unto ourselves as someone has said. We are a community of people who need one another for fellowship and to accomplish the ultimate purpose of every human being—to glorify God.

Jesus knew He needed people. He chose twelve men to be His intimate friends. They laughed and cried together, traveled day in, day out serving one another. Not only did the disciples serve Jesus. He served them.

God put the desire within us to serve just as His Son did.

Hebrews
10:25
NLT
*And let us not neglect
our meeting together,
as some people do,
but encourage one
another, especially
now that the day of
His return is
drawing near.*

When we isolate ourselves over an extended period of time something breaks down in our character, our desires become selfish and self-serving. Quite unlike the example Jesus set.

When someone separates themselves from others a gradual process of self-absorption takes place. They have no one to care for or be accountable to. Many come to a point where they even abandon their interaction with God because, well, 'they can take care of themselves.'

I'm not saying we don't need time alone. Not at all. It's important. Especially for those suffering from loss of any kind.

As a widow I have found being alone for too long brings on the propensity to live in my own gloomy dream world. When I don't share my thoughts and hurts, grief takes on the look of a martyr. Despondency and depression are not just a once-in-awhile acceptable part of the grieving process, they become a daily tendency to dwell in the state of poor me. I don't want to live there.

We were created for more.

Fear Of The What If People

Part 1

1 Kings
19:3
*And he [Elijah]
was afraid and
arose and ran for
his life and came
to Beersheba.*

Fear. We've all experienced it.

What causes the trepidation that immobilizes us? For Elijah it was death. Jezebel or Jezzy as my friend calls her, was out to get him. Today countless reckon with this fear through cancer, heart disease and numerous other threatening health conditions.

Don't let anyone tell you fear is a figment of your imagination. Those meddlers would have you believe you simply need to think positive thoughts. Nonsense. Fear is real.

How then are we, who profess to trust God, to respond to this very real emotion? Certainly not by questioning the unknown future. I mean what if the stock market crashes, what if I lose my job, what if my house burns to the ground, what if rain causes a mud slide? What if . . . what if . . . what if.

I call these folks 'what if' people. They explore every possible detail that could, might, may possibly go wrong and then ruminate throughout the day on into the wee hours of the night. These things might happen. Yet God reminds us *He* is our strong fortress.

There are those who fear the loss of a loved one, others the loss of position, possessions or property. Fear of discovery and repercussion from illegal, immoral or unethical acts paralyze some, as it should. False character assassination, the loss of status, gossip, the unknown give cause to many sleepless nights.

God is our shield and our strength. He would have us snuff out any flicker of fear before it causes a bonfire of anxiety attacks, stomach ulcers, migraine headaches, stress, loss of sleep and any number of other ailments that take over when fear reigns and God does not.

> Psalm
> 18:2
> GNT
> *The LORD is my protector; he is my strong fortress. My God is my protection, and with him I am safe. He protects me like a shield; he defends me and keeps me safe.*

God won't keep fear from entering our lives. But when it does He tells us to trust Him moment by moment and know He is always with us.

What's causes you to fear? Don't run from it. Identify the culprit and rely on God to rescue and redeem you. Just as Elijah and the Israelites learned to trust God, you can too.

Fear Of The What If People

Part 3

Psalm
42:5
Why are you in despair, O my soul? And why have you become disturbed within me? Hope in God, for I shall again praise Him for the help of His presence.

'What if' people live in fear.

The Israelites feared for sustenance in the desert. God provided for their needs, however only enough for each day. God wanted His people to trust Him for everything, just as He does today, even when we cannot see what tomorrow will bring.

Fear is nothing new, it began in the Garden of Eden. Adam and Eve hid because they were afraid of God's response when He found they had disobeyed. Jacob feared his brother would kill him for stealing his birthright. Moses was afraid to believe God wanted to use him. Joshua must have been afraid to take possession of the promise land or why would God tell him *four times* to be strong and courageous? Peter, John, Paul, all experienced fear. Every one of them was afraid of those pesky 'what ifs'.

The truth is, there are no 'what ifs' for Christians. We trust God is sovereign and take what is happening now, each frightening experience, every frustrating situation, and call on Him for wisdom and direction.

God always reveals Himself trustworthy.

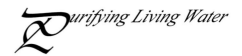

Hope words. Spoken by One knowing within days He would hang on a Roman cross.

Walking along the banks of the Rogue River, we listen. Moving swift, yet undisturbed, the cool water weaves around a gentle bend. Fallen logs and other rubble interrupt the easy flow, kicking up ripples, churning white water.

> John
> 16:33
> *"These things I have spoken to you, so that in Me you may have peace. In the world you have tribulation, but . . . .*

We stop. Watching. My wise friend, soul deep with spiritual insight, tutors on the purifying effects and aeration {life giving oxygen} of the water as it travels the river's path over, around and through natural obstacles. Living water.

Job said:
> *"Shall we indeed accept good from God and not accept adversity?"*
> *(Job 2:10)*

A.B. Simpson encourages in his book, *When the Comforter Came*:
"Nearly all the great examples of faith and victorious grace which we find in the Scriptures came out of situations of extremity and distress. God loves hard places, and faith is usually born of danger and extremity."

God, forever faithful through tribulations, trials, suffering; not punishment, rather purpose. Cleansing, purifying pools of new birth, but mostly persistent growth. Lives stirred to maturity made ready to receive the admonition.

JUNE 12

Psalm 73:25, 26
Who have I in heaven but You? And besides You, I desire nothing on earth. My flesh and my heart may fail, but God is the strength of my heart and my portion forever.

Life is all about God. Every frame, God-breathed.

God created us relational beings. Loving God first then pouring out His love to others. He continually places people in my path who receive me into their lives with kindhearted acceptance, allowing me to share in their trials, triumphs, joy. Making deeper heart connections while experiencing life together. Family and friends lavish time and love to help fill the barren places.

An integral part of embracing others is prayer. These days many of my prayers enfold a number of young couples, entreating God that they would love Him with a deeper passion and greater intensity than they love each other.

Seen through the lens of another I might appear to be one who now walks through life alone. That could not be farther from the truth. Yes there are lonely days. Times when the silent abandon of solitary rooms causes me to long for my husband's voice, his footsteps.

Yet I am not alone. There is One who satisfies my longings through His compassionate strength that never fails.

I will again praise the Lord. My truism as I walk through the aloneness and grief.

Psalm 42 recounts the psalmist's soul turmoil. While in this desperate place he remembers a time when God delivered him from his enemies. Reminded of God's faithfulness, the psalmist chooses to praise God for who he *knows* Him to be.

> Psalm
> 42:5, 8
> *Why are you in despair, O my soul? And why have you become disturbed within me? Hope in God, for I shall again praise Him for the help of His presence. . . The LORD will command His lovingkindness in the daytime; and His song will be with me in the night, a prayer to the God of my life.*

Whenever we recall God's character, the reality of His unwavering promises, we cannot help but praise Him. The psalmist gives the impression he wanted to shout his praises from a mountaintop.

Whenever I recall God's unreserved faithfulness I too cannot help but praise Him. I want to shout from my hilltop who He is, how much He loves me, what He did to save me.

Focusing our lens to a wide shot, we see not only does God walk with believers through every moment of our brief sojourn here on earth, but followers of Jesus Christ have the promise of eternity in heaven.

Expectation Smothers Grace

Ephesians 4:29
Let no unwholesome word proceed from your mouth, but only such a word as is good for edification according to the need of the moment, so that it will give grace to those who hear.

Mother Teresa:
"If you judge people, you have no time to love them."

Grace, unmerited favor. Receiving what we are not entitled to.

The pastor pounds his fist on the pulpit. Hellfire, damnation and God's mercy all in one breath. Elaborating how he put a man in his place when the man shared an opinion on a passage of scripture, the pastor arrogantly reminded the man that he was not a theologian and didn't know what he was talking about.

Where is the grace?

Grace is the giving away of the unconditional love God lavishes on us.

How we love to receive God's undeserved favor. But do we give it to others? Sometimes we think we're offering grace when in reality there are conditions attached. We extend the hand of favor only to judge.

Our eyes are clouded by what we think would be helpful:
"That's good, but . . ."
"If you would just . . ."
"It's really not that hard to understand . . ."

That's not grace. That's *our* expectation of how another ought to perform.

With a sigh of defeat. They give up.

Expectation smothers grace.

What does God have to do for us to listen *and* believe what He says?

How many, like the Israelites in the Old Testament, hear, but take hold of only a handful of bits and pieces? The bits and pieces we like.

God had a plan to take the Israelites on an amazing adventure. He not only delivered them from bondage through ten miraculous plagues, but He took care of their every need in the desert, promising to give them a fertile land and prosperous future. How did they respond? They grumbled and complained testing God's faithfulness. Sound familiar?

> Numbers
> 14:22, 23
> *"Surely all the men who have seen My glory and My signs which I performed in Egypt and in the wilderness, yet have put Me to the test these ten times and have not listened to My voice, shall by no means see the land which I swore to their fathers, nor shall any of those who spurned Me see it."*

Even though God proves Himself faithful time and again, how many of us are too stubborn to listen to His divine wisdom and trust Him?

So many wander aimlessly without a purpose, applying only the bits and pieces they've collected.

Wouldn't it be invigorating to jump *all in* and eagerly join God in His plan?

Root Diggers
Part 1

Hebrews
12:1
AMPLIFIED
*Therefore then,
since we are
surrounded by so
great a cloud of
witnesses [who
have borne
testimony of the
Truth], let us strip
off and throw
aside every
encumbrance—
unnecessary
weight—and that
sin which so
readily (deftly
and cleverly)
clings to and
entangles us, and
let us run with
patient endurance
and steady and
active persistence
the appointed
course of the race
that is set
before us.*

I am a root digger. My goal is to see every tiny weed pulled out by the roots never to show its prickly leaves again. Still, with twenty acres I've learned a weed whacker is an essential tool. In the flower garden. Root digger. Everywhere else. Whack em'.

However with whacking comes the certainty that the weeds will grow back, likely more dense than before. To skim the top is to allow the weed roots to spread and grow beneath the surface taking hold of other roots, rocks, debris.

Such a vivid picture of sin. When we cut off sin at the surface—determination not to touch, watch, imbibe—it would appear we have it under control. Really?

We can cut sin off at the surface, but what really lingers below the surface in the heart? What does it take to dig deeper? The Holy Spirit.

The rub? We don't just wake up one morning and decide from now on we're going to have a heart overflowing with the Holy Spirit's fruit; love, joy, peace, patience, kindness, goodness, faithfulness, gentleness and self-control.

Ephesians 4:22, 23
That, in reference to your former manner of life, you lay aside the old self, which is being corrupted in accordance with the lusts of deceit, and that you be renewed in the spirit of your mind.

The Holy Spirit alone produces this fruit. And as with any other fruit there is a process.
- seed planted = salvation
- fed, watered, nurtured = word of God
- pruned = Holy Spirit conviction
- growth = listening, put knowledge into action
- ripe—ready to give away = fruit of the Spirit

Okay, but how do we get rid of the garden weeds of bitterness, grief, unforgiveness, malice, immorality, deceit, rudeness, anger . . . .

Root Diggers
Part 3

Galatians
5:16, 18
THE MESSAGE
*My counsel is this:
live freely,
animated and
motivated by
God's Spirit. Then
you won't
feed the
compulsions of
selfishness . . . .
Why don't you
choose to be led
by the Spirit and
so escape the
erratic compulsions
of a law-dominated
existence?*

Good question.

Allowing the Holy Spirit to plant and nurture spiritual fruit He alone produces, brings it to fruition.

Our part is choosing to be led by the Spirit, daily living according to His direction and offering a well-prepared plot in our heart by uprooting those sin weeds.

For the fruit of the Spirit to grow there can be no intermingling with sin roots hiding just below the surface. How can love grow deep roots when it comes up against unforgiveness and bitterness? Or peace with fear and anxiety blocking the path?

Why, even this week God brought to mind someone I needed to forgive. That shocked me. I thought I'd forgiven this person years ago. Actually I had forgiven the sin, but not the carnage it waged on my life.

The Holy Spirit and me. Root diggers.

JUNE 19

From second grade through adulthood people called me names like hippo, elephant, even sumo. With those names seared into my subconscious I agonized for years with diets, pills, anorexia, insecurity. Even as a baggy size four that branding appeared when I looked in the mirror, linking my identity to the shape of my body, leaving deep scars.

> Hebrews 12:1
> *Let us also lay aside every encumbrance and the sin which so easily entangles us, and let us run with endurance the race that is set before us.*

There can be no fertile soil for the fruit of kindness and joy to grow when the roots of insecurity and unforgiveness threaten to choke and smother. The Holy Spirit transforms the mind, feeding, watering, nurturing, pruning. He cleanses the soil of the heart and pulls out, by the roots, no whacking here, the sin that so easily entangles.

It's essential to walk by the Spirit daily in order to be a cleansed vessel for His fruit to grow. Frustrating circumstances, impulsive family members, our own bitter roots affect our choices to be sure. But the writer of Hebrews gives us encouragement on how to overcome.

> *. . . . let us run the race that we have to run with patience, our eyes fixed on Jesus the source and the goal of our faith.*

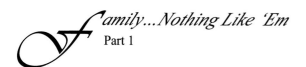

Family...Nothing Like 'Em

Part 1

Matthew
12:50
*"For whoever
does the will of
My Father who is
in heaven, he is
My brother and
sister and mother."*

Friday morning I sat on a bench outside a department store watching dozens of shoppers come and go. Parents, children, grands, cousins, aunts, uncles all looking for the perfect gift for that special someone. Babies cooed, children giggled. Okay, a few whined. Laughter, needling, even a little tickling was the norm.

There were a few grouchy grumps, but the greater percentage thoroughly enjoyed their loved ones. Some hurried, catching a glimpse of their watches. Others shouted, "On to the next store." An elderly couple strolled hand in hand, obviously cherishing every moment together.

What did Jesus mean when He said:

"For whoever does the will of My Father who is in heaven, he is My brother and sister and mother?"

Uppermost in the Father's heart is for us to believe He sent His Son as our Savior and to love Him with our whole being.

Jesus spent His time with what we might call, extended family. Men who ministered right alongside Him day in and day out for three years. Jesus deeply loved these men, even before He called them out of their chosen professions to follow Him.

JUNE 21

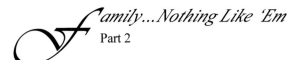

Love has a way of capturing our hearts, blocking inhibitions, doubts, uncertainties. We are powerfully drawn to love like no other emotion.

Of course, we all like being with people who are funny, even a little crazy, and those who have a positive attitude. Happy people just make us smile when we're with them. Still, that positive, funny, happy attitude may not hold up under the pressure and stress of another's pain or anxiety.

> John
> 1:12
> *But as many as received Him [Jesus Christ], to them He gave the right to become children of God, even to those who believe in His name.*

Love, however, real Holy Spirit-driven love, the kind Jesus gave away, has the power to listen to a broken heart, embrace a lonely soul, accept the short-comings and faults that glare under the scrutiny of gossip, pride, insecurity.

Sitting outside that department store watching the joyous family interactions did cause my heart to ache a bit. But God made a way for me to sit in the precious embrace of extended family during that weekend. Received, accepted and loved on; we laughed uproariously, cried joyous tears and gave praises to our Father who is in heaven.

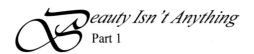

Beauty Isn't Anything
Part 1

Matthew
23:27
THE MESSAGE
"You're hopeless,
you religion
scholars and
Pharisees! Frauds!
You're like
manicured
grave plots, grass
clipped and the
flowers bright, but
six feet down it's all
rotting bones
and worm-eaten
flesh."

Hike our twenty acres and you'll discover a diverse accumulation of plants, shrubs, flowers, trees. One particular plant would add magnificent color to any floral arrangement. However outer beauty does not always reflect what lies within.

I know first-hand how deceitful outer beauty can be. In the Fall Southern Oregon's poison oak boasts a beautiful deep mauve. A minuscule drop of the plant's oil can trigger a severe rash, blister outbreak, intolerable pain and insufferable itching.

For me, the outbreak came on subtly, a little redness here, slight itching there. Ultimately I experienced the full effects; rash, blisters, pain and itching over seventy-five percent of my body. What would you expect when one hugs numerous bundles of this 'lovely' vegetation for three hours? Not a pretty sight.

Enslaved by the loathsome poison I was confined to bed for two weeks. In the span of a month the poison oak rebounded twice, each time with increased severity. It took potent medication to counteract the poison.

So like sin don't you think? Sin appears extremely attractive on the outside, but when we grab hold and indulge, sin's deadly poison contaminates our soul.

JUNE 23

Sin contaminates the soul. Even when we stop sinning the residue known as consequences remains. Sometimes sin is so intriguing it rebounds and entices us back, causing even greater corruption and guilt.

Most can relate to King David's prayer:

All my insides are on fire, my body is a wreck. I'm on my last legs; I've had it— my life is a vomit of groans. Lord, my longings are sitting in plain sight, my groans an old story to you. My heart's about to break; I'm a burned-out case. Cataracts blind me to God and good . . I'm on the edge of losing it—the pain in my gut keeps burning. I'm ready to tell my story of failure, I'm no longer smug in my sin
(Psalm 38:7-10, 17, 18 THE MESSAGE*).*

Psalm
38:3-6
THE MESSAGE
I've lost twenty pounds in two months because of your accusation. My bones are brittle as dry sticks because of my sin. I'm swamped by my bad behavior, collapsed under gunnysacks of guilt. The cuts in my flesh stink and grow maggots because I've lived so badly. And now I'm flat on my face feeling sorry for myself morning to night.

Freedom from the poison oak came through an extremely powerful antidote. Likewise freedom from sin comes through the most powerful antidote known to man—the blood of Jesus Christ.

Spiritual Complacency
Part 1

Revelation
3:15, 16
AMPLIFIED
*I know your
[record of] works
and what you are
doing; you are
neither cold nor
hot. Would that
you were cold or
hot! So, because
you are lukewarm,
and neither cold
nor hot, I will
spew you out
of My mouth!*

The state of being lukewarm or complacent is best described as indifference or apathy.

We cannot allow apathy to take root. Only stale words and platitudes come from it. God's creative glory is stifled in the cozy chair of complacency.

Spiritual complacency is like a weed that coils around the spirit and chokes the excitement and expectancy out of belonging to Jesus Christ. It discreetly sprouts, causing us to inconspicuously blend in. Like a weed, complacency depletes us of the energy and fervency we once had.

Remember as a new Christian how you couldn't wait to make new discoveries in the Bible? Everything you read became a revelation of immense proportions.

When was the last time you were excited over something God revealed from His word. You were so blown away that you set your Bible down and whispered in awe, "Wow."

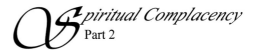

2 Timothy
1:6, 7
GNT
For this reason I remind you to keep alive the gift that God gave you when I laid my hands on you. For the Spirit that God has given us does not make us timid; instead, his Spirit fills us with power, love, and self-control.

Has corporate worship become mechanical? Does your mind wander from one thing to another rather then reflecting on the character, power, wonder of God? Has your heart become hollow, your soul sapped?

Complacency!

Like a weed that eclipses and chokes out the more desirable plants, the comfortable condition of complacency keeps us from encountering the more desirable works and experiences of God.

Why is it so difficult to break out of this comfy mold and jump headlong into the exciting world God has planned for our lives?

Fear. Laziness. Contentment with the ordinary. Lack of trust. Insecurity.

Fear keeps us frozen in the common everyday world of apprehension. Laziness leads to lethargy. Contentment with the ordinary is tedious boredom at its worse. Lack of trust is always a faith issue. Insecurity keeps us wringing our hands in anxious anticipation of 'what if'.

Oswald Chambers said:
"Self-complacency and spiritual pride are always the beginning of degeneration. When I begin to be satisfied with where I am spiritually, I begin to degenerate."

Spiritual Complacency
Part 3

2 Timothy
1:8, 9
GNT
Do not be ashamed, then, of witnessing for our Lord; nor be ashamed of me, a prisoner for Christ's sake. Instead, take your part in suffering for the Good News, as God gives you the strength to do it. He saved us and called us to be his own people, not because of what we have done, but because of his own purpose and grace. He gave us this grace by means of Christ Jesus before the beginning of time.

God has a spiritual adventure just waiting for us. He wants to use our surrendered lives to testify of, yes and even suffer for, the gospel. God reveals His glory through the gifts, talents, abilities He created in us when we were conceived.

You've heard it said God has a plan for your life. Do you know what that plan is? Are you living it to the fullest?

God is always at work. If we are not moving forward in our walk with Him {knowledge, understanding, experience, excitement} then we are growing lethargic and stagnant.

Anyone out there want Jesus to spew {or as the NASB says vomit} you out of His mouth? Living in a lukewarm spiritual state is not an option. Let's live the adventure!

How would you handle a devastating catastrophe?
Consider those financially 'secure' thanks to
lucrative jobs, dot.com techs for example. Many
computer technicians received six figure salaries,
living lavish lifestyles only to loose it all when their
profession went bust. Probably not in their business
plan.

> Proverbs
> 27:1
> *Do not boast about*
> *tomorrow, for you do*
> *not know what a day*
> *may bring forth.*

Some of us have difficulty managing today, let alone consider tomorrow.
Jesus said we are not to be anxious for tomorrow, today holds enough trouble
of its own. Are we borrowing trouble by planning ahead?

Certainly there are occasions when a plan is necessary. Say, vacation.
Without the initiative it's unlikely a seat will be waiting for you on the
airplane when it's time to depart.

As a good steward of the finances and possessions God provides, investing
for the future is often wise. Nevertheless you're playing the fool without
God's input. God alone knows the future and the plans He has for you.

You may not receive an immediate, clear directive from God. Be patient.
Wait on Him. It boils down to trusting God to handle your future. Don't let
yourself become weary in waiting and take on those projects yourself. Huge
mistake. Huge.

The point is, we should not spout off about how successful our future will be.
God would have us boast in knowing Him, not in our accomplishments.

Expectantly Excited
Part 1

Psalm
37:7
*Be still in the
LORD and wait
longingly for Him.*

We are a people of quickness. Do it now, get it done. Speed. Hurry. Rush to the next thing. Instant results and immediate outcomes. When our computer takes longer than a nano-second to pull something up, we drum our fingers, tap our feet, roll our eyes, mumble under our breath giving way to heavy sighs and annoyance.

When we make an effort to rest, read a good book, take a bubble bath, stroll through the park, write a letter, watch a favorite movie or take a nap {you're kidding, right} we feel guilty for not doing something productive.

Where did all this busy-ness, this listening and adhering to the expectations of others come from? Certainly not God. God wants us. Our companionship, not what we *do* for Him.

What does it mean to wait longingly or patiently for the Lord? I've heard some say, "Well, it doesn't mean we just sit by idly and do nothing." While others insist to wait patiently is to remain in readiness or expectation of what is to come.

When we wait expectantly {longingly} for the Lord we also listen intently for His voice in our spirit. We watch with eager excitement to see Him carry out His purpose.

Ever known a time when you felt the need to take things into your own hands and accomplish a task your way rather than wait on the Lord?

> Psalm
> 62:5
> *My soul, wait in silence for God only, for my hope is from Him.*

Are we really better at this than God? Ah, no. We may think we have the best strategy as we make a valiant effort to put it into action, but it's impossible to outmaneuver God's flawless purpose. In His perfect time.

God may choose to reveal His plan through something we would never have considered. He might use someone we don't even know or possibly wow us with unbelievable phenomenas. How and when are up to Him. I can think of several times when I waited on God and was awestruck by the results.

Paul wrote to the Romans:

> *but hope that is seen is not hope; for who hopes for what he already sees? But if we hope for what we do not see, with perseverance we wait eagerly for it (Romans 8:25).*

Real faith says—don't just wait patiently or longingly for God, wait expectantly, knowing His will always comes to fruition. Then eagerly watch to see how He does it.

July

Adoration

Inspiration

Awe

Elevation

Reverence

Relationship

Eternity

Faith

Grace

Truth

Life

Infinite Knowledge

Always

Forever

Never-ending

More of You
less of me
More of You
not more of what You can do for me

rowing In Faith
Part 1

Matthew
9:28
*When He entered
the house, the
blind men came
up to Him, and
Jesus said to them,
"Do you believe
that I am able to
do this?" They
said to Him,
"Yes, Lord."*

When I read this passage I thought, *is there any doubt*?

Has Jesus ever asked you if you believe He is able? Was your need so great that you answered as the blind men did, "Yes, Lord?"

How many of us *really* believe the Bible is the infallible, undisputable word of God? That God created everything in heaven and on earth, flooded the whole earth saving a small remnant, did and does miraculous things, i.e., plagues, manna, healing, protecting, providing for His people?

Do we believe Jesus is the prophesied Messiah, born of a virgin, lived a sinless life, died and shed His blood for all mankind so they could stand righteous and pure before the Father to have an intimate relationship with Him? That Jesus was raised from the dead and is God incarnate? That nothing is impossible for God?

Why then don't we live like it?

If we believe every word of the Bible is divinely inspired we ought to believe God will bring every promise and prophecy to pass.

If we believe Jesus is able to do all things why is it so difficult to trust Him, not merely with the big things we have no control over, but the small seemingly insignificant day-to-day issues?

> Matthew
> 9:29
> *Then He touched their eyes, saying, "It shall be done to you according to your faith."*

I remember a time when my husband and I were uncertain whether we were to buy property.
After making an offer we traveled several hours to perform 'due diligence'; checking taxes, building codes, county requirements, utility options. With only days before due diligence was to run out, our stress level was off the chart.

While at the county offices, diligently progressing from one department to the next, my husband was on the phone trying to find an engineer to check the slopes and details of the property. Things were not going well when I took a walk to the ladies' room. Alone in there, I heard in my spirit as clearly as if God had spoken aloud, "Do you trust Me, Anne?"

I looked around and responded out loud, *"Yes Lord I trust You."*

† "Do you *really* trust Me?"

"Yes Lord I really trust You."

I went to my husband and told him we needed to stop the process and withdraw our offer. He was beyond relief.

Mark
9:23
*And Jesus said to
him, " 'If You can?
All things are
possible to him
who believes."*

Nothing is impossible for God.

Even though disappointed and in tears after stopping the process of the purchase our twenty-acre 'dream' property, I knew if this was not the property for us then God had something better. I had no doubt this was what God wanted us to do. Maybe He was testing my faith. I don't know.

Some months later the property came to us at a reduced price and at the perfect time. We now reside in the beautiful home my husband built {he took on the general contractor position, something he had never done before} overlooking rich farmland with towering mountains in the distance.

My point is, if we believe Jesus is able, that all things are possible to him who believes, then we have to put shoe leather to our convictions and demonstrate it in our lives, even when we cannot see the end result.

Growing in faith sometimes requires testing. And absolutely no doubting.

Have you ever felt your life sinking into a miry pit? Panic to get free causes you to descend further into the bog, thinking if you devise an escape plan, your independence will be imminent. Unfortunately your struggles initiate a slippery descent into the cavernous abyss until you feel swallowed up by your circumstances.

Recently I chose to take matters into my own hands believing if I simply advanced through my well-thought-out steps of redemption, the climb out of the pit to freedom would be an easy task. Regrettably my plan failed as each movement 'to make it happen' caused me to slip deeper into the quagmire of my own destruction.

Why would God repeatedly rescue us when we cry out to Him?

The reasons for His interventions are limitless. This passage unveils five; to make our footsteps firm, put a new song in our mouths, sing praises to God, so many will see and fear and, last but certainly not least, to trust the Lord.

When our footsteps are made firm, we no longer struggle with *maybe* escaping the pit.

> Psalm
> 40:1-3
> *I waited patiently for the LORD; and He inclined to me, and heard my cry. He brought me up out of the pit of destruction, out of the miry clay; and He set my feet upon a rock making my footsteps firm. And He put a new song in my mouth, a song of praise to our God; many will see and fear, and will trust in the LORD.*

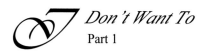

Exodus
3:11, 12
But Moses said to God, "Who am I, that I should go". . . . God answered, "I will be with You."

Responsibility. Fourteen letters clumped together to say we are liable, answerable, accountable. Not a word I've taken kindly to.

Webster's defines responsibility:
The quality or state of being responsible - moral, legal or mental accountability [an obligation or willingness to accept responsibility or to account for one's actions].

Not long ago God made it clear the phrase, 'I don't want to' could no longer be part of my stockpile of words. The word He gave to replace it? Yep you guessed it. Responsibility.

In all honesty I have run from that fourteen-letter word for years. Time to stop running *from* what I consider a burden and run *to* God. With that admonition God began the process of training me to answer for my conduct and obligations. It does not come natural to me.

Adam and Eve said the same thing. 'I don't want to' do what God instructed. I want to do what I want to do. Sin, plain and simple. No wonder God cut that phrase from my vocabulary. With those words, I was saying I want my way, not His.

Moses did not want the responsibility of speaking to Israel's elders or Pharaoh or leading millions out of bondage. Now *that's* responsibility. Right there at the burning bush God began the training process, preparing Moses for his destiny.

Moses needed to stop giving God 'I don't want to' excuses and allow God to accomplish His perfect, albeit overwhelming plan, by using His *not-so-sure-I-can-do-this* servant.

> Exodus
> 4:10
> *Then Moses said to the Lord, "Please, Lord, I have never been eloquent, neither recently nor in time past, nor since You have spoken to Your servant; for I am slow of speech and slow of tongue."*

Humm. Sound familiar? Uncertainty, fear of the unknown, situations we have no control over. How can we survive the process let alone reach our destiny?

Trust.

God told Moses, "I will be with you." Do we really believe that when dealing with the uncertainties of life? As with Moses, when God calls us, He promises to go with us. Step by tiny step. A truly transformed life requires us to stop telling God 'I don't want to'.

To reach our God-given destiny we must shout an unequivocal 'yes' to responsibility. Even when the direction seems completely out of our control.

Exactly. Precisely.

Responsibility. Trusting God even more.

Stepping Out
Part 1

Joshua
1:7, 8
*Only be strong
and very
courageous; be
careful to do
according to all
the law which
Moses My servant
commanded you;
do not turn from it
to the right or to
the left, so that
you may have
success wherever
you go. This book
of the law shall
not depart from
your mouth, but
you shall meditate
on it day and night,
so that you may be
careful to do
according to all
that is written in it;
for then you will
make your way
prosperous, and
then you will have
success.*

What exactly is success and how do we attain it? Success in the eyes of the world might consist of wealth, acquisition of a top position in the workplace, a university degree or two, reaching a set goal, overcoming adversity, paying off your mortgage and as they used to do in the old days, have a mortgage burning party.

Perhaps success is owning a business or when the book you've written reaches the bestseller list.

When I think of successful people my mind runs to the man who encourages the homeless into a new life, the hospice nurse whose compassion, kindness, patience, takes a grieving family through an extremely difficult time.

High on the list is the missionary who cares not about personal possessions, but to see lost souls find eternal salvation in Jesus Christ.

What is success?

Think about the handicapped woman who after years of struggle, at the age of thirty-five, receives her college diploma or the janitor who shows up every night for work for years, a smile on his face and a good word for his co-workers. There are doctors, nurses, teachers and others whose definition of success is caring for people.

> Joshua
> 1:9
> *"Have I not commanded you? Be strong and courageous! Do not tremble or be dismayed, for the LORD your God is with you wherever you go."*

Successful heroes in my eyes.

Joshua is one such hero. Joshua cared for God's people and trusted God to do the impossible; to enter, take control of, live in the promise land. The key to his success? Joshua knew God, loved Him with his whole being and trusted Him.

I heard a pastor suggest after Joshua's mentor, Moses, died he must have felt like, "I can't do this." God told Joshua *four times* to be strong and courageous. Along with that command God gave him three promises.

- Your future is secure
- I will provide all you need
- I will be with you

If we take heed, step out and *do* according to God's word we need not be afraid of what lies ahead or discouraged in the midst of seemingly impossible situations. For the Lord our God is with us wherever we go.

> Habakkuk
> 3:17-19
> *Though the fig tree should not blossom, and there be no fruit on the vines, though the yield of the olive should fail, and the fields produce no food, though the flock should be cut off from the fold and there be no cattle in the stalls, yet I will exult in the LORD, will rejoice in the God of my salvation. The Lord GOD is my strength.*

Today we would say, "Though . . . the stock market crashes, imports cause a decline in the sale of products, my company downsizes, my retirement is lost to embezzlement, a natural disaster wipes out everything I own, unemployment takes all my savings, my car is repossessed . . . I will exult in the Lord. He is my salvation. He has given me the hope of eternity and the promise to be my strength while here on earth."

Habakkuk would not allow any type of catastrophe to rob him of the one thing that mattered most, his relationship with God. Habakkuk desired God more than *anything*. He determined to love and praise God above all else. Can we say the same?

In the midst of the most horrific circumstances or when my petty, paltry, pathetic pride puts me in a panic, I praise God in the form of a poem or a song. Humbling my heart and praising God brings me into His presence.

We are a needy people in constant need of something.

Often unable to distinguish need from want. We want a new vehicle, we need contentment. We want a slimmer body, we need perseverance. We want a better position, we need humility. We want to escape pain, suffering, loneliness, we need I AM.

> Exodus
> 3:14
> *God said to Moses,*
> *"I AM WHO I AM";*
> *and He said, "Thus*
> *you shall say to the*
> *sons of Israel, 'I AM*
> *has sent me to you.' "*

Who is this I AM? Having pondered that question for years, I've considered some rather uncanny scenarios, injecting I AM to see if He is.

Lost in the forest no sense of which way to go – I AM the way
Arrested for a crime I did not commit – I AM your defense. I AM the truth
Attacked by terrorists, bomb in hand ready to detonate – I AM your peace
Down to my last five dollars, no place to go – I AM your provider. I AM
     your shelter
In a foreign country tortured for my faith – I AM the light that shines
     through you. I AM your covering. I AM your strong tower
Death of a spouse or child – I AM your comforter
Too much to do, not enough time – I AM your secret quiet place
What's next? What should I do? – I AM your shepherd

Allow your mind to deliberate the frailties of life. Hopeless situations. Impossible dilemmas. Unimaginable circumstances.

I AM is with you.

> **1 Peter 2:21**
>
> *For you have been called for this purpose, since Christ also suffered for you, leaving you an example for you to follow in His steps.*

We are instructed more than once in Scripture to abide by Christ's example. Jesus Himself charged us to do as He did and to learn from Him.

What would it look like to follow in Jesus' steps, to live according to His example? When we look through the gospel accounts Jesus modeled love, patience, kindness, humility, compassion, righteous anger, obedience, faith, joy, wisdom, trust, knowledge, leadership, strength, self control, authority, peace.

Whew.

One of the most remarkable examples Jesus set for us was His total surrender to the Father. Jesus did nothing apart from the Father. The things He spoke, His teaching, the miracles He performed, the power He displayed, came directly from His Father.

Looking at Jesus' example we have to admit there is no way we can live the same kind of life by our own means. Jesus said we can do nothing apart from Him. Any good work we aspire to accomplish for God is simply hay and stubble unless we abide in Jesus and accept and anticipate His power flowing through us.

We have no power of our own. Only the supernatural power of God working within and through us has kingdom value.

Imagine what our lives would be like if we followed Jesus' example and asked God to reveal His will through the power of the Holy Spirit in all we speak and do.

What an amazing adventure that would be. Not only that, God also promises to give us everything we need to accomplish His will.

Is it really possible for us mere mortals to follow Christ's example? Nothing is impossible with God. The apostle Paul said in order to live this kind of life we must walk by the Spirit, be led by the Spirit and live in the Spirit. It is a moment by moment thing.

There's a saying that goes like this: inch-by-inch everything is a cinch, yard-by-yard everything is hard. What if we began today with the small everyday things and determine in our hearts to do nothing on our own, but ask the Holy Spirit to do His supernatural kingdom work through us?

Imagine the possibilities.

John
14:12
NCV
"I tell you the truth, whoever believes in me will do the same things that I do. Those who believe will do even greater things than these, because I am going to the Father."

Live Not For Results
Part 1

Luke 6:46
"Why do you call Me, 'Lord, Lord,' and do not do what I say?"

John 12:26
"If anyone serves Me, he must follow Me; and where I am, there My servant will be also; if anyone serves Me, the Father will honor him."

A dear friend gave me an incredibly beautiful, thought-provoking book, *A Blossom in the Desert*. It is a compilation of the art and profound writings of Lilias Trotter, a missionary to the Arab people in North Africa in the late 1800's early 1900's.

While meditating on her exquisite paintings and divinely inspired insights, I learned that Lilias did not live to see results. She lived to serve God. Lilias had a spiritual mindset that caused her to garner significant wisdom from the everyday trials we all experience. Even though they may have been extremely difficult, demanding or challenging, she worked through them, then let them go.

A Blossom in the Desert has given thought to, "Am I 'doing' to further my agenda and see results or to serve God?"

The apostle Paul called himself a bond-servant {one bound and devoted to his Master by choice} of Jesus Christ in a permanent relationship of servitude for life. Paul wanted nothing to bring attention to himself, but wanted Jesus to receive every bit of glory.

Learning *and* living these lessons is not an easy task. Heavy sigh.

It seems no matter how hard I try to live a life that glorifies God, I continually revert back to what *I* want, not what honors God. Therein lies the rub . . . *no matter how hard I try.*

How do we give up our own right to ourselves and dedicate our lives to the purpose of serving and glorifying Jesus? Is it possible to live with this view in our media-filled, activity-based, accomplishment seeking, day-to-day lives?

Laying aside of self is accomplished only by the Holy Spirit. We are encouraged to keep on being filled with the Holy Spirit's power. This daily power filling gives us the ability to live not for results, but to serve God.

1 Peter
4:11
Whoever speaks, is to do so as one who is speaking the utterances of God; whoever serves is to do so as one who is serving by the strength which God supplies; so that in all things God may be glorified through Jesus Christ, to whom belongs the glory and dominion forever and ever.

So if God has called you to evangelize—evangelize lovingly. If He has called you to pray—pray fervently, to speak—speak as God's messenger. If you are to teach—teach wisely. Whatever God has put in your heart to do to serve Him, do it passionately. And do it now.

Matthew 14:23 THE MESSAGE

With the crowd dispersed, he climbed the mountain so he could be by himself and pray. He stayed there alone, late into the night.

S-L-O-W D-O-W-N

That's the message God has been impressing upon me lately. Sometimes I even make myself take slow, deliberate steps through the house to remind me to slow down. After all, what's the hurry?

I know, I know, places to go, people to see, deals to make, things to accomplish. And was Jesus' time any less hectic and demanding? He had just fed five thousand men plus women and children for goodness sake.

Thousands vied for Jesus' attention, numerous towns sought His presence. Still Jesus had one desire, to accomplish His Father's will. To know what that was He had to slow down, take time out of the busyness to hear His Father's voice.

Notice in those quiet hours Jesus didn't hang out with His pals or even read a good scroll. He went *alone* for refreshment, renewal, revitalization by His Father.

My friend says we ought to sit down alone every afternoon with a fresh brewed cup of coffee and talk to God about the day or anything for that matter. To thank Him for all His wondrous works.

A favorite anonymous quote comes to mind:
"In solitude I sit quietly and listen to whispers of His wisdom."

Being a widow you'd think I'd have plenty of idle hours to sit, pray, listen to God. Oh, the emptiness is there, all around me and in my heart, but as far as having *extra* time—not at all.

My responsibilities now include the few chores I had when my husband was here as well as the multitude he did. Every day is filled with what needs doing. Perhaps that is why God continually impresses upon my spirit to slow down. So I can hear Him, be refreshed, renewed, revitalized in order to accomplish His will.

Mark
1:35
In the early morning, while it was still dark, Jesus got up, left the house, and went away to a secluded place, and was praying there.

Yesterday afternoon while sitting on my porch, a fresh brewed cup of coffee in hand, I indulged my senses in the midst of a rain and hail deluge. Lightning flashed in the distant mountains, the boom and bellow of thunder shook the earth, the scent of wet hay in the fields nurtured thoughts of childhood days. Cool breezes encouraged me to slow down long enough to thank God for every bit of it.

I sat there and talked with God about life. It made me wonder if that's what Jesus did when He stopped His work, sent the crowds away and took time to be with His Father.

Unbearable Words
Part 1

Matthew 26:37
And He [Jesus] took with Him Peter and the two sons of Zebedee, and began to be grieved and distressed.

It's funny how words affect us. In the not too distant past, words like believe, trust, faithful flashed bold before me each time I read the Bible. Now as I read widow, heaven, grief, jump off the page.

Did you know at one time Jesus was so grieved and distressed he said, "My soul is deeply grieved to the point of death?" Jesus agonized over the burden he was soon to bear. Many would say He felt this way because He knew the horrific physical pain He would have to endure. Others think He understood the tremendous weight of the world's sin He would have placed wholly upon Him.

I tend to believe the separation between Jesus and His Father, something He had never experienced before, caused His agony. Even in this state, complete surrender of His will and His flesh ushered in redemption, hope and peace.

Note Jesus surrendered *before* the sacrifice and pain began. How many of us can say the same?

God will carry us. He walks with us through every trial and heartache. But are we willing to surrender our will and trust Him *before* the circumstances become unbearable?

God will carry us. He walks with us through every trial and heartache. But are we willing to surrender our will and trust Him *before* the circumstances become unbearable?

King David wrote:
> *Weeping may last for the night, but a shout of joy comes in the morning (Psalm 30:5).*

Hebrews 12:2, 3
NET
He [Jesus] suffered death on the cross. But he accepted the shame as if it were nothing because of the joy that God put before him. And now he is sitting at the right side of God's throne. Think about Jesus' example. He held on while wicked people were doing evil things to him. So do not get tired and stop trying.

He's right. Joy is not dependent upon circumstances or feelings. Joy, as Jesus experienced in the Garden of Gethsemane, comes through obedience to the point of death, surrender without holding anything back, giving up my will for God's *before* circumstances take their toll.

Joy is not a feeling, it is believing and trusting God before and in the midst of the worst possible conditions. Jesus trusted and obeyed for one purpose, to honor His Father.

Daily I look to Jesus' example in this dark aloneness of widowhood.

Words are powerful. God's word is the only thing I know that can supernaturally transform my mind, heal my heart and bring joy from sorrow.

Limited Power–Hardly

Numbers 11:23

The LORD said to Moses, "Is the LORD'S power limited? Now you shall see whether My word will come true for you or not."

How is it we question God's power, the very authority of His word? God is not man that He should lie. Whatever God says—happens. Still, haven't we all read something in the Bible and stopped to wonder, could that really be true? I know I have.

It's funny how even the tiniest doubt or unbelieving thought about what God says in His word brings disruption to the peace that was there only moments before.

Authentic peace comes when we trust God's immutable power no matter what's going on in our life. The good. Bad. Frustrating. Exhilarating. Exasperating. Exciting. Or even the dull and drab.

The Lord's power is *not* limited. It is limitless.

Good grief, He laid the foundation of the earth. Holds the stars, planets, universes {billions of them} in the sky. The Lord commands the morning and causes the dawn to know its place. He places boundaries upon the sea. He sends forth lightning and puts wisdom in the innermost being.

He is God Almighty. He created us to trust His word and to live securely in His peace.

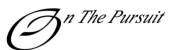

Success – the attainment of wealth, favor or eminence.

I wonder if God's definition of success agrees with Webster's?

Paul in his letter to the Corinthians reminds us we exist to love, know and honor God. As Jesus' example exhibits, the display of real love begins with a pure passionate pursuit of God.

> Romans
> 8:28
> *And we know that God causes all things to work together for good to those who love God, to those who are called according to His purpose.*

Sometimes we get so caught up in living life we forget the One who gives it. Suffering. Trials. Frustration. Persecution. God uses them not only to test and humble us, but to prepare us for what lies ahead. To cause us to diligently and passionately pursue Him.

God defines success as loving Him above all else.

May we never forget God continually lavishes His love in the midst of suffering, trials, frustration, persecution. All the while confirming His faithfulness. Nothing is ever wasted when ill-fated trials bring us closer to the realization that God really does cause all things to work together for good. And this good always points to God's grace.

If in the midst of life's struggles we can say as the psalmist did, "I will yet praise Him [God]," we are well on our way to success.

Proverbs 10:9

He who walks in integrity walks securely, but he who perverts his ways will be found out.

Integrity. Someone has said that integrity is who you are when no one else is around. That being said, how does your mind run and where do your actions lead?

One of the great benefits of living an upright life of integrity is the security that accompanies it. The Bible says when you live a life of integrity you will be secure in your conscience, your dealings with others, your standing in the community. An upright life is evident. There is never a doubt you can be trusted.

God is a shield to those who walk in integrity. Doesn't that give you a definite sense of security? This walking in integrity plays a major role in the lives of those who truly love God.

But I ask you, how can we possibly live this incorruptible life in today's world? Like most things, it's a choice. Sometimes a tough choice brought on by pressure to please someone other than God.

Do we want to express our love for God and honor Him or do we want the accolades and acceptance of others?

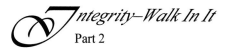

We walk in integrity by knowing and living according to God's word, not just occasionally, but continually. The Holy Spirit is with us to encourage, enlighten, decipher, discern, direct, convict, convince us of the necessity to listen, trust and obey.

> Job
> 31:5, 6
> *"If I have walked with falsehood, and my foot has hastened after deceit, let Him weigh me with accurate scales, and let God know my integrity."*

What joy to live securely and not have to constantly look over our shoulder or keep track of what's been said so we don't have to cover our not-so-honest words and actions.

Not one of us comes to Jesus with a perfect life of integrity. But once we belong to Him we have forgiveness for all past, present, future sins.

We have the opportunity to begin anew and determine to live a life of integrity. Oh, it won't be perfect by any means, but it can be a joy-filled life when our heart is wholly devoted to Jesus and His will.

Think of it, no matter what took place before, infused with the power of the Holy Spirit we can choose to walk in integrity from this moment forward.

$\mathcal{E}$nduring For Joy's Sake

Jesus encouraged his disciples to have faith and believe. He wanted them to follow His lead, to endure their sufferings to the death, emboldening them with the reality that after His death He would see them again. The grave had no hold over Jesus nor does it have a hold over those who trust in Him.

Many would question, "If God loved me He would rescue me from this horrible situation." The Bible is full of real life examples of suffering, the very things our lives are made of. And God *did* rescue us by allowing the brutal sacrifice and horrendous suffering of His Son so we could know redemption, reconciliation, the certainty of heaven.

The apostle Peter tells us to rejoice when we share in the sufferings of Christ. Could it be when we suffer loss, pain, sorrow, we are able to empathize, just the tiniest bit, with Christ's sufferings?

This joy James talks about does not come from the suffering or troubles. It comes from knowing Jesus and His assurance of the end result.

Someone once asked me, "What do you fear?" At the time I could not think of a single thing. Pretty naive. The absence of fear epitomizes courage. Right?

Proverbs
3:26
For the LORD will be your confidence and will keep your foot from being caught.

It has been said, "True courage is not the absence of fear—but the willingness to proceed in spite of it." This type of courage recently played out before my eyes.

A young man, probably mid-twenties, wearing dark glasses and a backpack, firmly clasped the handle of a leather harness attached to a seeing-eye dog that moved close alongside him. The two paused at a crosswalk where I waited in my car for the light to turn green.

Head up, face pointed toward the opposite side of the street, the young man spoke to his faithful Golden Lab. The dog moved forward and the man stepped off the curb into the street where traffic whirled furiously crosswise. He walked with confidence as if he could see everything around him. Exhibiting no fear, he put a tremendous amount of trust in his companion.

I was struck by the man's incredible courage and fortitude causing me to question if while trembling in emotional darkness do I put my confidence in Almighty God? Do I wear the same face of courage?

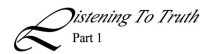

John
8:43, 44
NIV
Why is my language not clear to you? Because you are unable to hear what I say. You belong to your father, the devil, and you want to carry out your father's desire. He was a murderer from the beginning, not holding to the truth, for there is no truth in him. When he lies, he speaks his native language, for he is a liar and the father of lies.

Ladies . . . and . . . Gentlemen

Presenting the magnificent, colossal, creative, stupendous, inspiring, talented, unbelievably humble, {deep breath} the one and only . . . ME.

I saw a lot of this kind of ego at teen camp. I also saw a lot of healing breakthroughs only God could have orchestrated.

These kids come to camp with a shatterproof, impenetrable, laser resistant protective shield around their arcane insecurities and fragile sense of self-worth, only to leave with their defenses dismantled and hearts unlocked, wide open to the love, compassion, kindness, of God, their peers and *the* most incredible staff.

If our adversary, the devil, can't get us one way he'll use another. He prowls about intent on wreaking havoc on our souls. One day he leads us to believe we are the most astonishing human beings ever created.

The next he reminds us how despicably prideful, vile, undeserving we are, bringing to mind that we just cannot get it right.

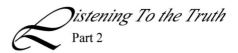

The devil uses every lie and devious scheme imaginable to get our focus off God, to distract us from His plan.

But it's not always the devil that 'made us do it'. There are other forces contributing to our distance from God. Our flesh, that old sin-filled man{woman} intended to be left behind at the cross, weasels its way into our thoughts ushering our actions into, shall we say, something less than hoped for—unholy and independent of God's influence.

The world around us and those in it seductively entice us into the pit of debauchery and sin where many reside. Isn't it supposed to be the other way around? Aren't followers of Jesus Christ meant to draw the world up out of the muck into His glorious presence?

1 Peter
5:9, 10
But resist him [devil], firm in your faith, knowing that the same experiences of suffering are being accomplished by your brethren who are in the world. After you have suffered for a little while, the God of all grace, who called you to His eternal glory in Christ, will Himself perfect, confirm, strengthen and establish you.

The battle is fierce, but God, through the power of the Holy Spirit, equips and leads us.

When tempted to believe the enemy's lies fill your mind with God's truth. Implant those crucial, imperative Bible passages in your memory. The truth of God's word has the power to thwart and overcome the enemy.

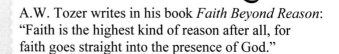

**1 Peter
1:8
NCV**
You have not seen Christ, but still you love him. You cannot see him now, but you believe in him. So you are filled with a joy that cannot be explained, joy full of glory.

A.W. Tozer writes in his book *Faith Beyond Reason*: "Faith is the highest kind of reason after all, for faith goes straight into the presence of God."

When tragedy strikes it can cause one to question, even doubt. November 2009 I bought a new Bible. On several occasions while reading I wrote in the margin; do you believe? Each time I asked myself that question along came myriad more.

• Did God really create the heavens and earth
• Is there a heaven
• Does God still love us even though we sin
• Is the Bible living and active as it says
• Is Jesus really the Messiah
• Am I saved
• Is God who He says He is
• Are God's promises true
• Will God always be with me
• What does the manifest presence of God look like

So I went searching for answers. Both the Old and New Testaments are filled with people who experienced God's manifest presence. Although described and experienced in different ways, the effect is always the same . . .

Speechless wonder.

"Do you believe?"

If you have ever sensed God's majestic presence right where you stood, you would shout, "Yes." In God's presence there is that sense of immense power, yet heart-bursting love consuming every thought.

> Matthew
> 1:23
> NLT
> *"Look! The virgin will conceive a child! She will give birth to a son, and they will call him Immanuel, which means 'God is with us.'"*

In His manifest presence one senses consoling peace, confident protection, unwarranted provision, excessive grace, eager anticipation, spontaneous excitement, sheer joy, unadulterated awe.

Christians always have God's presence in the person of the Holy Spirit living inside them. Some however, are wary of believing in God's manifest presence. They struggle to follow Jesus' example and live out radical faith. To believe for more then what they see or feel.

Yet those yearning for more of God, the Holy Spirit calmly, gracefully introduces His supernatural realm into their physical, natural world. Causing those who experience it . . .

Speechless wonder.

 Welcome Home
Part 1

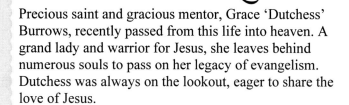

Precious saint and gracious mentor, Grace 'Dutchess' Burrows, recently passed from this life into heaven. A grand lady and warrior for Jesus, she leaves behind numerous souls to pass on her legacy of evangelism. Dutchess was always on the lookout, eager to share the love of Jesus.

Envisioning Dutchess' glorious welcome into heaven, I smiled when the words, "Well done," came to mind. Indeed my dear friend finished well for the glory of her Savior.

Leona Frances Choy's powerful words clearly describe Dutchess:
"Spirit-filled souls are ablaze for God. They love with a love that glows. They believe with a faith that binds. They serve with a devotion that consumes. . . . They rejoice with a joy that radiates." *

In Jesus' parable the master weeded out those who merely gave lip service. He wanted to see how well those who truly gave their lives to serve him put to use what he had entrusted to them.

Did they make the most of what he had given them charge? And did they do so with dread or enthusiasm?

* *Powerlines*

JULY 29

When they look at you do others see a soul ablaze for God? Does your love glow and faith bind? Do you serve with consuming devotion and radiant joy? Are you eagerly multiplying that which Jesus has entrusted to you?

> Revelation
> 3:21
> *'He who overcomes, I will grant to him to sit down with Me on My throne, as I also overcame and sat down with My Father on His throne.'*

Will each of us hear, "Well done . . .
- Child for honoring your father and mother with respect and obedience
- Husband for loving your wife, even through trying times, as I love My Bride
- Wife for respecting your husband, when money was tight and in the busyness of providing he lost sight of what's important
- Single for your resolve to remain pure until one comes to claim your heart
- Employee for your diligence and honesty

Certainly we all long to hear Jesus say, "Well done good and faithful servant for multiplying that which I entrusted to you" {your transparency in the pain, perseverance in the trials, strengthening the weak and feeble, remembering My joy, sharing it with those who have no hope}.

Even though I was unable to attend Dutchess' memorial, I could almost hear her say, "It's not how many show up to say good-bye. It's how many welcome you home."

Smile.

Romans 2:4

Or do you think lightly of the riches of His kindness and tolerance and patience, not knowing that the kindness of God leads you to repentance?

Can we even conceive the magnitude of the riches God lavishes upon His own? Treasures beyond our imagination. Wonderful things like:

- mercy
- power
- forgiveness
- provision for all our needs
- salvation
- eternal life
- regeneration
- renewal
- compassion
- true knowledge of Christ
- hidden treasures of wisdom and knowledge
- hope of glory
- kindness, tolerance, patience, forbearance
- redemption
- grace
- glory
- inheritance

The list is endless.

When Jesus Christ is our all in all, our Lord, King, Savior, Life—we are entitled to all this and much more. We have the opportunity to tap into this unreserved supply of riches continually.

And we ought not think lightly of all God has for us, but rather dance with abandon, sing joyous praises, shout glorious hallelujahs.

August

T – Total
R – Reckless
U – Unreserved
S – Surrender to
T – Truth

Matthew
14:31
NLT
*Jesus immediately
reached out and
grabbed him
[Peter]. "You have
so little faith," Jesus
said. "Why did you
doubt me?"*

Doubt can be paralyzing. We hum along knowing what we believe is truth and all of a sudden a tiny niggling captures our thoughts and we tumble into that mysterious rabbit hole of '*what ifs*'. Our thoughts run amuck with *maybe* and *this could happen*. Before long we forget the unfailing certainty of God's promises and sink in the hopeless riptide of doubt.

Faith, being the polar opposite of doubt, is:
being sure of the things we hope for and knowing that something is real even if we do not see it
(Hebrews 11:1 NCV*).*

Webster's defines doubt:
To distrust or have no trust or confidence in, an inclination not to believe or accept.

So what causes us to doubt God's word? I'm not sure I can explain the what, but I do know this debilitating agitator, doubt, has crept into my heart in the last six months more times than I'd like to admit.

For instance, never in all the years I've been a Christian have I questioned the existence of heaven. Whether it's the enemy's attack, the world's condemnation or just my mind trying to legitimize my thoughts, I've found myself asking, "Is there really a heaven?"

AUGUST 1

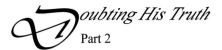

Part 2

In the logical thinker department, I would not be considered one by any stretch of the imagination. However this doubting heaven had me desperately needing to think it through.

My thoughts ran something like this. Since Jesus is a real person, proven through secular and theological history, and the Bible says Jesus is truth, I need to find what Jesus says about heaven.

Heaven is where our heavenly Father lives.
Jesus has all authority in heaven.
Jesus descended from heaven and after his resurrection was received up into heaven and now sits at the right hand of God in heaven.
And Jesus is coming to take His beloved there.

Just a miniscule glimpse of what Jesus has to say about heaven. No doubt, it's real.

So how do we overcome doubt? What does that look like in the real world where people are disillusioned and discouraged? We fix our eyes on Jesus through God's living word. It has a way of depleting our doubt, and in so doing, building our faith.

Hebrews
12:1, 2
Let us also lay aside every encumbrance and the sin which so easily entangles us, and let us run with endurance the race that is set before us, fixing our eyes on Jesus, the author and perfecter of faith.

It's Not Hard To Trust God

Part 1

Matthew
27:42, 43
*"He saved others;
He cannot save
Himself. He is the
King of Israel; let
Him now come
down from the
cross, and we will
believe in Him.
He trusts in God;
let God rescue
Him now, if He
delights in Him;
for He said,
'I am the
Son of God.' "*

Jesus knew obedience to His Father's will meant trusting Him even—no especially—in the painfully difficult times. As a man, Jesus agonized over giving Himself completely. Even so, His deepest desire was obedience to God's perfect divine will. Can we do any less?

Did it break God's heart to see His Son tortured, broken, bleeding, dying on the cross? More than we will ever comprehend. But God cared so much for the human race He gave His Son so that whoever believes in Him will have eternal life in heaven.

Jesus' example of trusting His Father shined throughout His time on earth. Yet on the cross, His wholly surrendered life gave new meaning to the word trust.

Elisabeth Elliot says in her book *The Music of His Promises*:
"Real trust yields utterly to the one trusted. All desire is turned over to that one, believing his ability to manage, control, and finally to accomplish what is best."

Do I trust like Jesus did?

Driving home from Eugene I had several hours to think, pray, cry. "Do you *really* trust Me?" kept coming to mind. I remembered when, a few years ago, I instantly answered, "Yes Lord of course I trust You."

Yet in the midst of this unbearable pain, loneliness, unknown future, I wondered if I would be so quick to respond now in like manner?

> Nahum 1:7
>
> *The LORD is good, a strong refuge when trouble comes. He is close to those who trust in him.*

We trust God because He is. Not because He does what we want Him to do.

To trust God means to believe that He is who He says He is. To have faith that His word is Truth, His promises reliable even when we cannot 'feel or sense' His presence. To praise Him even when His answer is not what we expected.

Is it hard to live in this state of grief? Yes. Very. But it's not hard to trust God.

As I gaze out my window admiring God's creation, writing this devotion, the sun is peeking over the mountains. Two airplanes full of people, rushing somewhere to do something, streak through the scattered clouds.

God is in no hurry to cause the sun to shine for our benefit, He does it every day. He simply wants us to have faith and believe *He* is the one who accomplishes this miraculous act.

$\mathcal{I}$ntimacy With The Three
Part 1

Psalm
21:1, 6, 7
ESV
O LORD, in your strength the king rejoices, and in your salvation how greatly he exults! For you make him most blessed forever; you make him glad with the joy of your presence. For the king trusts in the LORD, and through the steadfast love of the Most High he shall not be moved.

God recently gave me an acronym for the word trust.

T – Total
R – Reckless
U – Unreserved
S – Surrender to
T – Truth

Trust implies intimacy. Trusting God's faithfulness to do *all* that He says He will do. Trusting you can release every design, dream, desire, believing His truth. It's not about the project, it's about God drawing us to Himself.

God is calling His church, His people, into deeper intimacy with Him. These days the books I read, the messages I hear, continually bring that word to the forefront.

It's about intimacy . . . with *The Three*.

AUGUST 5

As we continue in obedience to God's plan the focus dramatically shifts from the fulfillment of the dream, to deeper intimacy with Him. We recklessly abandon all the hours of precious toil for Him to use—or not.

> **Psalm 16:8, 9**
> *I have set the LORD continually before me; because He is at my right hand, I will not be shaken. Therefore my heart is glad and my glory rejoices; my flesh also will dwell securely.*

Whatever we do whether it's write a book, paint a picture, compose music, have a passion for the lost, need a job, struggle at work, long for more knowledge, strive for peace and quiet, God is calling us into deeper intimacy.

Not to mention temptations and trials. Consider a struggle you're experiencing right now. If you presented it before God might you hear Him say, "I am using this to call you into a deeper intimacy with Me?"

Why? So God can break our hearts for what breaks His—the lost, afflicted, brokenhearted. So we will tell others the great things He has done in the midst of our suffering.

Bottom line—so many are brought into right relationship with God.

To Memorize Or Not To Memorize

Part 1

2 Timothy
3:16
THE MESSAGE
Every part of Scripture is God-breathed and useful one way or another—showing us truth, exposing our rebellion, correcting our mistakes, training us to live God's way.

Years ago, as a new believer, I attended a Bible study that encouraged us to memorize a new scripture verse every week. I tried, honestly I did. But for the life of me I could not embed those verses in my brain.

Not long after however, God spoke clearly to my spirit regarding Ephesians 4:29:

> *Let no unwholesome (rotten) word proceed from your mouth, but only such a word as is good for edification according to the need of the moment, so that it will give grace to those who hear.*

He pointed out I would need that verse and of course He was right. I had been experiencing that very thing and needed to stop passing on rotten unwholesome words. Rather I needed to speak words that edify and give life. In today's vernacular, 'stop talking smack.'

Over the years God has pointed out several verses that *needed* memorizing. He often allows me to *experience* the needed verses before expressing them.

*o Memorize Or
Not To Memorize*
Part 2

Colossians
4:6
THE MESSAGE
*Be gracious in your
speech. The goal is to
bring out the best in
others in a
conversation,
not put them down,
not cut them out.*

If you have ever experienced the bite of someone's caustic words you can understand why God repeatedly addresses our speech and our tongue.

Author and speaker, Gary Smalley, talks about word pictures, emotional pictures we paint so others *feel* the depth of our frustration or pain. Done well, word pictures emphatically get the point across.

Words have the power to deeply wound or powerfully heal. My friend uses the phrase, 'she stepped on my air hose.' That's a good word picture to express your feelings after someone has spoken tactless, cutting words that scald to the core and cut off life-giving breath to your spirit.

Who would have guessed that years ago when God had me memorize Psalm 138:8:

> *The LORD will accomplish what concerns me; Your lovingkindness, O LORD, is everlasting; do not forsake the works of Your hands.*

I would need it today to live though the experience of losing something so precious in my life?

*O*bedience Is A Heart Thing

John
14:15, 21
*If you love Me, you
will keep My
commandments . . .
He who has My
commandments
and keeps them is
the one who loves
Me; and he who
loves Me will be
loved by My
Father, and I will
love him and will
disclose Myself to
him.*

Wouldn't we all like to believe we love God with all our heart, soul, mind and strength? We say He is our Lord, our all in all, our purpose, our motive, our goal. He is our life. Still, what does Scripture say is the *proof* of our love? Obedience! Ouch.

But how do we know if we are being obedient? Oh, we know. Not to mention the Holy Spirit is faithful to search and reveal the truth that resides deep in the recesses of our hearts. His voice stirs our minds and burns in our hearts as to whether we are obedient or not.

Perhaps we ought to examine our heart and our actions to see if they align with our declaration of love for Jesus.

Obedience is not a difficult thing . . . it is a heart thing.

Forever the optimist, that's the apostle Paul. Often angered by fellow believers who strayed or disheartened with their self-centered attitudes, he still looked at the glass as half full.

> **2 Corinthians 4:8-9**
> *We are afflicted in every way, but not crushed; perplexed, but not despairing; persecuted, but not forsaken; struck down, but not destroyed.*

In the midst of heartache when your loved one is diagnosed as terminal do you despair of ever knowing why? When your integrity is under relentless attack do you feel like abandoning the Christian life? Does your mind say enough, but your heart says persevere?

No one likes suffering. Suffering from an illness or chronic pain brings about one of two responses; curse God for allowing the torment or praise Him for walking through the trial with You.

It's not a matter of *if* we will suffer, it's a matter of *when*. Paul suffered affliction, persecution, loneliness. Beatings, stoned, shipwrecked, constant danger did not divert his passion to serve Jesus Christ.

We ask God, "Why him, why them, why me?" Life should be neat and orderly with all the loose ends tied up. Right?

In the midst of life, as difficult as it is, we are not crushed or forsaken. Stand firm. Be strong.

Remain confident. After all—He is our hope.

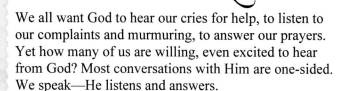

Psalm 55:16, 17, 19

As for me, I shall call upon God, and the LORD will save me. Evening and morning and at noon, I will complain and murmur, and He will hear my voice . . . . God will hear and answer.

We all want God to hear our cries for help, to listen to our complaints and murmuring, to answer our prayers. Yet how many of us are willing, even excited to hear from God? Most conversations with Him are one-sided. We speak—He listens and answers.

Suppose we do listen to what God is saying. Are we bold and courageous enough to first believe and accept that the Holy Spirit is speaking and then have faith to go forth?

The unknown can be frightening. But just as the certainty that God has spoken leads us to move in the direction of His purpose, we can be confident of His revelation for the next step.

Jesus said:

"My sheep hear My voice, and I know them, and they follow Me"
(John 10:27).

Is that an audible voice? Not usually. Is it writing on the wall like with Belshazzar? Rarely. God speaks to us in various ways.

Like when God uses another person to speak words of truth and wisdom into our lives. Do we listen or do we have our own agenda?

Has there ever been a time when you agonized over a situation, prayed fervently for help and the passage you were reading in the Bible had the exact words you needed or the perfect solution to the dilemma?

> **Psalm 57:2**
> *I will cry to God Most High, to God who accomplishes all things for me.*

Once my heart was so burdened for someone heavy into drugs, they could not break loose to find freedom from Satan's clutches {who comes to steal, kill and destroy} I did not know what to pray. 2 Chronicles 14:11, 12 nearly jumped off the page.

How about when a circumstance arises that never should have happened? Are you watching and listening to what God is saying? Ever been awakened from a deep sleep only to have a name come to mind with a strong sense they needed protection? You pray and find out later they narrowly escaped disaster.

Every true believer in Jesus Christ has the Holy Spirit living in them. His silent voice consistently speaks to their spirit to warn, convict, encourage, direct, comfort, reveal.

However it is difficult to hear God's voice on the run. In our busy lives we must slow down—no stop—to listen to God. Are you ready to listen?

God's Best
Part 1

Hebrews
11:18, 19
NCV
*God had said,
"The descendants
I promised you
will be from
Isaac." Abraham
believed that God
could raise the
dead, and really,
it was
as if Abraham
got Isaac back
from death.*

God told Abraham to take his son and go. I wonder if Abraham went through the doubting process we humans often experience when God gives us the directive to go. Even though the passage doesn't say it, might Abraham have battled with his faith?

"God You can't be serious. This is the son You promised. The very one I thought was a figment of Your imagination."

Remember when I told you to leave your home?

"Yes Lord."

Did I not lead, protect and provide for you?

"Yes but I love this boy!"

I love him too.

"Lord I just don't think I have what it takes to do this."

I promise to go with you and equip you for the journey.

"I don't know. I can't see how any good can come of this."

To obey is better than sacrifice.

"But isn't that what You are telling me to do, sacrifice my son?"

Trust Me.

Brennan Manning, in his radically insightful book, *Ruthless Trust,* defines trust this way: "Faith arises from the personal experience of Jesus as Lord. Hope is reliance on the promise of Jesus, accompanied by the expectation of fulfillment. Trust is the winsome wedding of faith and hope."

Abraham lived what he believed. He trusted God, obediently accepted God's testing and step by arduous step, found God to be faithful. Great blessings followed.

> **Genesis 22:16-18**
> *"By Myself I have sworn, declares the LORD, because you have done this thing and have not withheld your son, your only son, indeed I will greatly bless you . . . because you have obeyed My voice."*

Having just returned from an intense five-day writer's residency in Colorado with the Christian Writers Guild {CWG} I cannot tell you how many times I had to remind myself to obey God's directive for my life. To write. While talented authors critiqued my work I was tempted to toss my pen and hitch a ride on the next flight home.

There is no choice but to obey if I want to live what I profess—if I trust God to bless the very thing He has charged me to do.

The question is not whether we have a choice when it comes to obedience. Of course we do. The question is, do we want God's best?

Want More
Part 1

2 Chronicles
16:9
"For the eyes of the LORD move to and fro throughout the earth that He may strongly support those whose heart is completely His."

Show me Your glory Lord.

This is written throughout my journal entries. I watch and anticipate. I want more.

2 Samuel 5:14, 15 - And David was dancing before the LORD with all his might, and David was wearing a linen ephod. So David and all the house of Israel were bringing up the ark of the LORD with shouting and the sound of the trumpet.

King David was so captivated with the presence of the Lord he could not restrain his joy. He leaped, danced, shouted and probably sang.

But David wanted more.

More of God. David had known God as Shepherd. He had known Him as Protector, Provider, Deliverer. He knew Him as Lord of the heavenly hosts from Jacob and Joshua's stories. As Creator of heaven and earth and all they contain. He knew Him as faithful to His promises to Abraham, Isaac, Jacob and the nation of Israel. He knew Him as gracious, compassionate, slow to anger.

But David wanted more.

David wanted to live in God's glory.

I want more!

AUGUST 15

Show me Your glory Lord.

David danced before the Lord. Overjoyed and overwhelmed.

Psalm 24:7-10

David's Praise
Lift up your heads, O gates,
And be lifted up, O ancient doors,
That the King of glory may come in!

Who is the King of glory?
The LORD strong and mighty,
The LORD mighty in battle.

Lift up your heads, O gates,
And lift them up, O ancient doors,
That the King of glory may come in!

Who is this King of glory?
The LORD of hosts,
He is the King of glory.

Anne's Paraphrase
Open the doors wide my soul,
Lift your heart to the heavens,
So the King who illumines glory
may enter!

Who is the King whose glory
shines from everlasting to
everlasting?
My Warrior unsurpassed in
strength.
My Protector under whose
wings I rest.

Open O soul wider, Make room
for the King's majesty,
And the reality of my Beloved's
glory becomes mine!

I know this King of glory.
Savior, LORD, majestic and
resplendent in every way,
Sovereign who reigns over all.

The King is glorious!

Living In His Light
Part 1

Psalm
143:3
For the enemy has persecuted my soul, he has crushed my life to the ground; he has made me dwell in dark places, like those who have long been dead.

Darkness. Ever been there? Whether physical, emotional or spiritual darkness, the result is the same; depression, despondency, desperation, void of all peace and joy.

Have you ever been in a room where the light is completely blocked out, engulfed by darkness? You close your eyes and hope when you open them there will be light.

We do the same with emotional and spiritual darkness. If I do this it will get better. If I try that it will go away. When these things don't work we find ourselves in an even darker pit of gloom.

The Bible often addresses darkness. Sometimes using it to describe oppression, the enemy, a heaviness or place of anguish. David certainly had his bouts with darkness, describing it in detail in the Psalms. At times darkness overwhelmed him to the point of hopelessness.

How does one dispel this threatening foe? Light.

God knew we humans could not dwell in darkness for long without perishing. He gave the sun to illuminate the day and provide warmth, life, health. He gave Himself to enlighten us emotionally. His Son to shed light on our spiritual gloom.

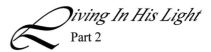

King Solomon said:
> *The fear {reverence} of the LORD is the beginning*
> *of knowledge (Proverbs 1:7).*

Psalm
119:105
Your word is a lamp
to my feet and a light
to my path.

In order to reverence God we must first believe He
exists and that He is the great I AM.

God enlightens our minds to grasp His immense love for us. So much love
that He sent His Son, Jesus, to die for us. Jesus, our Savior, is the Light of
the world.

As followers of Jesus Christ we receive more illumination through His Spirit
who indwells the believer, enabling us to walk in the light. Does that mean
we no longer have times of darkness? Unfortunately we still live in a dark
world, contending with our flesh and the enemy. Still God has given us
power to overcome while here on earth and the hope of His eternal light in
heaven.

Anybody out there shouting hallelujah besides me?

We conquer darkness and gloom by calling out to God, clinging to His
promises, counting on His faithfulness. If you are in the middle of a dark
time, persevere. Don't give up. Cry out to Jesus. Believe that He will light
your path.

AUGUST 18

He Is Worth The Journey
Part 1

Psalm 25:14
The secret [intimacy] of the LORD is for those who fear [reverence] Him, and He will make them know His covenant.

T – Total
R – Reckless
U – Unreserved
S – Surrender to
T – Truth

Little did I realize this TRUST meant giving up *everything*. Including and especially self.

What does it look like to give up everything and love God with all your heart, soul and mind?

Jesus pretty much put it out there saying if we want to follow Him, have a deeper intimacy, we must give up what is most precious to us.

People – Luke 14:26 THE MESSAGE - *Anyone who comes to me but refuses to let go of father, mother, spouse, children, brothers, sisters—yes, even one's own self!—can't be my disciple.*

Money – Matthew 6:24 NLT - *No one can serve two masters. For you will hate one and love the other; you will be devoted to one and despise the other. You cannot serve both God and money.*

Possessions – Luke 14:33 PHILLIPS - *So it is with you; only the man who says goodbye to all his possessions can be my disciple.*

I honestly thought I had surrendered everything until God asked me a question. My answer should have been a slam-dunk. It was not. My mind responded, "of course." But my soul was set on a tumultuous journey wrestling with God. For six days.

A friend wondered since I was seeking deeper intimacy with God, could He be taking me through a breaking process? Hadn't thought of that. Having gone through the painful purifying process before, had I known, I'm not sure I would have asked for deeper intimacy.

Journal excerpts that took place over several days:

It began with a conviction that my trials are miniscule compared to what Jesus faced. In the Garden of Gethsemane Jesus agonized, telling His Father He didn't want to go through all He knew lie ahead. Ultimately Jesus gave Himself to His Father's will. This offered a whole new perspective on my selfish and insignificant 'I don't want to (s)'. It is *so* not about me.

> 1 John
> 2:27
> *As for you, the anointing which you received from Him abides in you, and you have no need for anyone to teach you; but as His anointing teaches you about all things, and is true and is not a lie, and just as it has taught you, you abide in Him.*

The next day my heart ached with loneliness for my husband. I asked God to forgive me for wasting so much time living for me rather than appreciating and loving him while he was here. God teach me how to walk by the Spirit.

His message was clear – *Listen to Me. Truly listen.*

> **Ephesians 5:1, 2**
> *Therefore be imitators of God, as beloved children; and walk in love, just as Christ also loved you and gave Himself up for us, an offering and a sacrifice to God as a fragrant aroma.*

For days God walked me through the Bible providing priceless instruction from the Holy Spirit to confirm there were many things I needed to let go of before I could answer the question God kept asking me. I admitted to feeling alone, weak, vulnerable.

Not only was I fighting within myself to give up what God asked me to release, but also the enemy wanted to cause my focus to shift from the agony that must be experienced if I wanted to go deeper. I asked the Holy Spirit for strength, a voice of reason and assurance.

Digging deep I uncovered things I didn't realize were there. Things that were holding me hostage. Envy. Judgmental attitude. Resentment. Disappointment. Reliance on myself.

It was evident I needed to trust God and make a choice to give up my right to myself, my children, grandchildren, friends, finances, possessions, dependence on others, my pride.

"But God, I didn't have a choice in giving up my husband," I anguished.

† Yes Beloved. Are you willing to give up everything and everyone else by choice? Deeper intimacy requires sacrifice. COMPLETE SACRIFICE.

Do you know what the definition of complete is? Total – Absolute.

Sacrifice is an act of offering to God something precious – surrender of something for the sake of something else.

God didn't want a commitment from me. He wanted a covenant. A heart covenant.

My fear; what if I answer yes to Your question and I fail? What if I go back to what was? I'm weak, after all. Oh to be content in my weakness as Paul was.

> Psalm 31:7, 8
> *I will rejoice and be glad in Your lovingkindness, because You have seen my affliction; You have known the troubles of my soul, and You have not given me over into the hand of the enemy; You have set my feet in a large place.*

God's response

† Beloved, I love you and truly My strength is revealed when you are weak. I have not left you alone. You have the best of friends and helpers in the Holy Spirit.

His question.

† AM . . . I . . . Enough?

Finally, after six agonizing days I could give an honest answer.

"Yes Lord You are enough. Your grace is sufficient. When I am weak, You are strong. You have set my feet in a large place. I trust You. You are El-Shaddai, my Almighty, all-sufficient God. My times are in Your hand."

old Faith
Part 1

Joshua
1:8, 9
*This book of the
law shall not
depart from your
mouth, but you
shall meditate on
it day and night,
so that you may
be careful to do
according to all
that is written in
it; for then you
will make your
way prosperous,
and then you will
have success.
Have I not
commanded you?
Be strong and
courageous! Do
not tremble or be
dismayed, for the
LORD your God
is with you
wherever you go.*

God's law to the Jewish nation was spoken directly to Moses who was instructed to write it down for the people.

God reminds Joshua of the very thing Moses had instructed him earlier. If you do what I have commanded, according to all that Moses has written down, {My word} you will be prosperous, make wise decisions and have success.

Joshua, commissioned as the new leader of the Hebrew people, had been directed by Moses to be strong and courageous, not once, but four times. God reiterates those very words in the book of Joshua, also three times.

What would make Joshua strong and courageous? The same promise in both instances, "The Lord your God will go with you, He will be with you wherever you go." Reassuring words.

Yet in order to actually step out and go Joshua had to *believe* what God said. He had to have faith.

Non-Jewish believers in Jesus Christ are now included as 'God's people' for we have been grafted in. We have the privilege of being a part of His family and claiming His promises.

Today we have God's word {the Bible} in several translations and versions. Yet when we read God's word, do we believe it? Do we have faith that when God directs us to go He will be with us wherever that may be?

How often has God clearly shown us what He wanted to do through us, and we said, "I can't do that?"

Exactly. Precisely. We can't, but He can. That's the whole point. He doesn't assign us a task and then say, "Okay let's see what you're made of. Sink or swim."

For some reason God uses faulty, flawed, fearful people to accomplish His will. The Holy Spirit does this kingdom work through willing vessels, no matter what shape we're in.

We're like a collection of old art supplies resting under a table, dusty from lack of use. Until the artist picks up the canvas, paint and brush to use as they were designed, to create a beautiful work of art, they are useless.

AUGUST 24

Part 3

Psalm
31:23, 24
ESV
*Love the LORD,
all you his saints!
The LORD
preserves the
faithful but
abundantly repays
the one who acts
in pride. Be
strong, and let
your heart take
courage, all you
who wait for
the LORD!*

When the Master uses us to share His perfect picture of redemption for mankind, we are simply His instruments. I have been searching for years to find an old, beat up, bent, rusty, cracked lantern as a reminder of that point.

When I think of how God accomplishes His plan through His people, the lantern comes to mind. I see myself as that lantern in a cocoon of cobwebs, contentedly hanging in the corner of an old barn. One day I'm taken down from the rusty nail that bolstered me for years, and pressed into service to give light to the dark stable.

It isn't the lantern that makes a way for the farmer to see where he is going. It's the light inside. It's the same with God. I'm merely the cracked lantern *His* light shines through.

Are you apprehensive at the thought of speaking the good news of salvation to the unsaved or are you graciously bold because you believe God's word is true?

Be strong and courageous. God may send you places you had no intention of going. Do not fear. He goes with you.

Genesis 3:10 is the first mention of fear in the Bible:

He [Adam] said, "I heard the sound of You in the garden, and I was afraid because I was naked; so I hid myself."

John 14:27

"Peace I leave with you; My peace I give to you; not as the world gives do I give to you. Do not let your heart be troubled, nor let it be fearful."

Where did that come from? You guessed it, the father of lies.

My young friend beams with excitement at the new world Christianity has opened up to her. God saved her from depression, loneliness, abandonment, seeking love and acceptance in all the wrong places.

Her fear? "I'm afraid God will leave me like every other man in my life."

Another friend has an uncertain journey ahead of her. After twenty-three years of dedicated service she may soon be without a job. Although apprehensive, her faith in God has increased considerably during this time of uncertainty. She can't say she's excited {yet} about what lies ahead, but she's thrilled that she's learning to trust God more.

There is no fear, no obstacle, no threat that cannot be conquered through God's power.

May God, the source of hope, fill you with all joy and peace by means of your faith in him, so that your hope will continue to grow by the power of the Holy Spirit (Romans 15:13 GNT).

Memories Abound

Summer is fleeting. With it precious moments and memories.

Laughter. Cool breezes. Gardens overflowing fresh vegetables. Crisp watermelon. Camping trips. Homemade ice cream. Star-filled skies, shooting flames that disappear. S'mores. Getting lost time and again. Giggles. Sweltering heat. Iced coffee. Hikes to the beach. Al fresco lunches.

Games, winning and losing. Coffee on the porch, serious talks. Farmers harvesting hay. Lush green trees. Vibrant floral bouquets. Elated bees. Hummingbirds. Lounging lizards sunning, sharing lazy days. Papa quail leads, Mama shepherds from behind half dozen toddlers taking flight from a lofty mountain ledge.

Cherished memories etched, tucked away for a time when all is still, family and friends far away.

I wonder. Did we remember to make memories with God this summer? To seek and adore Him in the midst of all the various fun? Did we share quiet moments? Start each day praising? Thank and honor Him throughout?

Summer is fleeting. Yet our relationship with Jesus ought never be transitory, rather a continuous adventure with the King of kings. Remembering Him— our gift from Abba. Nurturing this priceless relationship relentlessly with our love and devotion.

Memories abound. Future adventures await.

Since the email went out asking for prayer to finish the novel, the devil has cleverly proved himself my adversary, prowling around like a roaring lion, seeking to devour.

There has been fear, distractions, apprehension, doubt, not to mention a major testing of my determination and faith. Of course my own poor choices and outside influences figure into the equation.

But God—reigns sovereign.

> Ephesians 6:12
> *For our struggle is not against flesh and blood, but against the rulers, against the powers, against the world forces of this darkness, against the spiritual forces of wickedness in the heavenly places.*

Satan had to ask God's permission to inflict Job and to sift Peter. It's comforting to know everything that comes into my life is no surprise to God. My courage comes from trusting Him to protect and defend me throughout the battle.

Have no doubt. God wins. Always.

Philippians 4:11, 12

Not that I speak from want, for I have learned to be content in whatever circumstances I am. I know how to get along with humble means, and I also know how to live in prosperity; in any and every circumstance I have learned the secret of being filled and going hungry, both of having abundance and suffering need.

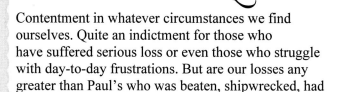

Contentment in whatever circumstances we find ourselves. Quite an indictment for those who have suffered serious loss or even those who struggle with day-to-day frustrations. But are our losses any greater than Paul's who was beaten, shipwrecked, had any number of dangerous encounters?

Over the years I've tried numerous ways to live in this contentment Paul talks about. Don't you find the necessary activities, pressures, 'what if's' and 'wish I would have's' deprive us of the ability to find contentment right where we are and enjoy the ordinary?

Elisabeth Elliot writes in her book, *Keep a Quiet Heart*: "St. Augustine said, "The very pleasures of human life men acquire by difficulties." There are times when the entire arrangement of our existence is disrupted and we long then for just one ordinary day—seeing our ordinary life as greatly desirable, even wonderful, in the light of the terrible disruption that has taken place. Difficulty opens our eyes to pleasures we had taken for granted."

Memories of ordinary things come to mind often as I walk through my days in this beautiful home my husband built. It's not that I'm longing for an extended vacation together, although those were always very sweet times. It's not even that I want to sit with him and plan out future goals. No I yearn for ordinary things:

- watching him ride his tractor
- receiving a surprise hug from behind while washing dishes
- a game of cards
- his smile
- his voice
- feeling his touch
- chatting over, re-visiting the events of the day
- laughter
- working in the garden together
- strolling together
- riding behind him on the motorcycle, giving him a squeeze now and then
- praying together

There are times I wonder why I'm here, when it seems my purpose has been taken from me. However I've come to the conclusion that my *only* purpose is to glorify God. Knowing He will reveal how that plays out in the everyday ordinary things.

The secret to contentment is looking to Jesus for the supernatural joy that comes from the reality that I really *can* make it through anything when I am surrendered to Him.

Let's Do The Ridiculous

Psalm
63:1
O God, You are my God; I shall seek You earnestly; my soul thirsts for You, my flesh yearns for You, in a dry and weary land where there is no water.

Do you hunger and thirst for more of God? When was the last time you put everything on hold and asked Him to meet with you?

One thing about meeting with God, the more we seek Him the more our soul thirsts and our flesh yearns for Him.

I know of someone who told God they would not budge until they heard from Him. This person knew they could not tackle all the frustrations, struggles, demands, of the day if they didn't first meet with and hear from God.

In the last several weeks I've been asking God to meet with me. He has uncovered amazing revelations, revealed prayers that needed praying, unveiled insights into the hefty job of transforming my character. He has even disclosed the next step of obedience in what He's called me to do. Even though it looks ridiculous and totally impossible.

Dave Patterson, a truly spiritually insightful pastor has said:
"God has consistently asked His people to do things that look ridiculous. When we do the ridiculous, God does the miraculous!"

Well, alrighty then. What am I waiting for?

September

God's best waits on the other side of obedience

Get On Board

Part 1

Haggai
1:1
In the second year of Darius the king, on the first day of the sixth month, the word of the LORD came by the prophet Haggai to Zerubbabel.

The Lord grabbed the Israelites by their spiritual shoulders and shook. He basically told them that *His* house had been left unfinished and forgotten. Enough is enough. Now is the appointed time.

Haggai 1:2, 4, 5

"Thus says the LORD of hosts, 'This people says, "The time has not come, even the time for the house of the LORD to be rebuilt."' Is it time for you yourselves to dwell in your paneled houses while this house lies desolate?

Now therefore, thus says the LORD of hosts, "Consider your ways!"

Anne's Paraphrase

My house. What do you not understand about those two words? Be obedient to what I have called you to do. And do it now!

What are you doing? Are you doing what I have said or what you think I said? Maybe you are doing what 'you' want to do.

Such a picture of complacency. Content with the status quo.

Webster's defines complacency as:
Self-satisfaction accompanied by unawareness of actual dangers or deficiencies.

Many of us live with the same contented indifference for the things of God as the Israelites did. We think only of what's going in in our own self-satisfied, smug life.

Is God saying to you, "Now is the appointed time?"

SEPTEMBER 1

Haggai
1:7
*Thus says the LORD
of hosts, "Consider
your ways!"*

Haggai 1:6, 7

"You have sown much, but harvest little; you eat, but there is not enough to be satisfied; you drink, but there is not enough to become drunk; you put on clothing, but no one is warm enough; and he who earns, earns wages to put into a purse with holes." Thus says the LORD of hosts, "Consider your ways!"

Anne's Paraphrase

You have been content living in complacency in the status quo. Not stepping out into the destiny I have for you. And what has it wrought? You work slightly, with little satisfaction and poor dividends. The results are spiritual food that feed only the surface cells of your soul with little nutrition. You can't even produce enough pure grapes to make a delicious potent wine to quench your thirst let alone take you over the top into a sweet spiritual stupor. The threadbare rags you use as clothing can't begin to protect you from the elements. They certainly won't keep you warm when freezing temperatures arrive.

You strive and work for what? You spend every last cent on what you consider important. Is this how you want to live? Is this the destiny I showed you? Now is the appointed time for what *I* have called you to. Get on board. Do it. Do it now! Go!

God would have us leave the complacency behind and go. He even promises to give us the tools to accomplish the task He has set before us. Do it. Do it now!

 What Promised Land
Part 1

> **Psalm 37:9**
> *But those who wait for the LORD, they will inherit the land.*

The Israelites longed for freedom from their bondage to the Egyptians. God saw the affliction of His people, heard their cry and was well aware of their suffering. Through Moses God delivered the Hebrew people from slavery and lead them to a good and spacious land flowing with milk and honey. The Promise Land.

What is your Promise Land? What does your heart long for more than anything else? Do you find yourself saying, "If I only had _____ I would be happy?"

Could that something be a better job, a comfortable house, college degree, good health, peace, reconciliation with a loved one, longevity of life, less responsibility at work, more responsibility at work, a good harvest, _____ {you fill in the blank}.

In Psalm 37:3 David wrote:

> *Trust in the LORD, and do good; dwell in the land and cultivate faithfulness.*

In other words, bloom where you are planted.

Feed on God's faithfulness. Seek His face continually, including and especially when it looks like the Promise Land is a dream that looms in the distance too far to ever inhabit.

How does one delight oneself in the Lord? Spend time with Him. Search the Scriptures. Pray. Seek to know Him intimately.

> Psalm
> 37:4
> *Delight yourself in the LORD; and He will give you the desires of your heart.*

Funny thing, when you delight yourself in the Lord the desires of your heart change. Your Promise Land is no longer that which fills the blank space. It becomes *Him*.

As you wait for, trust in, give yourself wholly to the sovereign Lord to deliver you from slavery to your wants and usher you into the Promise Land, note the changes He makes in your heart, mind, attitude, character.

Hebrews 11:6 says:
> *And without faith it is impossible to please Him, for he who comes to God must believe that He is and that He is a rewarder of those who seek Him.*

This journey takes a lifetime to complete, but the rewards are incredible. One day without even realizing it, you will have entered the land.

 rateful To Be His
Part 1

Ephesians
1:15, 16
For this reason I too, having heard of the faith in the Lord Jesus which exists among you and your love for all the saints, do not cease giving thanks for you, while making mention of you in my prayers.

Lavishly loved by God through others is having an extraordinary impact on me.

It's been a rough transition back into 'single' life having just returned from a visit with my aunt and uncle in Missouri. The two weeks passed quickly. We played games, watched movies, hiked, shopped, and talked almost nonstop, frequently sharing insights into God's word.

Missourians {is that even a word} won my heart when during one particular excursion to an outdoor mall we stepped out of a store and noticed that just about every person stood completely still looking in the same direction, some with their hand over their heart, others with hats in hand.

It seems, everyday at noon the local radio station plays the National Anthem and the fine people of Missouri take that seriously.

SEPTEMBER 5

Missouri, the *show me* state is a virtual classroom of learning experiences. Domestic and exotic animals and myriad colorful birds inhabit the lush countryside. Turtles {box and snapping}, opossum, armadillos, skunks, black snakes, fox, deer, raccoons, dragonflies, bobcats, ticks and chiggers roam freely. The latter are to be avoided at all costs.

> Ephesians
> 1:17
> *[I pray] that the God of our Lord Jesus Christ, the Father of glory, may give to you a spirit of wisdom and of revelation in the knowledge of Him.*

I'm told a redneck splint for a broken leg consists of PVC pipe, towels and duct tape. Did you know eight states border Missouri and in some the kudzu vine is known to grow one foot per day? This vine entwines and kills other plants and trees by smothering them under a solid blanket of leaves.

Interesting stuff.

Yet what I remember more than anything else is love, laughter—lots of laughter—and the reality that family extends far beyond blood, genes or DNA. When you belong to the family of believers in Jesus Christ, a helping hand is always there to give support. And hospitality is served up in heaping batches.

Grateful To Be His
Part 3

Philippians
2:3, 4
*Do nothing from
selfishness or empty
conceit, but with
humility of mind
regard one
another as more
important than
yourselves; do not
merely look out for
your own personal
interests, but also
for the interests of
others.*

Missouri . . . my home-away-from-home.

I was received with genuine warmth and love. Not only by my aunt and uncle, {who, by the way, graciously took two weeks out of their busy lives to love on and pamper my broken soul} but by long time and new friends who prayed for me before and after my husband's homegoing.

When God calls us into His family, adopts us as His own, thousands—no millions—of brothers and sisters stand ready to welcome us. To rejoice when we rejoice, weep when we weep, pray without ceasing, listen with a compassionate ear, lovingly point us to the One who knew us before the foundation of the world.

It's quite a phenomenon to experience the common ground we Christians share. All over the world because of one central figure, Jesus Christ, the comforting arms of spiritual family who love on one another with honest, transparent, unabashed abandon, stand eager to embrace us.

SEPTEMBER 7

I recently visited a lovely church in the country. Though I spoke with no one, I knew if the need arose this family of believers would, with just a simple request, hold and love me, pray and weep with me.

The Pastor taught on Acts 10, explaining that Jesus, the Messiah, came to save *all* nations, showing no partiality or prejudice. The apostle Peter demonstrated we ought to live likewise. As a Jew, Peter had been raised with years of prejudice against Gentiles. God turned Peter's world upside down with a vision and a visit.

Acts
10:28
And he [Peter] said to them, "You yourselves know how unlawful it is for a man who is a Jew to associate with a foreigner or to visit him; and yet God has shown me that I should not call any man unholy or unclean."

I wonder if we're ready to give up the prejudices and preconceived ideas we've accumulated over our lifetime? Are we willing to listen to God's directives, throw off what the world declares as sensible and reasonable and step into God's calling?

Do we view others with suspicion and judgment or do we extend unconditional love like I experienced in Missouri?

SEPTEMBER 8

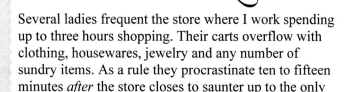

> **Hebrews 9:14**
>
> *How much more will the blood of Christ, who through the eternal Spirit offered Himself without blemish to God, cleanse your conscience from dead works to serve the living God?*

Several ladies frequent the store where I work spending up to three hours shopping. Their carts overflow with clothing, housewares, jewelry and any number of sundry items. As a rule they procrastinate ten to fifteen minutes *after* the store closes to saunter up to the only open register and check out.

One by one, they painstakingly examine each item. Hold it up to the light, turn it around, ask for an opinion from the cashier, decide whether to purchase it or not. Almost without fail, within a few days they return ninety percent of the items. Are these ladies crazy or just lonely women craving attention {albeit the wrong kind}? Or could it be their souls are searching for significance?

Every human being wants to be known, to leave their imprint on society. As you can tell the significance left upon my memory by these ladies is anything but momentous.

As Christians our search for significance ends with the saving, life-giving blood of Jesus Christ. From the moment we receive this precious gift of grace God offers through His Son, our significance is all about serving Him.

Oh yeah!

The search for significance. There are those to be sure who prove strong, intelligent, talented, giving. Some have a need for accolades, others applause. Unfortunately many end up humiliated and embarrassed.

> 1 Timothy
> 1:1
> *Paul, an apostle of Christ Jesus according to the commandment of God our Savior, and of Christ Jesus, who is our hope.*

Dreamers often believe unless their dreams are fulfilled they are doomed to never reach the height of their significance. Workaholics find their worth in achieving a professional goal, then moving on to the next. There are athletes who feel they have attained their pinnacle only when surpassing another's record.

Don't get me wrong I'm not saying we shouldn't excel at what we do. Of course we are to put forth our best effort. Still, I have to wonder for what purpose or ultimate goal? Significance? For who?

As Christians, every single thing we do in life should have one purpose, one ultimate goal—to point others to Jesus Christ. And how are we pointing them to Him? Through ourselves, our achievements, our dead works?

If we use {sometimes unknowingly} any means other than the power of the Holy Spirit to point people to Jesus, our efforts are merely hay and stubble.

ointing To The One
Part 3

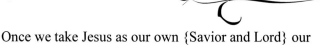

Once we take Jesus as our own {Savior and Lord} our significant search shifts to any means possible to know and honor Him.

Pastors, poets, purveyors of the pen and countless others tell us we ought to leave a legacy for those who come after. Certainly it's important to train up our children in the knowledge and admonition of the Lord, to teach, correct, discipline them. To help them learn to serve, give, put the needs of others before their own.

When someone asks what kind of legacy will you leave, one thing comes to mind—am I pointing people to Jesus? Our search for significance ought to cause a continually deeper longing to know, love and honor God.

In his letter to the church in Philippi, Paul is saying that once we find the joy of giving our life completely to Jesus our search has ended, and as I like to say . . .

The adventure begins.

SEPTEMBER 11

Remember Abraham. That admonition continues to ring in my mind.

1 Peter
2:21
*For you have been
called for this
purpose, since Christ
also suffered for you,
leaving you an
example for you to
follow in His steps.*

Abraham trusted God. Mostly. We tend to deify people in the Bible, thinking of them as paragons of virtue. We look up to them and their example. Still, Abraham was but a man and by no means faultless.

I wonder if God would have us look at the whole man, not just his flawless attributes. Abraham {Abram at the time} was basically unknown. We would call him an insignificant nobody. Yet God had a huge plan for him and his descendants.

Abraham began his journey of trusting God by setting out to a place he had never seen. During his travels however, he gave in to the clutches of fear and 'what ifs'. He trusted God with the *big* picture, but the trials and uncertainties of day-to-day life? Ah, no.

Even in the midst of Abraham's insecurities and sin God cared for him, continually reiterating His covenant promises. Abraham experienced God's protection, provision, prosperity.

Seeing Through New Eyes

Part 2

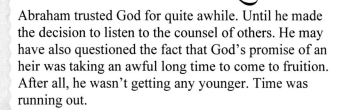

Abraham trusted God for quite awhile. Until he made the decision to listen to the counsel of others. He may have also questioned the fact that God's promise of an heir was taking an awful long time to come to fruition. After all, he wasn't getting any younger. Time was running out.

So, like any human who loses their focus, he caved. Abraham took matters into his own hands and ergo, Ishmael {*not* the promised child}.

Some time later God accomplished something only God could have done. He caused Abraham and Sarah, far beyond childbearing years, to conceive Isaac {the promised child}.

Years passed and God tested Abraham's faith with the command to offer up the very thing he treasured most, the son he loved. Almost as if God was saying, "Abraham, do you *really* trust Me?"

In the most recent release of the *Chronicles of Narnia* movie series, Aslan {symbolizing Christ} speaks words of truth into Lucy's soul. In a brief, but poignant scene, Lucy sees herself as plain when she longs to be as beautiful as her sister, Susan. Aslan tells Lucy that she has wished herself away.

> 1 John
> 2:5, 6
> *But whoever keeps His word, in him the love of God has truly been perfected. By this we know that we are in Him: the one who says he abides in Him ought himself to walk in the same manner as He walked.*

How many of us have spent years wishing ourselves away? After all, time is running out. We know God has a plan and we may even be in the midst of its fulfillment, yet we compare ourselves to others and wish we were as beautiful or smart or talented. If only we could sing like that one or paint with feeling or write with depth.

If only. Then we would be content, fulfilled. Our life would have meaning.

Major focus shift to who we are *not*, instead of who God *is*.

It's fine to admire the virtuous attributes of godly men and women like Abraham and Sarah. But when it comes to living in the here and now, the only example worthy of following is Jesus.

SEPTEMBER 14

God's Next Surprise
Part 1

Hebrews
11:8
THE MESSAGE
*By an act of faith,
Abraham said yes
to God's call to
travel to an unknown
place that
would become his
home. When he left
he had no idea where
he was going.*

Don't you just love unexpected jaw-dropping surprises, especially when they come from God? We find it hard to believe He would show favor in such unbelievable ways.

When we tell God we've planned our destiny with a completely different outcome, He will forever surpass our expectations exponentially.

What if we went forward with the dream God planted in our spirit with no plans, strategies or expectations? You know, the dream that is impossible for us to accomplish because it's something we have absolutely no talent for and we've never done anything even remotely like it? Yeah, that's the one. Like Abraham.

I am on that journey now. Originally with no training, talent or expertise, I moved forward and watched God bring to fruition bits and pieces of the dream that looked *way* beyond my grasp and abilities.

God has now encouraged me to go forth into an arena I never thought would be part of the dream He planted in me.

Writing a book is one thing, getting it published is another. It's been said expectation kills the surprise.

I love being surprised by God. He brings about events, ideas, adventures that cause me to stand in awe. It's really pretty exciting to go into this new venture, into this next step in the fulfillment of the dream, with no expectations.

> Hebrews
> 11:9
> *By faith he [Abraham] lived as an alien in the land of promise, as in a foreign land, dwelling in tents with Isaac and Jacob, fellow heirs of the same promise.*

The act of obedience takes us step by step walking in the Spirit into the unknown, when all of a sudden God brings in another dimension that is completely beyond our grasp.

Are you feeling incapable, unqualified, ill equipped? Me too. Having just received a major rejection—fed by my own expectations—God clearly spoke to my spirit that I was to; *Wait. Stand and see the salvation of the Lord.*

Moses said to the people:
> *"Do not fear! Stand by and see the salvation of the LORD which He will accomplish for you today . . . . The LORD will fight for you while you keep silent (Exodus 14:13, 14).*

No more expectations here. Rather listening and moving forward as God leads, even if trepidation haunts.

I'm excited to see God's next surprise.

Isaiah
61:1
The Spirit of the Lord GOD is upon me, because the LORD has anointed me to bring good news to the afflicted; He has sent me to bind up the brokenhearted, to proclaim liberty to captives and freedom to prisoners.

Every day we are surrounded by people. Each has a story. Each a past, present, future. Many would like to erase their whitewashed past. Others clamor for help to overcome the insurmountable present. Almost all desperately hope for a better future.

Have you ever sat in a courtroom to observe the proceedings? Observe the poor, blind, oppressed captives? I have. It pains me to admit my emotions ran the gamut. Apprehension. Frustration. Disgust. Anger. Grief. Irritation. Empathy. Disappointment.

One judge poured out abundant grace. Firm, yet caring, he encouraged hope for those appearing before him to overcome their present circumstances and build a better future.

Another judge delivered plentiful condemnation. Harsh and unmoved, he demanded the gravest debt be paid to the full extent of the law. This judge passed on to those cowering on the other side of the bench, deplorable bondage.

et The Captives Free
Part 2

Many have bought into Satan's subtle, destructive lies.

DUI, no big deal. Burglary, you had every right. Violence, necessary for justice. Domestic abuse, deserved. Murder, the only way out. The enemy has convinced some they have no worth and others they are better than everyone else and somehow above the law. It takes very little persuasion either way.

Jesus Christ is the fulfillment of Isaiah's prophetic declaration of the One who would come to proclaim the good news. God's salvation for all. Jesus came to release the captives, give recovery of sight to the blind, free the oppressed. Jesus died to set us *all* free.

Over and over in that courtroom, a prayer of freedom for lost souls rang out from my heart. Freedom from insecurity. Oppression. Arrogance. Pride. Drugs. Alcohol. Lawlessness. Chaos. Feeling unlovely and unwanted.

A cry for the love of Jesus to touch each soul. To reveal how valuable they are.

SEPTEMBER 18

$\mathcal{K}$eep Calling Us Lord
Part 1

Psalm 16:8, 11

I have set the LORD continually before me . . . You will make known to me the path of life; in Your presence is fullness of joy; in Your right hand there are pleasures forever.

God is calling us to a deeper intimacy with Him. It's a choice. The outcome—fullness of joy and pleasures forever.

Not long ago I sat down, closed my eyes and asked God about this deeper intimacy. In a matter of minutes He spoke several things to my spirit.

Our life holds *no* meaning if not to live each moment to glorify . . . ABBA—JESUS—HOLY SPIRIT

Loneliness is a dangerous state of mind redeemed only through communion with and complete trust in God. Otherwise we sit in the sullen chambers of darkness and isolation we have created. Freedom comes through worship and adoration for . . . ALMIGHTY GOD

Purpose depends solely on the disposition of the heart. To whom or what will we give our heart? To the physical reality of what we see around us or to the truth of a dimension we cannot see? Our purpose and the giving of our heart are one in the same . . . *THE THREE*

SEPTEMBER 19

Make us deaf and blind Lord if only for a moment, that we might truly know You. Cause the scales to fall from our eyes, that we might fully grasp Your beauty. Encase us is the presence of Your majesty that we might in awestruck wonder behold . . . THE BRIGHT MORNING STAR

> Psalm
> 73:28
> *But as for me, the nearness of God is my good; I have made the Lord GOD my refuge, that I may tell of all Your works.*

Time is fleeting even as the years slip away. Yet You Lord are Eternity. Always. Forever. Our sovereign King who reigns over the eternal. Calling Your servants to gather up lost souls that You might hold them tenderly in Your arms. Time passes quickly, leaving little to bring them before . . . ETERNAL FATHER

Strength wanes. Energy depleted. Truth replenished. Courage revealed. Temptations overcome. Faith strengthened. Trust restored. Desire complete . . . I AM

Distractions turn our heads and hearts from God. Pleasures to be sure, but at what cost? A carefully designed shifting of devotion—bit by tiny bit. God is able to tear off the leeches that drain our desire for Him and remove the muck that keeps us bogged down in the mire of this world.

May we wholeheartedly lay down our will for His.

UTTERLY DISTRACTED BY HIS GLORY.

SEPTEMBER 20

> Psalm 32:5
> *I acknowledged my sin to You, and my iniquity I did not hide; I said, "I will confess my transgressions to the LORD"; and You forgave the guilt of my sin.*

The judge's gavel hammered the elevated podium with thundering force. "Guilty as charged."

The shackled man sobbed unashamedly, pleading for mercy. "Give me another chance. I promise it won't happen again."

"Young man, you have stood before this bench on four previous occasions for the same grievous crime. I warned you last time if I ever saw you in my court again, you would receive the full penalty allowed. You are hereby sentenced to fifty years, ten for each offense, in the state Penitentiary."

Each of us has an invisible placard hanging above our heads that reads 'guilty as charged'.

> *For all have sinned and fall short of the glory of God (Romans 3:23).*

According to God's righteous standard we deserve nothing less then eternal separation from Him.

But God . . .

> *For God has imprisoned everyone in disobedience so he could have mercy on everyone. Oh, how great are God's riches and wisdom and knowledge! How impossible it is for us to understand his decisions and his ways! (Romans 11:32, 33 NLT)*

God's love far outreaches our finite comprehension. God gave His Son.

Jesus received the penalty for our sin. His death paid the debt in full.

SEPTEMBER 21

"Guilty as charged."

Those who live in a world of self-made guilt fear God's wrath for their habitual sin while they desperately try to end their unholy habits. Without the power of the Holy Spirit they're fools doomed to return to their own vomit {sin} as the proverb so graphically describes.

Guilt is ever present with the perpetual practice of sin.

Then there is the guilt better described as self-reproach. Like Paul, we say:
> *For the good that I want, I do not do, but I practice the very evil that I do not want. But if I am doing the very thing I do not want, I am no longer the one doing it, but sin which dwells in me (Romans 7:19, 20).*

Guilt causes us to believe we are beyond hope with our imperfections. Wrong.
> *Thank God! The answer is in Jesus Christ our Lord (Romans 7:25 NLT).*

> Romans
> 3:24
> THE MESSAGE
> *God did it for us. Out of sheer generosity he put us in right standing with himself. A pure gift. He got us out of the mess we're in and restored us to where he always wanted us to be. And he did it by means of Jesus Christ.*

The Power Of Weakness
Part 1

Ephesians
1:18, 19
*I pray that the eyes
of your heart
may be enlightened,
so that you
will know what is
the hope of His
calling, what are
the riches of the
glory of His
inheritance
in the saints, and
what is the
surpassing
greatness of His
power toward us
who believe. These
are in accordance
with the working of
the strength of His
might.*

The power of God is more real to me these days than at any time in my life. I've stood in awe of His miraculous works from time to time and asked myself, "Why are you surprised?"

It's humbling and liberating when you come to the end of yourself and realize, God is *all* you've got and God is *all* you need.

Lilias Trotter wrote in *A Blossom in the Desert:* "The miracle of Cana has been shining out these days. "Fill the waterpots with water" has been their watchword. Undiluted weakness transmuted with undiluted strength. It seems to me as if the first thing we expect of God is that He will tinge our water with the wine of His power. Then as we progress in our faith understanding we look for its wine, but feel it must still have an admixture of our water. It is but slowly that we come to see that the mingling is not His way with us. It is "all weakness"—up to the brim—**exchanged** for His "all power.""

God is opening my eyes each day to behold His miraculous, powerful works in even the tiniest of details.

Each time our weaknesses are made obvious by the lack of ability to accomplish even the most minute, insignificant task, God doesn't take our weaknesses and work His power through them.

> 1 John
> 1:9
> *If we confess our sins, He is faithful and righteous to forgive us our sins and to cleanse us from all unrighteousness.*

No. God depletes, drains, exhausts every bit of weakness from us and diffuses the empty space with His Almighty power. There is nothing of our weakness or us involved. It is *all* God's supernatural might and force.

Where did we ever get the idea that God would use any kind of weakness to display His power? That's a negative added to a positive, water and oil, they don't mix.

It's God's potent power infused into His willing, eager, cleansed servant that accomplishes His perfect will. When He takes us out of the equation *He* is magnified. God minus our weakness, multiplied by the Holy Spirit's power, equals miraculous works for God's glory.

It's no wonder we are to ask for forgiveness and be cleansed of all unrighteousness. God then has an uncontaminated, untainted, unpolluted vessel for His pure, perfect, pristine power to indwell.

SEPTEMBER 24

The Poignant Affect Of A Listening Ear

Part 1

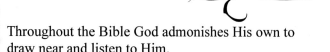

Ecclesiastes 5:1, 2

Guard your steps as you go to the house of God and draw near to listen rather than to offer the sacrifice of fools; for they do not know they are doing evil. Do not be hasty in word or impulsive in thought to bring up a matter in the presence of God. For God is in heaven and you are on the earth; therefore let your words be few.

Throughout the Bible God admonishes His own to draw near and listen to Him.

When God revealed Himself to Moses He told him he was standing on holy ground. Was God intimating for Moses to listen up, questioning if he knew Who he was dealing with?

I AM

Listening with no personal agenda encourages others to speak from the heart and work through issues that might otherwise brew into a steaming cauldron of anger and frustration.

Not many years ago my telephone was connected to the wall by a short pigtail cord. When having a conversation I could not do dishes, surf the net, make the bed, pull weeds. I sat on my steps and gave the person calling my undivided attention. It was great.

The Poignant Affect Of A Listening Ear

Part 2

Recently while speaking to someone on my cell phone, my attention was drawn to the computer and the plethora of events happening there. I asked questions, but do you think I can remember the answers? No. Flat out rude.

> Mark
> 4:9
> NCV
> *Then Jesus said, "Let those with ears use them and listen!"*

I came away from the conversation wondering, "What did they say?" Disgusted with myself I swore never to do that again. I was determined to listen intently to every new conversation.

I have an acquaintance who, when she calls, talks almost continually about herself. When she does ask about my life, within two sentences she interrupts and says something like, "Oh yeah, I know what you mean, that happened to me. Did I tell you about . . .?"

Ever have someone stare into space, probably thinking of all the things they *could* be doing, while you pour out your heart hoping for an occasional encouraging response? Or how about those who shy away from any kind of contact for fear of saying the wrong thing?

Be a listening ear for someone. Ask the Holy Spirit to give you direction when to speak and what to say. Make the call. Ask questions. Jesus did.

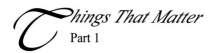

Isaiah
54:10
GNT
*The mountains
and hills may
crumble, but My
love for you will
never end; I will
keep forever my
promise of
peace." So says
the LORD who
loves you.*

Reality is a tough taskmaster.

Gloria Gaither wrote:
"We deal with reality at two points in our lives—
birth and death. If only we could always live our
days with as clear a vision of the things that matter as
we do at those two times." *

Gazing at the maple tree my husband planted, I'm
reminded how not long ago we watched the leaves turn
brilliant red. Today I observe its beauty alone.

The aloneness is intense. Sitting quietly at Jesus' feet it
slips away with a little less pain.

The hurried busyness of the next thing that must be done takes a back seat to
the tenderness the Holy Spirit brings through a deeper intimacy with *The
Three*.

After a death, life goes on, so they say. That's true. But never as we once
knew it.

Never again to experience the things that mattered. Hear the voice. See the
smile. Feel the touch. Share laughter, trials. Make up after a fight. Stroll hand
in hand. Sip coffee on the porch. Praise God for the promise of His rainbow.

Reality is a tough taskmaster.

* *We Have This Moment*

The changing leaves remind me I too am changing. I'm learning to forgive. Deciding to love.

Allowing disappointment and disillusionment to carry me through each day does not leave the choice to let go of hurtful criticism and condemnation. To forgive.

There is no real forgiveness without first understanding God's forgiveness. Receiving God's *unconditional* love and forgiveness enables me to love and forgive others.

> 1 Thessalonians
> 4:9
> ESV
> *Now concerning brotherly love you no need for anyone to write to you, for you yourselves have been taught by God to love one another.*

The supernatural work of the Holy Spirit is causing me to see with new eyes. I linger now to watch leaves slowly drift to the ground, hummingbirds draw pollen from flowers, a lizard warm himself on a sun-drenched rock.

I'm listening more to frogs croak at dusk, to the breeze-tossed wind chime fashion a new tune, the rushing river in the distance.

I'm living in the moment and resisting new activities to replace unnecessary ones I've given up. I've stopped the hurried pace to take time to reflect. To share with, pray for and love on people.

Remembering the precious time spent with my husband, hopefully I won't forget to capture every moment with those who are still here.

Every moment matters.

SEPTEMBER 28

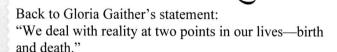

Isaiah
41:10
GNT
*"Do not be afraid—
I am with you! I am
your God—let
nothing terrify you!
I will make
you strong and
help you; I will
protect you
and save you."*

Back to Gloria Gaither's statement:
"We deal with reality at two points in our lives—birth and death."

Birth brings joy, excitement, anticipation. A whole lifetime of discovery. On the other hand, a notable heaviness accompanies death. Disappointment, sorrow, fear, all wrapped around a fragile heart enduring excruciating pain. Death feels so unnatural.

Before long you're caught up in the vague reality of 'now what'. The nineteenth century artist, Alfred Stevens, captured this thought in his exquisite painting of a beautiful young woman entitled *The Bath*. I know that look in her eyes. I've seen it my mirror.

Sometimes when we are in the midst of a tumultuous storm our vision is so blurred by fear and insecurity we can't *see* Jesus, let alone trust Him enough to step out of the boat. When my husband died I could not sense God's presence. Fear kept clawing at my spirit of ever sensing it again.

When we cannot see or sense, we are called to believe. Not easy, but absolutely essential if we are to trust Jesus in the fragile realities of life.

Some call me courageous. I have to wonder.

Not long ago, God used an experience to uncover my fear of going forward with writing. My home is in the country and one morning while walking I saw a horse having, what looked to me like a tantrum. He repeatedly bucked and ran from one end of the corral to the other. Each time he came to the electric wire that separated his corral from the next one, he skidded to a stop. I felt as if God was saying, "That's you Anne."

2 Timothy
1:7
DARBY
For God has not given us a spirit of cowardice, but of power, and of love, and of wise discretion.

"Me? What do You mean?"

† For years you've picked up the novel. You get going on it and time and again something causes you to skid to a halt and give up.

"Why do I do that Lord?"

† Fear. Fear of rejection. Fear of failure. Fear of what other people will say.

Ouch. Major dose of reality.

Charles Spurgeon wrote:
"How can you glorify God if you act like a coward?"

Isn't that the truth? We cannot allow fear to keep us from glorifying God in the things that truly matter. Loving God. Loving others. Wholly surrendering our lives for God's service.

Let's make every moment matter.

 ctober

His Healing Touch
It comes in a moment
Complete . . .
Guilt cannot withstand
Anger has no choice
Uncertainty and fear take flight
Pain hidden deep is vanquished
His Healing Touch
Secure in His nearness
Safe in His promises
Mind renewed
Heart restored
Accepted . . .
It lasts forever

Exciting Adventures Await
Part 1

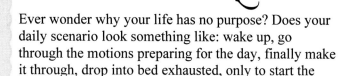

> **Romans 12:1, 2**
>
> *Therefore I urge you, brethren, by the mercies of God, to present your bodies a living and holy sacrifice, acceptable to God, which is your spiritual service of worship. And do not be conformed to this world, but be transformed by the renewing of your mind, so that you may prove what the will of God is, that which is good and acceptable and perfect.*

Ever wonder why your life has no purpose? Does your daily scenario look something like: wake up, go through the motions preparing for the day, finally make it through, drop into bed exhausted, only to start the next day doing the same thing all over again?

We go year after year looking forward to what? It's easy to understand the line in Peggy Lee's song, "Is that all there is?"

When my husband graduated to heaven I knew my purpose for living had vanished along with him. There's this sense of hopelessness when life has no purpose. You go through the motions and end up right back where you started. Hopeless.

King Solomon said, "Vanity. All is vanity." Vanity suggests uselessness, having no real value. All is vanity, unless of course, our lives are spent serving and glorifying God.

After a lot of soul searching I finally comprehend the reality that *God* is my purpose. Serving Him. Whatever that looks like.

Lack of purpose has been linked to depression, physical illness, even suicide. We humans were created to have purpose. Most however, never realize their purpose because they search with the wrong emphasis, motive, goal.

> Matthew
> 14:29
> NCV
> *Jesus said, "Come."*
> *And Peter left the*
> *boat and walked on*
> *the water to Jesus.*

Christians enjoy the unique advantage of having the power of the Holy Spirit residing within them. He encourages, excites, equips, executes all that is needed when our emphasis, motive, goal, is God's glory.

But are we willing to surrender our lives, let go of our own pre-conceived ideas, give of our time, talent, treasure allowing God to direct us in His perfect plan? We are an instant gratification society. Even when we do let go we want to see results *now*. God doesn't work that way.

If simply existing from day to day, floundering through life with no purpose has you longing for more, why not receive God's gift of salvation through His Son, Jesus Christ? Then ask God to reveal *His* purpose for your life. No matter how far God stretches you, don't be afraid to take the first step to making your true purpose a reality.

Come join the adventure.

God's Agenda
Part 1

Following Paul's description of the excellence of love, we are commanded to *pursue* love. In the Greek pursue is to follow or press hard after with earnestness, diligence. One who pursues love does so with the objective of obtaining it at all costs.

God is love and when we press in to know Him more, we are pursuing the purest love there is.

In this particular passage Paul is referring to spiritual gifts, infused by the Holy Spirit. Isn't Paul saying if we do not pursue love first, the gifts simply draw attention to the gift and ourselves, not to the Gift-Giver?

I have repeatedly failed in this pursuit. There have been glimpses of my gaining on the reality. Like when I complied with detailed instructions in a three-inch-thick binder, assembled a team, a site, advertising and more, for a two-day seminar featuring a nationally celebrated Bible study group. Selfishly undertaken for one reason only, so *I* could learn how to study the Bible in depth.

A call from my Mom informed me that my Dad's aorta surgery was scheduled for the first day of the seminar. Crushed, after an entire year of intense planning, scheduling, arranging, God graciously showed me that love is about people, not seminars.

od's Agenda
Part 2

To pursue love is to press hard after it, at the expense of all else.

> 1 Corinthians
> 16:14
> *Let all that you do be
> done in love.*

It means we want love more than our own way. It's a paradigm shift, changing our agenda from our own to God's. A shift to being, so the Holy Spirit can work— in the spiritual realm. We continue to move forward by His leading in the physical, but we look at circumstances through eyes and hearts of love.

In her book, *We Have This Moment*, Gloria Gaither writes about a morning observing the sights and sounds of London, England:
"Women of the night scurried past the proper ladies doing their morning shopping, never giving each other a glance of recognition of what they share in common."

Her perspective caused me to pause and wonder, what does that mean? These are women with the same needs. Doing what it takes to survive. Sadly, ignoring the realities of each other's lives.

Are we not to see broken, struggling survivors through eyes of love? Give them a smile, a touch, even stop everything in our own lives, at the expense of all else—to love them. God allows us the privilege of not just chasing love in the cerebral dimensions of our minds, but as Jesus demonstrated through His example, in our actions.

OCTOBER 4

$\mathcal{A}$ nxiety–What Anxiety
Part 1

1 Peter
5:7
AMPLIFIED
Casting the whole of your care [all your anxieties, all your worries, all your concerns, and for all] on Him, for He cares for you affectionately and cares about you watchfully.

That verse makes my stressed out, hair pulling, fist shaking, worrisome heart shout, "Thank You God."

To think He cares that much about *me*. To know I am God's *personal concern* encourages me to take a deep breath and release the pent up frustration inside. It gives me reason to smile and loosen my tense, tight, hunched-up shoulders.

An unfamiliar peace settles upon my soul urging me to rest securely in God's promises, knowing He is accomplishing much, even if it's not within my grasp to touch or catch sight of it.

In this world of inflated gas and food prices, the closure of countless businesses, massive layoffs, numerous homes in foreclosure and the probability of impending national financial disaster, can we really throw the whole weight of our anxieties completely and unreservedly upon God?

Absolutely. But how?

By becoming familiar with God's character and learning to trust the One who is concerned about every detail of our lives.

OCTOBER 5

Wouldn't it be great if we could hand over our worries, uncertainties, anxieties, one time and be done with it? Unfortunately everyday life creeps in and we tend to go right back to fretting and fussing.

> 1 Peter
> 5:6, 7
> *Therefore humble yourselves under the mighty hand of God, that He may exalt you at the proper time, casting all your anxiety on Him, because He cares for you.*

This act of surrender to God is a daily decision. It's a moment by moment choice to unshackle our concerns and relinquish them, believing He is faithful. Consider how much less stress we would suffer if we gave God every anxious thought.

Webster's defines anxiety as:
An abnormal and overwhelming sense of apprehension and fear often marked by physiological signs (as sweating, tension, and increased pulse), by doubt concerning the reality and nature of the threat, and by self-doubt about one's capacity to cope with it.

What a relief to rid ourselves of that.

We can't change another's attitude or response, only determine to relinquish our own anxiety and thank God that:
> *"The Lord your God is in your midst, a victorious warrior. He will exult over you with joy, He will renew you in His love, He will rejoice over you with shouts of joy" (Zephaniah 3:17).*

Does it get any better than that?

No Surprise To God

Part 1

I met a woman in the park the other day quite 'by accident'. I'll call her Betty.

Betty has lived through extreme hardship and is determined to overcome. As she puts it, "Through the power of the Holy Spirit."

For Betty, it's a moment by moment decision, as it ought to be for all of us. She chooses to cling to Jesus and His word as her very breath, to make it through just one more day.

Raised in the east by alcoholic parents Betty was abused in every way imaginable. Even so, she felt it could have been worse. Sickly, her parents' abuse turned more to her siblings than to her. Married to an alcoholic, Betty became one herself.

Diagnosed with a type of mental illness, for the past year Betty has had surgery twice on her bleeding brain, been hospitalized for numerous serious afflictions and had surgery to remove a mass from her pancreas. During this time her husband died. After all she has endured her family cannot understand her faith and joy.

It's encouraging to know that God's eye is upon us so we can triumph over whatever may come. Betty certainly has.

OCTOBER 7

"This is no surprise to God." That's been on my lips a lot lately.

Most mornings I open my eyes wondering what the day will hold. Quiet solitude. Hectic chaos. Happiness. Sorrow. Will calamity and confusion consume the hours or will serving others make up my day? How will I handle the obstacles? Frustrations. Anxious moments. Uncertainties.

> Jeremiah
> 17:10
> *"I, the LORD, search the heart, I test the mind, even to give to each man according to his ways, according to the results of his deeds."*

God searches the heart and tests the mind. Nothing happens that He is not aware of. We have everything we need to spread God's love to others no matter what our circumstances. Just look at dear Betty, my new friend from the park.

Bible in hand and walker to steady her pace, Betty's goal that day was to minister to me, a stranger. Even though difficult to think clearly and speak precisely Betty did not get frustrated, but rather apologized for her failure to communicate well. Her smile was luminous especially when she talked about the love of her Jesus.

If you believe God's hand is upon you no matter what happens, like Betty you too can experience profound peace when uncertainty threatens or calamity strikes.

After all . . . it's no surprise to God.

OCTOBER 8

 o You Believe

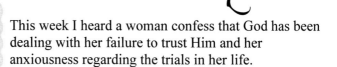

1 Peter 1:3-5

Blessed be the God and Father of our Lord Jesus Christ, who according to His great mercy has caused us to be born again to a living hope through the resurrection of Jesus Christ from the dead, to obtain an inheritance which is imperishable and undefiled and will not fade away, reserved in heaven for you, who are protected by the power of God through faith for a salvation ready to be revealed in the last time.

This week I heard a woman confess that God has been dealing with her failure to trust Him and her anxiousness regarding the trials in her life.

"It's hard to believe what I'm reading in the Bible. How can I trust God and be obedient if I don't really know Him? How can I know Him unless I believe His word?" she asked.

Good questions. Time and again the Bible reminds us who God is. Protector. Shield. Strong Tower. Defender. Refuge. Fortress.

Like an eagle that stirs up its nest, that hovers over its young, He [God] spread His wings and caught them, He carried them on His pinions (Deuteronomy 32:11).

Look at Gideon and the three hundred, David and Goliath, King Asa, Peter, Paul among many others. The Bible is full of encouraging confirmations to relieve an anxious heart . . . if only we believe.

Believe it. God is trustworthy.

Exactly what are we able to overwhelmingly conquer? Paul provides a list: tribulation, distress, persecution, famine, nakedness, peril, sword.

Overwhelmingly. What a great word. In the original language it means more then conquer, it means to utterly defeat. We have the power of Christ within us to utterly defeat everything on Paul's list.

How do we defeat them? Once we know the immense love of God and receive it through His Son we have the power of His Spirit to overcome. Knowing absolutely nothing will ever separate us from His love encourages us to believe we can prevail over every obstacle.

There is no other power like God's love.

Romans 8:37-39
But in all these things we overwhelmingly conquer through Him who loved us. For I am convinced that neither death, nor life, nor angels, nor principalities, nor things present, nor things to come, nor powers, nor height, nor depth, nor any other created thing shall be able to separate us from the love of God, which is in Christ Jesus our Lord.

Catch The Vision
Part 1

Acts
1:8
"But you will receive power when the Holy Spirit has come upon you; and you shall be My [Jesus] witnesses both in Jerusalem, and in all Judea and Samaria, and even to the remotest part of the earth."

Lord break our hearts for what breaks Yours.

Life is hard. Jesus knew that. He lived it. Even so, He said:

> *"I came that they may have life, and have it abundantly" (John 10:10).*

Jesus is not asking us to do anything He didn't do as a man, fully human. But many would say, "He was God. Of course He made it through the tough stuff." Really? Do we not, as Christians, have God living inside us in the person of the Holy Spirit?

Jesus was a man full of joy who loved life. He loved people. We see Him in the company of and giving worth and value to all kinds of people; men, women, children, lepers, prostitutes, tax collectors, shop owners. People were drawn to Him. Was it because of the miraculous works He did? No.

Jesus demonstrated authentic joy. And from the joy that filled His being, He exuded love. Pure, unadulterated love. Have you ever known anyone who was not drawn to that kind of love? They may appear untouched, but in time watch how their hardness and resistance melt under love's miraculous power.

OCTOBER 11

atch The Vision
Part 2

Last week I received a letter from a friend who lives on the other side of the valley. Sensing a serious battle, her parting word was a plea to pray for pastors in the valley.

> My response: You asked me to pray for the pastors in our valley and actually I been praying for some of the pastors. There *is* a major battle going on and it's being fought by God's mighty warriors. I sense a protective army around some of them. And sadly, there are others who don't need the army.

Matthew
23:37
THE MESSAGE
"Jerusalem!
Jerusalem! Murderer
of prophets! Killer of
the ones who brought
you God's news! How
often I've ached to
embrace your children,
the way a hen gathers
her chicks
under her wings, and
you wouldn't let me."

As I look out over the valley this morning, tears flow.
God is breaking my heart for what breaks His. Those who think they know Him, but don't.

A precious saint, Miss Betty, who is now in glory with her sweet Jesus, pointed out how much Jesus loved those religious leaders who condemned and hated Him. The ones who thought they were living in the fullness of God, but sadly were not. His heart ached to gather those with hardened hearts and pious knowledge.

OCTOBER 12

Hebrews
12:2
THE MESSAGE
*Keep your eyes on
Jesus, who both
began and finished
this race we're in.
Study how he
did it. Because he
never lost sight of
where he was
headed—that
exhilarating finish
in and with God—
he could put up
with anything along
the way: Cross,
shame, whatever.*

If we are to catch Jesus' vision, it begins by allowing the Holy Spirit to do a heart search and break down all pretense, cover-up, false beliefs within us. For how can we be filled with abundant joy with all that other rubble in there?

Through the power of the Holy Spirit we are able to love the unlovely with honest compassion. Others are then drawn to that joy-filled love that emanates from us.

My friend's letter brought to mind the reality that many churches are lukewarm. Stuck in a dead rut. Going through the motions. *Doing* church.

It's comfortable. That may be, but it is certainly not the example Jesus set. He rocked the world of the religious leaders as well as those who had no religious training. It was not comfortable. Yet joy radiated from His very being.

Jesus did not *do* church. He loved people.

Come on everybody. Catch the vision. Let's stop just *doing* church and start loving people.

I've recently recorded a number of passages that refer to what God sees. I seem to 'stumble' on them at least once a week.

> Psalm
> 32:8
> *I will instruct you and teach you in the way which you should go; I will counsel you with My eye upon you.*

It's as if God is saying, "I'm here, this is no surprise to Me. I know the frustration, heartache, joy, you feel. I see every detail of your life. I'm here."

Contented sigh. Peace to my soul.

Some would argue they don't want God to see everything going on in their lives. Why not? Sure, I don't like it when He sees me act like a putz or when I flippantly say something that should have been left unsaid. It's not pretty when my anger gets the upper hand or my pride stands up straight and stiff.

Ultimately, I'm grateful God sees everything. For then the Holy Spirit lovingly speaks to me. Confirming, convicting, transforming my heart. Confessing my sin, God is faithful to forgive me.

It's exciting to chronicle passages of how God watches over us. Here's one to dwell on today.

> *For the eyes of the LORD move to and fro throughout the earth that He may strongly support those whose heart is completely His (2 Chronicles 16:9).*

What's In Your Hand
Part 1

Luke
24:47-49
NLT
It was also written that this message would be proclaimed in the authority of His name to all the nations, beginning in Jerusalem: 'There is forgiveness of sins for all who repent.' You are witnesses of all these things. And now I will send the Holy Spirit, just as my Father promised. But stay here in the city until the Holy Spirit comes and fills you with power from heaven.

Once a person comes to the startling revelation of who Jesus is, and who they are in light of that discovery, most stand awestruck and humbled, as were the two men on their way to Emmaus.

This true knowledge of and love for Jesus causes us to eagerly live each day obedient to His call. Filled with the Holy Spirit, His fruit {love, joy, peace, patience, kindness, goodness, faithfulness, gentleness, self-control} overflows as evidence of our desire to serve Jesus.

On our own we do not possess the power to accomplish this work. However, the Holy Spirit teaches, endows with gifts, gives us courage to address others providing the appropriate words to speak with boldness.

Look at the apostle Paul. He was always asking for prayer knowing he could do nothing of kingdom value without the Holy Spirit's power.

To catch the vision where it begins; in our hearts, families, church, community, means learning how to live out our faith and care for others. Jesus cast His vision even farther into all of Judea and Samaria. For us, our county, state, nation.

We may well ask, "But what can I do?" The ripple effect of our faith commitment to obedience spreads wide. We simply say yes. Make ourselves available and use whatever God has put in our hand. Then we step out and hurl the first stone into the water.

> John
> 14:26
> *But the Helper, the Holy Spirit, whom the Father will send in My name, He will teach you all things, and bring to your remembrance all that said to you.*

Filled with the Holy Spirit's supernatural power we hear and obey, sometimes timid and unsure, often not knowing where that might lead. We take up our sword and go. Trusting His presence, favor, mercy, go with us.

Wouldn't it be great to have the fortitude to trust God and go forth like Jonathan? One man along with his armor bearer against thousands, determined to move out, despite impossible odds, to honor his God.
    "For the LORD is not restrained to save by many or by few"
    (1 Samuel 14:6).

 Part 1

Late one night I sat reading a book. For more than a quarter of an hour the agonizing honk of a single goose kept disrupting my thoughts. Walking onto the porch, unable to discern the reason for the distraught cry, I asked God to help the poor creature.

Back with my book I listened. The honking stopped. Smile.

The next morning I wrote in my journal:
Thank You Lord for helping that lonely, hurting, lost, confused goose last night. Its cry was heart wrenching. You do care for Your creatures.

God's response to my heartfelt gratitude:
† That goose is a picture of Israel—had a compelling impact, seeing that an increasingly deeper love for the Jewish people has been growing in my heart since first visiting The Beautiful Land. My global missionary heart aches for Israel.

Many would say if you can't go then give, pray. True, but I wonder if some of us hear those words and breathe a sigh of relief sensing we're off the hook. We no longer fear having to serve in Africa or Iceland or Russia.

Have we really offered all we have and all we are to God? Are we doing everything we possibly can so those in all the world hear the gospel?

OCTOBER 17

Some cannot go. Still, it's possible to write letters of encouragement to those in foreign lands even as the apostle Paul did. Shouldn't we be asking ourselves, "What do I have in my hand?"

I know two incredible women who asked that very question.

Aleta, artist extraordinaire, used her art to teach, encourage, pray with others, bringing many into an intimate encounter with Jesus. When she became bedridden, Aleta felt as if she had nothing left in her hand, until she realized she could still teach art and strengthen others in their faith from her bed.

> **Romans 10:14, 15 NCV**
> *But before people can ask the Lord for help, they must believe in him; and before they can believe in him, they must hear about him; and for them to hear about the Lord, someone must tell them; and before someone can go and tell them, that person must be sent.*

Tosha Zwanziger wondered what she had in her hand. As a worship leader, together with husband, Joseph, they cut a CD with the sole intent that all proceeds would go to organizations fighting injustice around the globe. *

Moses had a staff, Jonathan a sword, Paul a pen, Aleta a brush, Tosha a keyboard. Though they carry diverse objects in their hands, they all embrace and exhibit the same faith and trust in their hearts.

And . . . they went.

* http://www.pagesforjustice.com

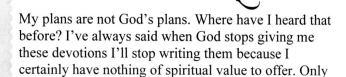

Psalm 66:5
Come and see the works of God, who is awesome in His deeds toward the sons of men.
*THE MESSAGE -
Take a good look at God's wonders— they'll take your breath away.*

My plans are not God's plans. Where have I heard that before? I've always said when God stops giving me these devotions I'll stop writing them because I certainly have nothing of spiritual value to offer. Only God's word does.

It's been said confession is good for the soul. Although it would not be my choice, it seems God wants me to share a bit of my journal notes, at least during this incredible time here at Oasis of Hope Hospital—God's little taste of heaven on earth.

Thank You Lord for:
- *This place - You got us here in such quick time, what an adventure it's been*
- *Another day with my husband - for his perseverance - what an inspiration he is*
- *Time yesterday morning with You, time to prepare myself for this journey*
- *Your incredible word, for speaking sweet words of promise and truth to my spirit*

You alone are God! Awesome, giving, loving, gracious.
I feel like I've crawled into Your lap, Abba. I'm resting in the comfort of Your strong arms. You whisper Your word into my spirit and remind me of who You are and the wonder of Your works.

OCTOBER 19

Lord, You are bathing me in the deepest, most secure kind of peace I've ever known. There is no fear, no anxiousness, no questioning Your wisdom. Sheathed in Your strength I am protected from the attacks of the enemy.

It feels like Your warring angels and a supernatural impenetrable barrier of protection surrounds this hospital. You are doing miraculous works every moment in, through and for the people who are here. How good You are God. How awesome Your works.

> Colossians
> 3:15, 16
> *Let the peace of Christ rule in your hearts, to which indeed you were called in one body; and be thankful. Let the word of Christ richly dwell within you.*

To think it was only one week ago I spoke to Dr. L and here we are after The Passport Tour smack dab in the midst of Your awesome works. Thank You for the opportunity to be here, to see and experience Your hand at work. Bless the patients with encouragement and hope. Infuse them, Holy Spirit, with the truth of Your power.

Lord, You are answering my prayers in ways I never could have imagined. Humbling my heart. A deeper intimacy with You.

Open my eyes to see Your supernatural hand at work, give me all You have. I've known for some time there is much, much more. I want whatever that is.

OCTOBER 20

Words Of Promise And Truth

Part 3

> Psalm
> 66:8-10
> Bless our God, O peoples, and sound His praise abroad, who keeps us in life and does not allow our feet to slip. For You have tried us, O God; You have refined us as silver is refined.

Nothing like a dramatic wake up call to reveal what is really important.

Lord Jesus, show me how to shower my husband with the tremendous love You demonstrated and left behind as an example.

Give me the heart and attitude of a true servant, one that says, what can I do for you? This seems such a daunting task Lord. After all the years I've lived to make my needs known and met rather than giving every one to You, allowing You to accomplish what concerns me.

In his heart a man plans his course, but the Lord determines his steps. You make me smile Lord. You are teaching me to slow down and savor each moment. Even with the hair dryer, it overheated on high. Slow down Anne.

It is not good for a person to be without knowledge, and he who hurries his footsteps makes a mistake.

You make me smile Lord.

Your promises are true.

Blackberry bushes are prolific here. A strong, hearty plant, they grow wild. Cut them down, they come back thicker and heartier. Salvaging the tasty treat encaged in the dense foliage is not for the faint of heart.

> Psalm
> 119:105
> *Your word is a lamp*
> *to my feet and a*
> *light to my path.*

Sharp thorns and massive undergrowth invariably thwart the first time treasure hunter from claiming the juicy, succulent bounty. However, determined perseverance is often rewarded with a triumphant bucket of black gold. The perilous hunt is well worth the effort when savoring the first luscious cobbler of the season.

Life has its own prickly barbs, impenetrable barriers, insurmountable obstacles. Disappointment. Sadness. Division. Pride. Guilt. Frustration. Unmet dreams.

The psalmist reminds us it is God's word that illumines our hearts and minds to clear the confusion. Like supernatural clippers lopping the clutter and uncertainty in our lives until we sense . . . Encouragement. Joy. Unity. Humility. Confidence. Contentment. Fulfillment.

Deep within the dense jungle of the heart and the treacherous dark undergrowth of the soul, lies a pearl of great value.

Jesus waits for the slightest invitation to begin the pruning process, to cut through all the barriers and clear away the obstacles that smother our spirit, allowing His light to flood the darkness and direct our path.

God Is Doin' Something
Part 1

Ecclesiastes
5:1, 2
Guard your steps
as you go to the
house of God and
draw near to
listen rather than
to offer the
sacrifice of fools;
for they do not
know they are
doing evil. Do not
be hasty in word
or impulsive in
thought to bring
up a matter in the
presence of God.
For God is in
heaven and you
are on the earth;
therefore let your
words be few.

More instruction from God to share my journal notes. I came across this conversation with God that took place some time ago. Amazing how He prepares us for whatever will come in order to take us even deeper.

Guard your steps – remember you are in God's holy presence
Have a clean heart rather than to offer the sacrifice of fools
I think I am doing the right thing when in reality I am being a fool – doing my thing, not God's

Exodus 3:5-6
† Do you really know who I AM?

Exodus 30:18-20
† Come to Me with a clean heart ready to give your life to and for Me

Jesus my High Priest, You have cleansed my heart with Your blood Holy Spirit do this in my heart make it truly pure, do Your work, WHATEVER it takes to get me to this point - Protect me from the lies and attacks of the enemy

OCTOBER 23

Ecclesiastes
5:3, 4
For the dream comes through much effort and the voice of a fool through many words. When you make a vow to God, do not be late in paying it; for He takes no delight in fools. Pay what you vow!

Sharing conversations with God through my journal notes is revealing and humbling.

Isaiah 1:12, 16, 18-19; 1 Samuel 15:22
† I desire a pure heart, washed clean of everything that is not of Me – a heart that is ready to be no matter what I ask

† Once your heart has been cleansed of everything else it is a clean slate for Me to write on
Listen and talk to Me – Keep close – Watch as I do the writing
Be strong and courageous to do what I write on your heart - do not doubt it

REMEMBER—LISTEN TO GOD—TALK TO GOD

Not by my might or my intellect or my dreams or my drive or my strength or my plans but by YOU

Remember God is holy – listen don't talk – don't give what I think God wants, listen to what HE wants

Don't give Him a bunch of flowery words that sound impressive, give Him what truly flows from my heart

Choose your words well before you speak them and don't hurry your heart to believe this is God's will

WATCH—LISTEN—LISTEN—LISTEN to His good, holy, true words

Holding On Tight

Part 1

> Isaiah
> 43:2
> NLT
> *"When you go through deep waters, I will be with you. When you go through rivers of difficulty, you will not drown! When you walk through the fire of oppression, you will not be burned up; the flames will not consume you."*

I will be with you.

What more comforting words are there? In the midst of any situation we can count on God to be there, holding on tight. Whether in need of comfort, encouragement, healing, refreshing, courage, restoration, or even just a friend with a listening ear, God promises to be with us.

God told His people through Moses:

> *"Be strong and courageous, do not be afraid or tremble at them, for the LORD your God is the one who goes with you. He will not fail you or forsake you . . . The LORD is the one who goes ahead of you; He will be with you"* (Deuteronomy 31:6,8).

We as God's people can take hold of His word and cling to His promises. No matter our circumstances, we need not be afraid. We can count on God.

OCTOBER 25

This has been a particularly difficult week of battling fiery darts and flaming arrows from every direction. Battling my flesh {succumbing to pride}, the world {gratifying whoever}, the devil {devious liar}, all of them consuming my thoughts and actions.

My prayers have centered on the word *help*, repeating this passage over and over to myself.

God brought to mind events that took place in the Bible where He was with those who trusted Him. The prophet Elisha, surrounded by the king of Aram's army, encouraged his petrified servant:

> *"Do not fear, for those who are with us are more than those who are with them" (2 Kings 6:16).*

Can you imagine what the servant thought as he looked around and saw only the two of them standing there?

Elisha, confident God was with him, asked God to relieve his servant's fear:

> *"O LORD, I pray, open his eyes that he may see." And the LORD opened the servant's eyes and he saw; and behold, the mountain was full of horses and chariots of fire all around Elisha (2 Kings 6:17).*

Oh yeah. We can trust God.

OCTOBER 26

Holding On Tight

Part 3

> Esther
> 5:13, 14
> *"Yet all of this does not satisfy me every time I see Mordecai the Jew sitting at the king's gate." Then Zeresh his wife and all his friends said to him, "Have a gallows fifty cubits high made and in the morning ask the king to have Mordecai hanged on it; then go joyfully with the king to the banquet."*

The evil, jealous Haman, prime minister to king Ahasuerus, had a gallows built to hang Queen Esther's guardian, Mordecai. God's divine intervention caused the king to have a restless night. For some strange reason {we all know what that was} Ahasuerus asked for the book of records of important kingdom events.

Lo and behold Ahasuerus finds a previous incident where Mordecai's intercession saved the king's life. Now he wants to honor Mordecai:

> *So Haman came in and the king said to him, "What is to be done for the man whom the king desires to honor?" (Esther 6:6)*

Brings a smile to my face how God intervenes on our behalf. I can trust Him with every detail of my life.

You too, can trust God to battle those flaming arrows, to be with you through the valley of the shadow of whatever overwhelming trouble, difficulty or oppression you're facing. You can know without a doubt—God is with you.

OCTOBER 27

Webster's defines praise:
To regard with great or extravagant respect, honor or devotion

I love the word extravagant. It brings to mind unrestrained and lavish worship.

This month marks the anniversary of my Beloved's death and home-going. At times it's been a horrendous storm of uncertainty and loneliness. Each day has felt like an eternity, yet the months have passed swiftly. The Lord has continually carried me, through every first experience and major learning curve. Teaching me humility, dependence, thankfulness, grace, mercy, love.

> Isaiah
> 12:4, 5
> NCV
> *At that time you will say, "Praise the LORD and worship him. Tell everyone what he has done and how great he is. Sing praise to the LORD, because he has done great things. Let all the world know what he has done."*

Casting Crowns, sings a song, *Praise You in the Storm,* that pretty much describes my journey.

The chorus goes like this:
I'll praise You in this storm
And I will lift my hands
For You are who You are
No matter where I am
Every tear I've cried
You hold in Your hand
You never left my side
And though my heart is torn
I will praise You in this storm

Anyone can praise God when life is moving along like a gentle breeze. But do we choose to give Him extravagant praise while living through the frightening, uncertain storm?

> 1 Corinthians
> 15:55
> *"O death, where is your victory? O death, where is your sting?"*

Although the pain remains, the list of praises continues to grow as the anniversary of my Love's home-going approaches.

We have a choice when tragedy strikes. We can become resentful and wallow in self-pity or resiliently look for God's beauty that rises out of the ashes. We have the opportunity to grow and reveal God's transforming power.

In the gospel of John, Jesus, having told His disciples He would soon be leaving, wanted them to know He would see them again. If they believe. *Jesus said to him, "I am the way, and the truth, and the life; no one comes to the Father but through Me" (John 14:6).*

The truth is death has no victory or sting for those who intimately know the Way [Jesus] to the Father in heaven. Fear of death is annihilated, replaced by glorious anticipation.

I've heard it said of those who belong to Jesus; the first breath they take after their last breath here, is in heaven. That is where my Love resides. Face to face, breathing in the presence of Jesus.

Heaven or hell? The Truth or the lie? Will death have its stinging victory? Or will your last breath here, usher you into the presence of Jesus?

OCTOBER 29

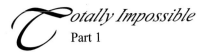

Can we, like Mary, exalt and glorify God in the midst of uncertainty and difficult circumstances? Mary must have felt confusion, fear, doubt, when the angel Gabriel announced she was the woman who would give birth to the Messiah. Yet most assuredly, there would also have been awe and humility in her heart as she listened to the certain proclamation.

> Luke
> 1:46, 47
> *And Mary said: "My soul exalts the Lord, and my spirit has rejoiced in God my Savior."*

Imagine the reassurance Mary experienced when Gabriel confirmed *nothing* will be impossible with God. That statement is another one of those that has a 'do you believe' written beside it in my Bible. Do I really believe *nothing* is impossible with God?

God revealed this truth to Abraham, Job, Jeremiah, Zechariah and many others. Thousands believed nothing was impossible when Jesus healed the sick, cast out demons, spoke life into the hearts of those who had given up hope. After Jesus raised Lazarus from the dead there had to be countless who believed.

Are we convinced today that nothing is impossible with God? Once He has given us direction are we determined to believe, trust and exult Him as Mary did, without seeing the end result?

OCTOBER 30

Totally Impossible
Part 2

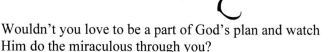

Wouldn't you love to be a part of God's plan and watch Him do the miraculous through you?

Certainly Mary never thought her part would include divine conception and giving birth to the Son of God. Mary's faith {the promise, confidence, guarantee of things hoped for, the evidence, certain persuasion, strong belief of things not seen} caused her to trust God completely.

We serve a living God and those who believe have the opportunity to experience in real time, right now, what we might be tempted to call the impossible.

What word has God spoken into your life that you've pushed back in your mind because it seems ridiculous, impractical, unachievable? Is there something that appears totally impossible?

Like Mary you may be thinking, how can this be? You might wonder what God is doing. This is definitely not the direction you thought He would take with regard to your life.

Ah, been there. Living that.

November

We endure not because we are
determined and resolute
but because of our love
for the Invisible King
and the supernatural strength
and power of the
Holy Spirit within

$\mathcal{A}$ lone In God's Presence
Part 1

Exodus
33:15
*Then he said to
Him, "If Your
presence does not
go with us, do not
lead us up from
here."*
GNT - *Moses
replied, "If you
do not go with us,
don't make us
leave this place."*

Have you ever had such an intense desire for God's presence that you said, "Lord I'm not leaving this place until I sense Your presence?" Adamant, Moses was not going anywhere without God. I wonder if we are ever that hungry for God.

Every once in awhile, the need for God's presence wells up so strong inside of me that I go and spend a day with God. Some of you are saying, "What are you talking about? God is with us all the time, every minute of every day. He's everywhere."

True. However, the manifest presence of God, the sense that He is right there talking to my spirit seems to take on deeper intimacy when it's just Him and I in a quiet solitary place. There are no distractions. He has my undivided attention. I tend to listen more intently.

Does that deep yearning for God persist in you to such an extent that you only find solace outside your normal environment with extended one on one time with Him? When was the last time you deliberately set aside a whole day just to be with God?

NOVEMBER 1

Notice everyone who sought the Lord went outside the camp away from the everyday things of life. Verse nine goes on to say:

> *Whenever Moses entered the tent, the pillar of cloud would descend and stand at the entrance of the tent; and the LORD would speak with Moses (Exodus 33:9).*

When we go out, take time away from the day to day just to be with the Lord, He comes and speaks with us. We have heart communication with Him. Through the Holy Spirit, His word, perhaps an inspirational book, singing praises, exploring His creation.

> **Exodus 33:7**
> *Now Moses used to take the tent and pitch it outside the camp, a good distance from the camp, and he called it the tent of meeting. And everyone who sought the LORD would go out to the tent of meeting which was outside the camp.*

As the discussion progresses in this Exodus passage, Moses' desire for God intensifies. He basically tells God, if I cannot sense Your presence I don't want to go, I won't go! Lord, only when You are with me and *Your* presence is seen, not mine, will others believe and see that You are. Moses is so overwhelmed with the majesty of God's presence he asks God to show him His glory.

Imagine time alone with God as He reveals His glory.

In The Dark Hours

Part 1

2 Corinthians
12:9, 10
And He has said to me, "My grace is sufficient for you, for power is perfected in weakness." Most gladly, therefore, I will rather boast about my weaknesses, so that the power of Christ may dwell in me. Therefore I am well content with weaknesses, with insults, with distresses, with persecutions, with difficulties, for Christ's sake; for when I am weak, then I am strong.

You never truly recognize how weak you are until something completely out of your control takes place.

My husband had a great knack for creating a sense of security for me here in the physical realm. A detail person with lots of energy, he cared for me in ways I did not fully appreciate until he was gone. Today my life is one *major* learning curve.

I have a whole new view of being strong. When my husband died, people told me Jesus would meet me were I am, that He would hold and comfort me, pull me up out of the pit when I fell in over my head. They said He would be my strength when mine was spent.

In the dark hours of sorrow I wasn't so sure I believed them.

One night after a particularly difficult day of grieving long and hard, I needed to stop crying or face the very real possibility of making myself sick. Someone had said when life is overwhelming speak out the name of Jesus. Hoarse whispers uttered the only two words I could get out, "Jesus help."

Within seconds it felt as if a warm quilt rested upon me. Sensing Jesus' nearness my sobbing stopped. Surprisingly I fell asleep and slept all night.

> **2 Corinthians 13:4**
> *For indeed He was crucified because of weakness, yet He lives because of the power of God. For we also are weak in Him, yet we will live with Him because of the power of God directed toward you.*

It's not false modesty when I say I no longer want to be strong. It is Jesus' strength alone that carries me through this horrendous experience. Without His strength it's nearly impossible to perform even the most menial task. To get out of bed, take a shower, make myself presentable, go out among people, breathe.

People have called me brave, courageous, an inspiration. I am none of those things. What they see is Jesus' tremendous strength. His hand working to humble my heart, to grow my character.

Am I really all that weak? Oh yeah. And believe me when I am weak Christ's power is all-sufficient.

> **1 John 4:16**
>
> *We have come to know and have believed the love which God has for us. God is love and the one who abides in love abides in God, and God abides in him.*

God is love. John states it twice to make a vital point. God is love. Whatever concept we might have of love, God personifies it.

1 Corinthians 13:4-8 gives a glimpse of what unconditional love looks like. Certainly a standard we ought to strive for. Still, true unconditional love is bestowed by only one person—God.

Okay . . . so . . . grandparents, mothers, fathers, wives, husbands, brothers, sisters are saying, "I love unconditionally." Really? You love another and expect *nothing* in return? Not even love, respect, an understanding word, a listening ear, a sweet smile from a tiny face?

Someone asked me, "If God loves me how can He inflict so much pain on me and my loved one(s)?" Does God inflict pain? That's not what love does. *Love is patient, love is kind and is not jealous; love does not brag and is not arrogant, does not act unbecomingly; it does not seek its own, is not provoked, does not take into account a wrong suffered, does not rejoice in unrighteousness, but rejoices with the truth; bears all things, believes all things, hopes all things, endures all things. Love never fails (1 Corinthians 13:4-8).*

Love is faithful and just.

NOVEMBER 5

It is love that saves us from hell and eternal separation from God.

I recently met a man who is into mystical religions. He said for the first thirty years of his 'faith walk' he read only the Bible. In the short time I spoke with him it became apparent he was extremely knowledgeable about what the Bible says.

> 1 John
> 4:17
> *By this, love is perfected with us, so that we may have confidence in the day of judgment; because as He is, so also are we in this world.*

This man now reads books on transcendental thinking and every kind of religious experience. It seemed to me he picked something he liked from each, including the Bible, and made that his religion.

He told me when he looks at people he sees love and the good that was created in them. That the ultimate goal is to see that love in every person he looks at, to pray {I'm not so sure who he prays to} that the Holy Spirit would do His miraculous work in them so they could live a good, prosperous life. I pointed out not every person has the Holy Spirit living within them.

He smiled.

We also talked about pain and suffering, Adam and Eve and how sin came into the world and God's plan of salvation for humanity.

NOVEMBER 6

> 1 John
> 4:18, 19
> *There is no fear in love; but perfect love casts out fear, because fear involves punishment, and the one who fears is not perfected in love. We love, because He first loved us.*

During our lunch hour exposition of the Bible, this man said he didn't like the 'bloody' Old Testament, but preferred the New Testament.

I told him when I was a new Christian I didn't care much for the Old Testaments either because I didn't understand it. But the more I learned about Jesus, I could see the Old Testament pointed directly to Him. Jesus is on every page of the Old Testament as God's plan of salvation for mankind.

This searcher told me he didn't care much for the book of Revelation either, feeling it's all about an angry God. My response—I don't see God as angry, rather just. A just, loving God.

He nodded thoughtfully.

The point is, God is love and love does not inflict pain. Pain, whether physical, emotional or mental is a direct result of the fall of man. From Genesis to Revelation we see every horrendous sin man has ever committed and many of the repercussions and consequences for those sins.

For now we still live in a fallen world. But God—sent His Son and promised believers in Jesus Christ a beautiful future, eternity with Him.

Now that's pure, unconditional love.

Consider God's peace encountered by 'some' of the Israelites while living through their desert experience. Knowing God carried them in His unseen arms through the entire ordeal, they learned to trust Him even when they could not see the end result.

God considered their every need as a father would his child. He not only supplied physical provisions, but spiritual sustenance as well. The Israelites' faith increased as they walked through difficult wilderness trials and experienced God's presence and deliverance.

> **Deuteronomy 1:31**
> *And in the wilderness where you saw how the LORD your God carried you, just as a man carries his son, in all the way which you have walked, until you came to this place.*

Can you envision God carrying you through your darkest hour, your most bleak desert plight? Picture God lifting you in His strong arms when your heart is broken, your health is progressively getting worse, your hope is gone.

Even if your earthly father did not care for you as he should have, you can be assured your heavenly Father is trustworthy.

When God promises security, peace, unfathomable love—He delivers.

Passionate To Shine

> **Matthew 5:14, 16**
> *"You are the light of the world. A city set on a hill cannot be hidden . . . Let your light shine before men in such a way that they may see your good works, and glorify your Father who is in heaven."*

I live in a white two-story house that sits on a hill clearly seen from the highway. It never ceases to amaze me when I forget to leave a light on and return home after the sun goes down that in the darkness of the valley there is no hint a house or even a hill exists.

On the other hand, when expecting company the house is illuminated from inside and by porch lights as well. No exaggeration, when driving down the highway in the dark, you can see the lights shining from my house a mile and a half away.

In this passage, Jesus, talking to His followers, those who have believed and received the truth of who He is, tells them to live their lives in such a way that their actions glorify the Father.

The light radiating through us ought to shine so bright that others have no problem seeing. Our passion for *The Three* ought to illuminate our lives.

NOVEMBER 9

Just how is this spiritual light illuminated? The Holy Spirit infuses believers with His power, illumining our hearts so that it's as impossible to hide the joy and excitement of our faith as it is to hide an entire city built on top of a hill. We may have no idea how bright His light shines through us, but others see it.

> 2 Timothy
> 1:14
> NLT
> *Through the power of the Holy Spirit who lives within us, carefully guard the precious truth that has been entrusted to you.*

I admire A.W. Tozer's resolve to set out on a lifelong pursuit of God. He says of the Holy Spirit in the book *Tozer on the Holy Spirit*:
"[He] loves us so much that when we insult Him, He is grieved; when we ignore Him, He is grieved; when we resist Him, He is grieved; and when we doubt Him, He is grieved."

I do not want to grieve the Holy Spirit. There is a dogged tenacity in me to intimately know this One who fills me with His power. My heart's desire is to exalt and honor Him as I do the other two members of the Trinity.

Tell me, does your life lack passionate illumination? Or does the power of the Holy Spirit permeate your life so joy and excitement shine bright?

A God Of Details
Part 1

Exodus
25:10, 11
"They shall construct an ark of acacia wood two and a half cubits long, and one and a half cubits wide, and one and a half cubits high. You shall overlay it with pure gold, inside and out you shall overlay it, and you shall make a gold molding around it."

From creation to salvation, the Garden of Eden, to Noah's ark, manna in the desert, constructing the Tabernacle, division of the promised land, blessings, curses, building Solomon's temple, the lineage of Messiah, fulfillment of every Messianic prophecy, the Cross, death, resurrection of Jesus, to the new Jerusalem; God is into details.

God created us for moment by moment fellowship with Him, to walk and talk with Him in the cool of the day, seek His will, live it out with great joy, excitement and anticipation.

Our God longs for intimacy with us. An intimacy that grows deeper with knowledge of and continuous interaction with Him.

In the book of Romans, Paul shows us how to die to the old sin nature and live a new victorious life in Christ Jesus. He reminds us that new life is a futile act of 'just trying real hard' until we comprehend that only a moment by moment intimacy with God gives us victory in the details.

NOVEMBER 11

A *God of Details*
Part 2

God cares about the details of our lives. Yes, every tiny facet, component and aspect. It's not that we draw Him into or leave Him out of the details, He is actively involved in every one of them. We just choose not to acknowledge that He is working.

Does God really care about where you work, who your friends are, what school you attend, the spouse you choose, the home you live in? Does it matter to Him what you eat? Do your frustrations, fears, anxieties concern Him? Can He understand the pain of not being able to get out of bed in the morning because of the desperate sorrow deep in your soul?

> Deuteronomy
> 5:32, 33
> NLT
> *So Moses told the people, "You must be careful to obey all the commands of the LORD your God, following his instructions in every detail. Stay on the path that the LORD your God has commanded you to follow. Then you will live long and prosperous lives in the land you are about to enter and occupy."*

Yes.

It's your choice whether you embrace every moment with God or head off on your own tangent, putting your plans into action. God wants to interact, encourage, care for and direct you in the seemingly small details of your life.

He is a God of intimacy who cares about every minute detail.

NOVEMBER 12

Let's Do This
Part 1

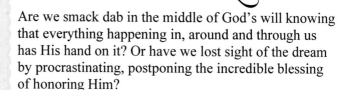

> 2 Corinthians
> 3:5, 6
> *Not that we are adequate in ourselves to consider anything as coming from ourselves, but our adequacy is from God, who also made us adequate as servants of a new covenant, not of the letter but of the Spirit; for the letter kills, but the Spirit gives life.*

Are we smack dab in the middle of God's will knowing that everything happening in, around and through us has His hand on it? Or have we lost sight of the dream by procrastinating, postponing the incredible blessing of honoring Him?

Is the task far beyond what we are capable of doing? Of course it is. How can God be glorified if we are entirely capable for the task?

God's calling is *always* bigger than us. And when we do put our hand to the task—we will definitely see God's hand at work.

For the last seven weeks a rebellious disposition of disobedience has grabbed hold of me. I set aside writing, giving myself permission to take a respite. But with that choice came reality.

Reality of *not* putting my hand to something far bigger than the scope of my imagination or ability to accomplish, brings with it a distance from God.

I feel God's pleasure when I'm in the center of His will, doing what He called me to do. Even if it's difficult and I don't have a clue what I'm doing.

When I'm not in the center of His will I feel lost, unfulfilled, unsettled. There is a sense of confusion and aimless displacement.

> Philippians
> 2:13
> *For it is God who is at work in you, both to will and to work for His good pleasure.*

God always leads us to the place where we seek more of Jesus to experience triumphant lives. Triumphant in that every place we go the joy of a life lived for Christ is made known.

We don't create the sweet aroma Paul talks about in his letter to the Corinthians, God does. Paul asks, *who is adequate for these things?* Our adequacy comes from one place. From God through the work of the Holy Spirit.

When I procrastinate in obeying God I show my inadequacy by standing still, not only in engaging in the journey God has set forth for my life, but in my relationship with Him.

With stillness comes stagnancy, a stale, foul, lifeless reality.

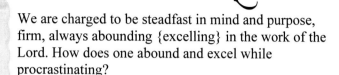

2 Corinthians
12:9
AMPLIFIED
*But He said to me,
My grace (My
favor and loving-
kindness and
mercy) is enough
for you
[sufficient against
any danger and
enables you to
bear the trouble
manfully]; for My
strength and
power are made
perfect (fulfilled
and completed)
and show
themselves most
effective in [your]
weakness.
Therefore, I will
all the more
gladly glory in my
weaknesses and
infirmities, that
the strength and
power of Christ
(the Messiah)
may rest
(yes, may pitch a
tent over and
dwell) upon me!*

We are charged to be steadfast in mind and purpose, firm, always abounding {excelling} in the work of the Lord. How does one abound and excel while procrastinating?

I remember asking, "Lord what happened to my desire to do what You called me to? To get on with it no matter the difficulty or inadequacy for the task? The goal is not publication, it's obedient diligence and abounding in the work."

Have I been beating myself up? Yes.

Is that necessary? Not necessary, but definitely human.

Paul, in his humanness, always encourages me to action . . . to obedience to Christ.
> *So for the sake of Christ, I am well pleased and take pleasure in infirmities, insults, hardships, persecutions, perplexities and distresses; for when I am weak [in human strength], then am I [truly] strong (able, powerful in divine strength)*
> *2 Corinthians 12:10 AMPLIFIED.*

Why would God proclaim His actions beforehand? To show that He alone is God and knows all things. To reveal His mighty power. For God to speak out what will ultimately happen tests our faith.

Many new things were revealed to the nation of Israel. Most important were the teachings and prophecies regarding the coming Messiah, which came to fruition in the person of Jesus Christ.

The truths in the Bible are given further proof through documented historical and archeological facts. Ever wonder what Jesus meant when He said, "I tell you, if these become silent, the stones will cry out?" Could it be archeologists' findings have proven what God has said all along? Historical scholars, Jewish writings and the ruins of ancient cities continue to prove God's word true.

Documented historical events give evidence that God's proclamations took place. Search the scriptures. What God stated throughout the Bible, He has already completed or will accomplish in the future.

Try this exercise, read Revelation 21. Make a list of the new things God declares. Will these things come to pass? You can count on it.

Isaiah 42:8, 9
"I am the LORD, that is My name; I will not give my glory to another, nor My praise to idols. Behold, the former things have come to pass, now I declare new things; before they spring forth I proclaim them to you."

Endurance
Part 1

Webster's defines endure:
To undergo {as a hardship} especially without giving in - to remain firm under suffering or misfortune without yielding.

Moses certainly didn't begin his journey strong and courageous, rather full of fear and doubt. But because of his love for and trust in God, Moses did not fear Pharaoh's rage, instead he went forth in what the Lord called him to do.

Having confessed how in my weakness Jesus' strength carries me through each moment, like Moses, frightened and uncertain, I too can be strong and courageous and go forth as God directs.

In his book, *Sir Gibbie*, George MacDonald tells why the young boy, Gibbie, is not afraid when facing a terrible situation head on:
"He is not terrified. One believing like him in the perfect Love and perfect Will of a Father of men, as the fact of facts, fears nothing. Fear is faithlessness . . . A perfect faith would lift us absolutely above fear. It is in the cracks, crannies, and gulfy faults of our belief, the gaps that are not faith, that the snow of apprehension settles and the ice of unkindness forms."

We know the facts. It's just hard living with them.

Endurance and perseverance equate to a loving trust that transcends circumstances. I have seen true courage and bravery in those who ventured to Oasis Hospital in Mexico, in friends and family who live in chronic pain and in an ever-increasing number of those who have experienced loss. They remain firm in their faith and love for God without yielding.

> Hebrews
> 11:27
> PHILLIPS
> *By faith he led the exodus from Egypt; he defied the king's anger with the strength that came from obedience to the Invisible King.*

We endure not because we are determined and resolute, but because of our love for the Invisible King and the supernatural strength and power of the Holy Spirit within.

Elisabeth Elliott said:
"Courage is not the absence of fear but the willingness to do the thing we fear."

So day-by-day we bravely put one foot in front of the other and go forth. We fix our eyes on Jesus, on *Him who lives,* who is the perfect example of endurance. And because He lives, we have absolute assurance that our loved ones taken home to heaven live as well.

We endure during our brief sojourn here on earth having the hope—no certainty—that the Lord our God is with us wherever we go.

NOVEMBER 18

Greater Clarity

2 Kings
6:16, 17
*So he answered,
"Do not fear, for
those who are
with us are more
than those who
are with them."
Then Elisha
prayed and said,
"O LORD, I pray,
open his eyes that
he may see."*

The story of Elisha's servant always makes me smile. Elisha, walking tight with God, calm and confident, encourages his uptight, fearful servant by asking God to reveal the invisible army sent on their behalf. God unveils a mountain full of horses and chariots of fire.

There's a lot more going on then the eye can see. We can't see what tomorrow has in store or for that matter what the next minute holds. Still we fret and make up any number of scenarios. 'What if' and 'how come' is not conducive to trusting God with your whole heart.

You may not be able to see beyond the immediate crisis, but God promises to carry and protect you. In today's vernacular— He's got your back.

Is it easy? No.

Does it mean fear becomes extinct? No.

But you can go through impossible circumstances, confront overwhelming obstacles as Elisha did and come away fully trusting God.

I'm reminded of Elisha when I gaze at the mountains surrounding my home. Majestic indeed. And who is to say there aren't thousands of angelic warriors up there right now protecting me?

Wait . . . I think I see a little movement up along the ridge.

NOVEMBER 19

"I should be making a lot more money for all I do."
"Listen, this two-bit job doesn't pay enough for me to
take verbal abuse from the customers." "I'm makin'
minimum wage here. What's the big deal if I take a
little extra from the till now and then? I deserve it."

> Luke
> 3:14
> *. . . be content with*
> *your wages*

As one who supervised cashiers at a department store, this mentality always
surprised me. I witnessed many an employee ushered out in handcuffs for
what they considered just compensation.

For one thing, when you accept a position at a certain wage you know before
you begin work what that job entails and what the compensation will be.

Second, when you work face to face with the public you can expect
discontented, annoyed, hurried people.

Third, never accept a position for minimum wage if you can't live with that
salary. The alternative? Find a job that offers more money. Stealing is never
justified.

God promises to meet our needs. Those who serve their own desperate
desires and not God become resentful, defensive, greedy. The apostle Paul
encouraged his young friend, Timothy, to live a pure, unadulterated life of
dedication and service to Jesus Christ, reminding him that the love of money
is a root of all sorts of evil.

Who do you serve? It's your choice.

Words–Gotta Love 'Em
Part 1

Words—a writer's tool to: Stir emotion. Embrace the mind. Depict a scene. Rend the soul with a good cleansing. Illustrate the profound. Caress the heart. Create laughter where there is none.
Perfect the imperfect. Express myriad facets of ones intellect.

God's word—Supernatural. Infallible. Enduring.
For the word of God is living and active and sharper than any two-edged sword, and piercing as far as the division of soul and spirit, of both joints and marrow, and able to judge the thoughts and intentions of the heart (Hebrews 4:12).

God's word pierces the outer glitz portrayed to others, exposing the very essence of our being.

Foolishness to the unbeliever, the Bible is seen as a collection of stories, some helpful, even encouraging, others not so much. They cannot comprehend the Bible because it's spiritually appraised.

Yet those who have received Jesus as Savior are given the Holy Spirit who reveals the truth and depth of God's word so they might comprehend the magnitude, majesty, magnificence, of the incredible God they serve.

Believers are made spiritually alive to serve their King.

NOVEMBER 21

God has offered me various words to contemplate, understand, appreciate, live out.

Redemption

God continually reveals how Jesus Christ paid my ransom in full, setting me free from the sin that strives frantically to keep me enslaved in its web of deception and guilt. Freedom means liberation from slavery. No longer under sin's restraints, ensnared by its lure, Christ has set me free to be all God would have me be. I need never allow sin to have dominion in my life.

> **1 Timothy 2:5, 6**
> *For there is one God, and one mediator also between God and men, the man Christ Jesus, who gave Himself as a ransom for all, the testimony given at the proper time.*

Revive

Whenever I see the word revive in my Bible, I circle it. Revive reminds me God is always encouraging me to become more active, to flourish in my faith through the intense work the Holy Spirit is doing.

Responsibility

Not my favorite word. It's important to do the things I *can* and ask for help with the things I can't. It would be much easier to hire someone to do all the things I don't *want* to do. God is stretching me beyond what I ever thought, calling me to answer for my conduct and obligations. To petition Him with every detail.

I am growing up—bit by bit.

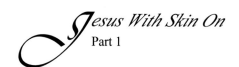

Jesus With Skin On
Part 1

Acts
4:13
Now as they observed the confidence of Peter and John and understood that they were uneducated and untrained men, they were amazed, and began to recognize them as having been with Jesus.

What do people see when they observe you, especially when you have no idea they're watching?

Several months ago my friend made a profound declaration. "It's not about us, it's about the people around us." How we live our lives and interact with others makes a huge statement about our relationship with Jesus Christ.

What do people see when you experience trials? How do you react when the things you've planned don't work out? How do you wear joy, sorrow, excitement, frustration, anger?

Peter and John were not prophets or learned men, they were fishermen. Yet they displayed absolute confidence and certainty when they proclaimed Jesus as the long awaited Messiah, the Savior of the world.

Peter and John wore their intimacy with Jesus well. Whenever a healing took place through their touch or word, they were quick to remind people it was not by their hand, but by the powerful name of Jesus of Nazareth.

When people watch you do they see Jesus with skin on?

NOVEMBER 23

Do you look like you've been with Jesus even in the trials?

Sometimes not.

Believe me, there are times I've wanted to shed the garments of righteousness Jesus shrouded me with, to let loose and assault someone for what they've said or done. Like the doctor who spewed out dismissive, destructive words after proclaiming his cancer death sentence. Or the insensitive person who sent a cold, unsympathetic email.

> 1 Corinthians
> 1:27
> *But God has chosen the foolish things of the world to shame the wise, and God has chosen the weak things of the world to shame the things which are strong.*

My flesh wanted to slap a generous piece of duct tape over the doctor's mouth before another hopeless, disparaging word fell from his lips. I was beyond tempted to elucidate to the writer of the brief, heartless email my angry fervor of what might have been conveyed to a grieving heart.

However that is not how Jesus would have me respond. After the initial rage with the doctor subsided and my wounded heart had time to mend from the email, I prayed. God impressed upon me these people needed to know and experience the love of Jesus. Whether I saw them again or not, I was to commit them to Him and pray for them.

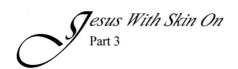
Galatians
5:22, 23, 25
*But the fruit of the
Spirit is love, joy,
peace, patience,
kindness, goodness
faithfulness,
gentleness, self-
control . . . If we
live by the Spirit,
let us also walk
by the Spirit.*

Oswald Chambers in *My Utmost For His Highest* said: "We become so abandoned to God that the consciousness of being used never enters in . . . all consciousness of ourselves and of what God is doing through us is eliminated. A saint is never consciously a saint; a saint is consciously dependent on God."

Paul did not go about his day consciously showing off his intimate friendship with Jesus. He simply lived life, moment by moment, honoring his Lord, giving away what the Holy Spirit poured into him.

I wonder if we take every opportunity to give away the love, joy, peace, patience, kindness, goodness, faithfulness, gentleness, self-control that is ours through the Holy Spirit? When people watch us in the midst of trials do they wonder what or Who has caused us to respond differently than others would?

May our lives cause people to stand wide-eyed amazed at what knowing Jesus and being with Him does for, in and through us.

NOVEMBER 25

Ever been in 'the depths of despair' as *Anne of Green Gables* would say? Not poor me despair, rather anguish that leaves you hopeless. Perhaps you're in turmoil this very moment. You see no end to the desperation.

> **Psalm 59:16**
> *But as for me, I will sing of Your strength; yes, I will joyfully sing of Your lovingkindness in the morning, for You have been my stronghold and a refuge in the day of my distress.*

If you're like most of us you follow the pattern of Psalm 59. When under attack we want retribution and we want it now. We beg God to rescue us. We don't care what it takes, just make the pain go away.

Helpless to deliver himself, David pleaded with God to save him. His fervor escalated as he demanded revenge on those who persecuted him. He insists God make an example of the evil men surrounding him.

No, that's not enough—David wants God to annihilate them. At the end of his tirade David remembers God's faithfulness and praises Him.

Difficult times? In the depths of despair? Hopeless? Want God to zap someone? Don't be afraid to tell God your true feelings. Pour out your grief and frustration. Ask Him to rescue you. After you've exhausted your anger and aggravation, praise Him with all your heart. Even if the results are yet to be seen.

Hebrews 4:12 NLT
For the word of God is alive and powerful. It is sharper than the sharpest two-edged sword, cutting between soul and spirit, between joint and marrow. It exposes our innermost thoughts and desires.

In all honesty, there are days in this grieving process when I'd just as soon stay in bed with the covers over my head.

But God . . .

In God's desire for all to come to repentance, He chooses to involve believers in His plan to reconcile the human race to Himself. His design for every individual, through the direction and power of the Holy Spirit, is to accomplish His divine purpose. I have to get out of bed to do that.

We hear a lot about surrendering our lives to God in order for Him to accomplish His work through us, but what does that look like?

- Realization and confession I am a sinner separated from a holy God by my sin
- Receive God's Son, Jesus Christ as my personal Savior
- Humility of spirit – give up my right to myself, to a self-absorbed life and make Jesus Christ Lord of everything
- Become wholly yielded to Jesus serving Him and others

Missionary to North Africa, Lilias Trotter, wrote in *Parables of the Cross*:
"We ourselves are "saved to save"—we are made to give—to let everything go if only we may have more to give. The pebble takes in the rays of light that fall on it, but the diamond flashes them out again: every little facet is meant, not simply of drinking more in, but of giving more out."

> 2 Timothy
> 3:16
> THE MESSAGE
> *Every part of Scripture is God-breathed and useful one way or another—showing us truth, exposing our rebellion, correcting our mistakes, training us to live God's way.*

In order to live the servant life, God's living word comes before the work, before any action is taken toward the goal. We read, capture, embody, live out, those things God speaks to our hearts daily, without which there can be no true divine purpose accomplished.

This is *so* a word of conviction and confirmation for me. Timely to say the least. As I undertake this journey of writing a novel, I can *never* forget it is not by my might, not by my power, but by God's Spirit, who gives wisdom, counsel, strength, through God's word, that anything of eternal value is gained.

> **Psalm 37:4, 5**
> *Delight yourself in the LORD; and He will give you the desires of your heart. Commit your way to the LORD, trust also in Him, and He will do it.*

The daily choice to surrender to God's power and direction is vital if we are to be a useful vessel for His divine purpose.

Jim Reimann, in his book, *Look Unto Me, The Devotions of Charles Spurgeon*, responds to Spurgeon's writing on Psalm 37:4:
"Not only should you "delight yourself in the Lord," but you should also delight yourself in His Word. And since Jesus is the Word incarnate, delighting yourself in the Lord and in His Word are actually synonymous. Therefore, it stands to reason we are incapable of delighting in the Lord without spending quality time in His Word."

This delighting takes time. Devoted, dedicated time with the One who means more to me than anyone or anything else. Time of quiet reflection to hear the Holy Spirit speak to my spirit through God's Word.

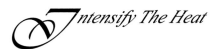

It warms my heart to know God calls me His beloved. Makes me wonder {I tend to wonder a lot} just who are those today God deems His beloved?

God loves all His creation. Yet He calls those who love Him with all their heart, soul, mind and strength . . . beloved. Jesus states it clearly, those who love His Father in this way keep His commandments.

> Psalm
> 127:2
> *It is vain for you to rise up early, to retire late, to eat the bread of painful labors; for He [the LORD] gives to His beloved even in his sleep.*

A wonderful thing about being dearly loved by God, although often uncomfortable, is He graciously tests our faith as with a refiner's fire. God calls His beloved to a life of purity and holiness so that *The Three* are glorified through our lives.

It's a process. If needed, God adds more fuel to intensify the heat, causing it to become almost unbearable. The outcome? A stronger, more pure vessel, ready for His use.

God may have you in the fire reducing the impurities. He may have you on the shelf all fired up waiting for use. Or He could be pouring out to others what He has poured into you.

December

There is absolutely no faith in
doing what you are already good at

> **Mark 14:36**
> *And He [Jesus] was saying, "Abba! Father! All things are possible for You; remove this cup from Me; yet not what I will, but what You will."*

Ambrose Redmoon said:
"Courage is not the absence of fear, but rather the judgment that something else is more important than fear."

Jesus Christ personifies authentic courage.

The other day a friend said she admired my courage to travel alone and to do what she only dreamed of doing with regard to writing, finishing and actively seeking a publisher for my book. I told her I didn't consider it courage, rather obedience. I couldn't not do what God had undeniably called me to do. Trust me, fear enters at the most inopportune moments.

Allow me to point you to truly courageous people I know who:
- have had cancer *twice* and determined to survive at all costs
- ran a 5K when blood sugar levels bounced all over the Richter scale
- stayed committed to a spouse when they had given up
- spoke out when it was not popular or politically correct
- kept quiet when railing against someone was the desire
- trusted when receiving a large unexpected bill, with no money to pay it
- had a family member arrested when they threatened the safety of others
- looked past the palpable—believed the inconceivable
- admitted pride, insecurity, judgmental attitudes to another

Authentic courage.

DECEMBER 1

Having pondered the truly courageous people I know, God encouraged ways to exhibit courage in my own life:

- get out of bed each day even though my life has been altered forever
- overcome the obstacles of *firsts*
- step into the unknown
- no longer say 'I don't want to'
- choose obedience in the face of excruciating pain
- have faith to believe all this is no surprise to God
- trust that God is enough
- never give up

How do we gain the mettle and tenacity to walk in this kind of courage?

The prophet, Micah, associated his being filled with power with the Spirit of the Lord. According to the apostle Paul, Christ followers are filled with power through the Holy Spirit and we are to keep on being filled {present tense}.

What does courage look like in your life? Is it forgiving someone when the offense is unforgivable or even asking for forgiveness yourself? Is courage taking the first step to do something you've only dreamed of doing? Is it being obedient by stepping into the unknown?

The Love of God Encapsulated
Part 1

Romans
8:37-39
NLT
*No, despite all
these things,
overwhelming
victory is ours
through Christ,
who loved us.
And I am
convinced that
nothing can ever
separate us from
God's love.
Neither death nor
life, neither angels
nor demons,
neither our fears
for today nor our
worries about
tomorrow—not
even the powers
of hell can
separate us from
God's love. No
power in the
sky above or in the
earth below—
indeed, nothing in
all creation will
ever be able to
separate us from
the love of God
that is revealed in
Christ Jesus our
Lord.*

The love of God. How can one encapsulate it? Impossible.

Authors and poets attempt to capture it with words, artists struggle to paint it into the fiber of every stroke, theologians give it their best shot through verbal illustrations.

Archbishop Fenelon writes:
"Be persuaded, timid soul, that He has loved you too much to cease loving you."

Some have the misconception that God has abandoned them. They believe His love is only available when they're good. His love does not cease because we sin time and again. God's love never ceases.

Sadly, they cannot comprehend the depths of God's love until He takes drastic measures to get their attention. Yet even in the midst of those drastic measures God encases them in His immeasurable love.

What more must God do to convince us of His unfathomable love?

> **Romans 5:8**
> *But God demonstrates His own love toward us, in that while we were yet sinners, Christ died for us.*

Even during—no especially—in the suffering, God's love is there. For had we not known His love in the suffering how could we praise Him in the happiness? This incredible love does not negate the pain. It validates it. In this way God demonstrates His intense love just as He did through the suffering of His Son on the cross.

Sometimes, in those painful moments when we find ourselves crying out to God, it's then we grasp the magnitude of our own sin. When this happens we can't help but fall down before Him with thanksgiving and praise, coming from somewhere so deep inside, we could not imagine that much love ever existed in our being.

Much as Paul and Peter were forever changed because of God's demonstration of love, James too, experienced Love in the flesh and gratefully wrote:

> *Consider it all joy, my brethren, when you encounter various trials, knowing that the testing of your faith produces endurance (James 1:2).*

The love of God. How can one encapsulate it?

Two words—Jesus Christ

Luke
2:19
*Mary treasured
all these things,
pondering them in
her heart.*

John
19:25
*Now there stood
by the cross of
Jesus his mother.*

I wonder if Mary recalled the things she pondered in her heart after the birth of Jesus, when she stood at the foot of the cross.

Three decades earlier this woman had treasured the shepherds confirming words proclaimed by an angel, that this baby was indeed their Savior, Messiah, Lord. Even before the divine conception God sent the angel, Gabriel, to tell Mary she had been chosen to bear the Son of the Most High, the long-awaited King.

Throughout the years Mary must have wondered what her son's kingdom would look like. It's doubtful however, she conjured in her mind his reign included a vicious, brutal beating, with His body marred, disfigured, nailed to a Roman cross.

How could Mary have known that God's Son and His kingdom were not of this world? God's promises to her all came to fruition, although certainly not as she had imagined.

Every promise in God's word is truth. He promises the reality of heaven. His peace which transcends all understanding. Mercy and compassion. His presence continually.

God promises those who belong to Him that He will bring good from all things. Really? Even this severe pain and harsh suffering, Lord?

Over the years I've thought about Paul's encouragement to believers in his letter to the Romans. More times then I can count I've experienced this truth through situations so devastating, at the time I thought there was no way God could use them to bring about something good. Wrong.

> **Romans 8:28**
> *And we know that God causes all things to work together for good to those who love God, to those who are called according to His purpose.*

Looking back I agree with Paul and give praise to God for the events in my life, even the extremely difficult ones. Today however, I've pondered how God can cause good to come from death. Then He reminded me of all the good He has accomplished through the death of His Son.

Just as with the death of Jesus, God knows the purpose(s) and the outcome of even our most heinous experiences. Somehow He uses every one to accomplish His perfect plan for the ultimate purpose of His glory.

Mary had no way of knowing the baby nestled in her arms would one day hang on a cross shedding His blood to transform the lives of mankind forever. Still, she along with many others, saw the good God brought through His Son's resurrection from the dead.

We, on the other hand, receive this gift by faith—believing without seeing.

DECEMBER 6

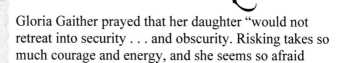

Luke
9:23
AMPLIFIED
*And He said to all,
If any person
wills to come after
Me, let him deny
himself [disown
himself, forget,
lose sight of
himself and his
own interests,
refuse and give up
himself]
and take up his
cross daily and
follow Me [cleave
steadfastly to Me,
conform wholly to
My example in
living and, if need
be, in dying also].*

Gloria Gaither prayed that her daughter "would not retreat into security . . . and obscurity. Risking takes so much courage and energy, and she seems so afraid sometimes . . . and weary." *

Release. One of the six 'R' words the Lord has given me in the last few years. I've been under the false assumption that as the next word came the previous had been fulfilled. Ah, no. It's a continual retracing and growing up with each of these words.

When I first received the word, *release*, I realized I was to let go of anything and anyone that prevented me from total reliance upon God. That's not to say, sell all my possessions, say goodbye to family and friends and take up residence in a convent.

Release means relinquishing any emotional, physical or spiritual holds. Surrendering anything that dominates my desires, so that loving God consumes my heart, soul, mind and strength.

Alrighty then.

*We Have This Moment

I awoke from a dream angry and confused. After transcribing the details, I asked God to clarify. Bottom line? The dream had to do with my past and recognizing that justified responses, reasonable reactions, judgmental attitudes, self-absorbed actions, were *all about me.* As my friend says, "I can't like that."

Luke
4:18
"He has sent me to proclaim release to the captives."

After a revealing two and a half hours, it became clear God wanted me to release the past in order to move forward. Time to release: Hurt. Anger. Judgments. Guilt. Myself. Family. Expectations {both given and received}. Uncertainty. Fear. The Future.

Journal excerpt:

Why do You bless me so much Lord, knowing who I am inside?

† I love you.

I don't know why.

† I made you. And you love Us.

I do love You and want to be worthy to serve You. I am not.

† You are under the blood of My Son—cleansed – perfect – forgiven – worthy. Follow Him. Release what was and look to Him for the future. Trust Us {*The Three* as you call Us – Smile} to take you on this journey. Let go.

How about you? Are you content living in security and obscurity? Or will you join me and take a risk? Let's release anything that entangles and causes us to grow weary. Let's move forward into the future God has for us.

DECEMBER 8

Keep Going
Part 1

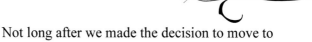

Genesis
12:1, 2
*Now the LORD
said to Abram, "Go
forth from your
country, and from
your relatives and
from your father's
house, to the land
which I will show
you; and I will
make you
a great nation."*

Not long after we made the decision to move to Oregon, God spoke these words into my spirit, *Remember Abraham.*

Naturally, in the course of moving and living in a fifth-wheel for eighteen months, I thought God wanted me to remember that Abraham trusted Him when he traveled to a place he didn't know and lived in a tent along the way. After all, that's what we were doing. Almost.

On the other hand, God also told Abraham He would accomplish impossible things through him. Things God alone could do. Abraham's trusting example humbles me to think of how I question God's wisdom in directing my life. God will accomplish His perfect plan. Even when I take a detour.

It has been said confession is good for the soul. Here goes.

Last week was a nightmare. Had two meltdowns, one as a widow and one as a writer. Missing my husband's hand in decorating the house for Christmas left me sad and lonely. Included in the nightmare were doubts about the word God gave me that the novel is a reality.

DECEMBER 9

Keep Going
Part 2

Having received my now functioning computer from the computer guy, it took precious time to re-program all that had been unprogrammed.

Frustration mounted. My cell phone died. The printer gave a continual error message. Bought a new printer, had to install it. The re-program thing again.

This month's lesson for my online writing course was two days late, read the date wrong. My writing ability seriously came into question from my mentor.

It's Christmas time. I miss my husband like crazy. I can't see the forest for the trees.

In the midst of the turmoil and meltdowns I asked Jesus why He chose me to write. "I don't know what I'm doing or how to do it."

His response . . .
† Exactly.
  Do you trust Me, Anne?
  There is absolutely no faith in doing what you are already good at.
  Faith is following Me.
  Believing I am in those things you cannot do.
  I have given you direction.
  Keep going.

> Genesis
> 18:17-19
> NCV
> The LORD said,
> "Should I tell
> Abraham what I am
> going to do now?
> Abraham's children
> will certainly become
> a great and powerful
> nation, and all
> nations on earth will
> be blessed
> through him. I have
> chosen him so he
> would command his
> children and his
> descendants
> to live the way the
> LORD wants them to,
> to live right and be
> fair. Then I, the LORD
> will give Abraham
> what I
> promised him."

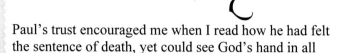

Luke
1:45
"And blessed is she who believed that there would be a fulfillment of what had been spoken to her by the Lord."

Paul's trust encouraged me when I read how he had felt the sentence of death, yet could see God's hand in all that took place. Paul said:

> *But this happened so we would not trust in ourselves but in God, who raises people from the dead (2 Corinthians 1:9 NCV).*

Aha. Humility. I had been asking God for a humble heart. It begins by realizing and accepting I can't. It's only by God's grace that I'm able to do anything.

After protesting and complaining for an entire week about the frustrations in my life, I woke up one morning thinking about the women and children who have been sold into human trafficking. My heart sank. What is wrong with me?

I thanked God for safety, freedom, protection and asked for forgiveness for all the whining about my piddling, so-called trials.

Started fresh with hope in my heart, joy in my spirit. Thanked Him for every happening in my life, including the trials and frustrations.

I'm trusting God to accomplish those impossible things He alone can do. Heal the grief and loneliness and make the novel a reality.

While I just do the next thing.

DECEMBER 11

How many times have I read Philippians 4:7 asking for God's incomprehensible peace? Funny, I just noticed an 'and' at the beginning of verse seven. That led me to believe it's connected to verse six. Did you know God's peace has conditions?

First, we are to be anxious for nothing—*no thing* . . . Ah, that's a pretty tall order Lord.

In *everything* by prayer and supplication with thanksgiving . . . I don't know about you, but when I am in the throes of an anxious fit it's a little difficult to thank God.

> Philippians
> 4:6-7
> *Be anxious for nothing but in everything by prayer and supplication with thanksgiving let your requests be made known to God. And the peace of God, which surpasses all comprehension, shall guard your hearts and your minds in Christ Jesus.*

Yet whenever we become troubled we are to ask for God's help at that very moment. We lay aside anxiety and thank Him for His hand in the details. Whether we see it or not. It's at this point we receive God's unfathomable peace.

Listen to J.B. Phillips translation:
> *Don't worry over anything whatever; tell God every detail of your needs in earnest and thankful prayer, and the peace of God, which transcends human understanding, will keep constant guard over your hearts and minds as they rest in Christ Jesus.*

God is constantly in the details.

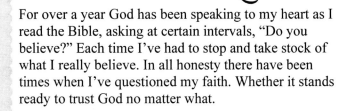

Matthew 9:20, 21

And a woman who had been suffering from a hemorrhage for twelve years, came up behind Him and touched the fringe of His cloak; for she was saying to herself, "If I only touch His garment, I will get well."

For over a year God has been speaking to my heart as I read the Bible, asking at certain intervals, "Do you believe?" Each time I've had to stop and take stock of what I really believe. In all honesty there have been times when I've questioned my faith. Whether it stands ready to trust God no matter what.

Sometimes I try to put myself in the place of the person I'm reading about. It's easy to 'pretend' to understand what they experienced from this side of history. Mostly I'd say yes I believe. Yet there were stories that left me wondering.

At one time I sensed the tiniest whisper in my spirit asking the same question He asked long ago, "Do you *really* trust Me?"

"Yes Lord, of course I *really* trust You."

Paul told the Corinthians:
   We walk by faith, not by sight (2 Corinthians 5:7).

Now that's a major test of faith. Believing God is faithful and accepting without seeing the final outcome.

Jesus said to the woman who touched the fringe of His cloak:

> *"Daughter, take courage, your faith has made you well" (Matthew 9:22).*

Jesus never said we had to be super saints with faith the size of a bowling ball, rather the size of a mustard seed.

> Matthew
> 17:20
> *"For truly I tell you, if you have faith like a grain of mustard seed, you can say to this mountain, 'Move from here to there,' and it will move, and nothing will be impossible for you."*

A few nights ago, concerned over the lack of faith of others, God reminded me about the size of a mustard seed and what He can do with the teeniest bit of faith.

Besides, it's not for me to fret over what *others* believe. It's knowing what I believe.

Because of my husband's death, I know now why God asked me if I *really* trust Him. To prepare me for this time.

Do I believe? Absolutely. More every day.

Do I wonder how He will reveal His power? Sure.

Do I question His ultimate answer to my fervent prayers? No.

He is my Abba Father. He continually bathes me in His love, assuring me of His grace and wisdom.

His word is as real and true for us today as it was for the leper or the woman with the hemorrhage.

What's On Your List
Part 1

Psalm
63:1
O God, You are my God; I shall seek You earnestly; my soul thirsts for You, my flesh yearns for You, in a dry and weary land where there is no water.

When we no longer crave what God can give us, but hunger for Him alone, we are truly ready to be filled up to all the fullness of God. When we stop seeking answers to our prayers and seek *Him*.

Augustine wrote:
"Thou has made us for Thyself, O God, and our hearts are restless till they find rest in Thee."

We are restless, anxious, fretful, impatient, apprehensive, uncertain people—until God reigns supreme in our heart, mind, soul and spirit. In every cell of our body.

There is a beautiful line from an old hymn: *Jesus, I am resting, resting in the joy of who Thou art; I am finding out the greatness of Thy loving heart.* *

Who is God to you?

* *Jesus, I am resting, resting.*

DECEMBER 15

Of all the names of God, I AM is my favorite. This personal name for God says it all.

This year while reading through the Bible I've chronicled who *The Three* are to me. Below is an ongoing list I hope to add to significantly in the coming years.

> Genesis 3:14
> *God said to Moses, "I AM WHO I AM"; and He said, "Thus you shall say to the sons of Israel, 'I AM has sent me to you.'"*

No matter the situation I AM is my:

Refuge	Joy	Covering
Deliverer	Praise	Worship
Adoration	Awe	Forgiver
Longing	Desire	Hearer of prayer
Trust	Provider	Savior
Lord	Hope of glory	God
Father	Counselor	Teacher
Friend	Helper	Love
Hope for eternity	Strength	Courage
Life	Example	Pledge
Home	Redeemer	New thing
Reconciler	All in all	Help
Answer	Sovereign King	Rescuer
Bright Morning Star	Mighty God	Grace
Mercy	Restorer	Reviver
Rest	Wonderful Counselor	Shepherd
Hope	Confidence	Rock of Habitation
Prince of Peace	Fortress	Sustainer
Salvation	Righteousness	Eternal Father
Power	Truth	Interceder
Way	Faithful	Fulfiller of His promises
Justice	Most High	Portion
Guardian	Guidance	Creator
Compassionate Father	Hiding place	Healer
Avenger	Atonement	Victor
Triumph	Goodness	Nearness
Holiness	Champion	

What's on your list?

A Rare Treasure

Isaiah
6:8

Then I heard the voice of the Lord, saying, "Whom shall I send, and who will go for Us?"
Then I said, "Here am I. Send me!"

Time. One of the rarest treasures on earth.
Do I hoard it?
Invest it?
Give it away freely—begrudgingly?
Do I find excuses why it must be saved for 'the big event'?
Do I give it away bit by tiny bit so that it is all used up in serving God and others by the time my head hits the pillow each night?

God has me in His hand for all eternity. Are there human words of gratitude? Hardly. Not at all.
Out of the heart comes . . .
Jesus said:

"For the mouth speaks out of that which fills the heart"
(Matthew 12:34).

Thanksgiving for the most expensive gift ever given—eternity with God—that is what flows from my heart these days.
Thankful for the days while here.
I realize more and more every minute is precious.
This day will *never* happen again.

Lord how would You have me spend this rare treasure today? Here am I. Send me!

DECEMBER 17

Webster's defines a promise as:
A declaration that one will do or refrain from doing something specified. It is the guarantee or assurance {something that inspires confidence} it will happen, giving ground for expectation.

We know God cannot lie. God does what He says. Always. Every time. I would venture to say there's not another living creature that can make that claim.

Why is it important we believe not one word will fail of all God's promises? If we cannot trust the validity of everything God has promised then how can we believe Him for the most important decision of our lives, eternal salvation through faith in His Son?

If we cannot believe God when He says, "I will or I will not," there is no basis for us to suppose justice will come to all that is evil.

Where is the hope, the changed hearts, transformed lives without the absolute assurance of God's promises? Without faith in God's promises there is no guarantee the Holy Spirit dwells in believers to accomplish His miraculous works.

I guess like most things it all comes down to faith. Do we believe God or not?

The Lord Reigns
Part 1

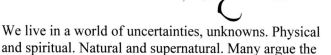

1 Corinthians 2:12, 14 NCV
Now we did not receive the spirit of the world, but we received the Spirit that is from God so that we can know all that God has given us. And we speak about these things, not with words taught us by human wisdom but with words taught us by the Spirit . . . A person who does not have the Spirit does not accept the truths that come from the Spirit of God. That person thinks they are foolish and cannot understand them, because they can only be judged to be true by the Spirit.

We live in a world of uncertainties, unknowns. Physical and spiritual. Natural and supernatural. Many argue the supernatural does not exist. I disagree.

Every one of us will live longer in the supernatural world than in this natural world. Eternity is a L-O-N-G time.

There is more evidence to the supernatural then most realize. If we have eyes to see, the supernatural is at work all around us. Good verses evil.

I knew a man, a regular church attender, who did not believe in the unseen world forces. Although he believed in the supernatural realm of God and heaven, he refused to accept one as evil as Satan exists.

DECEMBER 19

Do not be deceived, Satan is real and working overtime to disgrace and discredit God and His People.

Ephesians
6:12
For our struggle is not against flesh and blood, but against the rulers, against the powers, against the world forces of this darkness, against the spiritual forces of wickedness in the heavenly places.

God created all things including the most beautiful of all angels, to worship and serve Him. The prophet Ezekiel describes the magnificence of God's creation and also reveals that Satan's pride and arrogance caused him to be thrust out of heaven and thrown down to earth, taking one-third of the angels {now called demons} with him.

Don't be fooled thinking the devil is an ugly monster.
Part of his deception is his beauty. He is able to draw the unknowing and unsuspecting and convince them of his sincerity simply by twisting the wisdom God originally granted him.

The first glimpse we have of this tempter–accuser is in the Garden of Eden. The Bible describes him as the serpent. Revelation reveals this serpent has many names; the great dragon, the devil and Satan who deceives the whole world.

DECEMBER 20

John
8:44
"You are of your father the devil, and you want to do the desires of your father. He was a murderer from the beginning, and does not stand in the truth because there is no truth in him. Whenever he speaks a lie, he speaks from his own nature, for he is a liar and the father of lies.

This father of lies is also known as:

tempter
adversary
evil one
accuser of the brethren
angel of light – disguising himself as an angel
    of light
ruler of this world
god of this world
he who is in the world
the prince of the power of the air
murderer
Beelzebul – ruler of demons

In 1 John, the apostle writes to those who are born of God making it clear only those who are believers in Jesus Christ are of God. Those who are not, lie in the power of this clever enemy, the evil one.

No matter how hard Satan fights to win his war against God, the Bible reveals God's victory and Satan's ultimate defeat. To be sure the devil hates believers, but we who belong to Jesus Christ are protected by the power of Jesus' name. Jesus the Christ—who *will* one day crush the enemy.

The truth is, our all-powerful, supernatural God reigns supreme over our adversary and all creation.

DECEMBER 21

The writer of Hebrews encourages believers when they draw near in prayer and worship to God they must grasp the fact that He is a real being. He exists as the One true God and Sovereign over all creation, *and* He is a rewarder of those who diligently seek Him.

> Hebrews
> 11:6
> NCV
> *Without faith no one can please God. Anyone who comes to God must believe that he is real and that he rewards those who truly want to find him.*

Don't you just love that word, reward? It conjures up all sorts of lovely visions of the gifts God lavishes upon us. Gifts such as His Son. Unconditional love. Eternal life. The Holy Spirit. Spiritual gifting. Grace. Mercy. Peace. Righteousness. Knowledge. Wisdom. Humility. Provision. Protection.

As I searched the Bible for the word *reward*, my eyes were opened to how very giving our God is to those who believe He exists and trust in His word.

In one instance, the book of James says:

> *Every good thing given and every perfect gift is from above, coming down from the Father of lights, with whom there is no variation or shifting shadow (James 1:17).*

As we share gifts with others this Christmas season, let us not forget the greatest gift ever given.

God's own Son—Jesus the Christ.

Jesus–The Gift
Part 1

1 John
4:10, 11, 19
NCV
*This is what real
love is: It is not
our love for God;
it is God's love
for us. He sent his
Son to die in our
place to take
away our sins.
Dear friends, if
God loved us that
much we
also should love
each other. . . .
We love because
God first loved us.*

Love is . . .
A feeling?
An action?
A decision?
All consuming?

Movies often portray love as a rapturous emotion that thrives on the attention of another person. Whether it's an adult, a child or even a memory, many live primarily to experience the fulfillment of their definition of love through the presence, acceptance or remembrance of someone special to them.

The decision to love as God loves us, even—no especially—in the most difficult odious cases, has the capacity to break down walls of resentment and bitterness and to transform the heart of the giver.

Real love is authenticated by actions as displayed through God's example when He *gave* His Son. Jesus touched the untouchable, showed compassion to the weak and poor. He even cared about the pious.

Love is Jesus who died for *all*.

DECEMBER 23

Love costs something . . .
The giving up of our right to have it our way, allowing
   another to excel.
Holding in words of retaliation when under attack.
Moving into an awkward situation when we'd rather
   stay comfortable.
Giving when everything in us says, 'I want'.
Remaining faithful to a commitment no matter how
   difficult.

> Ephesians
> 2:4, 5
> *But God, being rich in mercy, because of His great love with which He loved us, even when we were dead in our transgressions, made us alive together with Christ (by grace you have been saved).*

My brother thought a parting 'I love you' a flippant
salutation. Eddie felt those words were
spoken too easily and loosely. Even so, I told him I loved him each time we
brought our infrequent telephone calls to an end.

When I visited Eddie while he lay in a Denver hospital awaiting a heart
transplant, we talked of what real love looks like. It's not a flippant good-bye
or a phrase to win acceptance. Real love is the example Jesus set of giving
until it hurts and then giving more.

When I explained how powerful Jesus' love is, as evidenced by His brutal
sacrifice on the cross, Eddie changed his opinion. He finally understood why
we give love away. With tears streaming down his cheeks Eddie whispered,
"And to think He did that for me."

Love is Jesus—*THE Gift*

Matthew 2:11

After coming into the house they [magi from the east] saw the Child with Mary His mother; and they fell to the ground and worshiped Him. Then, opening their treasures, they presented to Him gifts of gold, frankincense, and myrrh.

Imagine the excitement of the magi as they neared their destination. Scholars believe it took more than two years for them to travel to Bethlehem. Why did they journey so far to worship a Jewish baby? After all, these men were Gentiles. Had they seen something while studying the stars that led them to believe this was a monumental moment in history?

Oh yeah.

Who is this Child we worship and adore? ***Messiah!*** Do we truly know the One to whom we present our gifts and offerings? The Son of the Most High. Wonderful Counselor. Mighty God. Prince of Peace.

What are the offerings we bring to the Savior? ***Everything!*** Some say it's enough to take the only real day of rest they have to attend church. Maybe give a little money here and there. Really? This is Immanuel. God with us. The One who sits on the throne of heaven. The Risen Lamb. Praised and honored forever.

When is the appropriate time to present our offerings to this Wonderful Counselor? ***Always!*** Praise Him all day for the incredible ways He accomplishes His miraculous work in our lives and in the lives of others.

DECEMBER 25

Traveling from afar as they did to honor and worship the newborn King, surely the magi understood the birth of this child was indeed a monumental moment in history.

Where are we to worship the Prince of Peace? *Everywhere!* A huge part of our worship offering is sharing the truth of who Jesus is wherever we go. Look at the magi, they announced to evil King Herod that they had come to worship the King of the Jews.

> Romans
> 12:1
> *Therefore I urge you, brethren, by the mercies of God, to present your bodies a living and holy sacrifice, acceptable to God, which is your spiritual service of worship.*

Why do we bring our offerings to the Lord? *Love!* Pure and simple. He poured out His love and His life for us on a cross. To fully understand the meaning of God's indescribable gift we must look to Easter. It was for this reason Jesus Christ was born.

How do we offer our King honor? *Humbly!* With our whole being. We are talking about Jesus—The Christ—King of ALL kings.

The magi were in awe of this King before them. They presented Him with the most formidable gifts they could find. We, on the other hand, have the opportunity to offer Him something far more valuable.

Our lives.

DECEMBER 26

Gracious Responses
Part 1

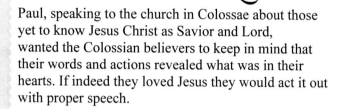

Colossians
4:6
*Let your speech
always be with
grace, seasoned,
as it were, with
salt, so that you
may know how
you should
respond to each
person.*

Paul, speaking to the church in Colossae about those yet to know Jesus Christ as Savior and Lord, wanted the Colossian believers to keep in mind that their words and actions revealed what was in their hearts. If indeed they loved Jesus they would act it out with proper speech.

These faithful saints would be among those who obeyed one of Jesus' last commands, to go and preach the gospel to all the world. They may not have been able to travel far from their own little town, but they could share the good news that Jesus shed His blood and died to redeem the world from sin, right where they were.

Paul's words of exhortation are for our ears as well. How do we put this command into practice so those who do not know Jesus Christ want to hear about Him? Grace.

Gracious responses to slander, revilement, accusation, cause others to wonder how and why. Our natural tendency is to defend ourselves, protect our honor with excuses or persuasive responses. God says He will take up our defense. We are to respond with grace.

Gracious Responses
Part 2

It's easy to spout off and think afterward, *I set them straight*. When in reality we have turned people away from the very thing they need most—God.

If we reply improperly and our words are not peppered with grace, we haven't been much of an example of trusting God. It comes down to this, do we trust God to come to our defense or do we feel He needs our input and assistance?

It's a choice to think before we speak, so that wisdom and grace are passed on.

I confess to being far from gracious in my speech. My heart is saddened because of my poor example and the breach in fellowship with the One I love most.

> Ephesians
> 4:29
> *Let no unwholesome word proceed from your mouth, but only such a word as is good for edification according to the need of the moment, so that it will give grace to those who hear.*

DECEMBER 28

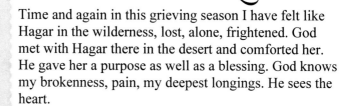

Genesis 16:13 NLT

Thereafter, Hagar used another name to refer to the LORD who had spoken to her. She said, "You are the God who sees me." She also said, "Have I truly seen the One who sees me?"

Time and again in this grieving season I have felt like Hagar in the wilderness, lost, alone, frightened. God met with Hagar there in the desert and comforted her. He gave her a purpose as well as a blessing. God knows my brokenness, pain, my deepest longings. He sees the heart.

God is here with me every moment. He sees everything happening in my life. All of this is no surprise to Him. He truly is Elroi {God who sees}.

God also *feels* what I'm feeling. The Holy Spirit, living in me, *feels* my excruciating pain, my desolate loneliness. He knows me intimately and sees my circumstances.

Jesus, my strong and gracious Savior, is here to carry me when I'm incapable of moving forward.

What comfort to know when I'm unable to see through the cloak of darkness that surrounds my broken heart, God sees *and* feels my pain. What encouragement and assurance that in those moments He holds me for as long as I need.

God meets with me. He gives me purpose and a blessing.

Nothing is too difficult for Him.

DECEMBER 29

othing Is Too
Difficult For God

I have this sense, this anticipation, that this coming year, even though wrought with challenges, will bring us closer to the destiny God has for us. There is an excitement in my soul of inescapable fulfillment and realization.

Things seen only as shadows, unfocused, disjointed scenes of impossibilities are soon to become clear. Pristine. Evident. Observable. We are about to embark upon an unimaginable adventure.

Jeremiah
32:17
*'Ah Lord GOD!
Behold, You have
made the heavens
and the earth by Your
great power
and by Your
outstretched arm!
Nothing is too
difficult for You.'*

In gaining deeper understanding of God's word we learn to trust His character. Knowing His character brings praise and worship from the heart. A tremendously grateful heart wants nothing more than to obey God's direction. Especially when the unknown lies ahead.

It seems every book I pick up these days challenges the reader to take a risk. And isn't that what God asks of us when we cannot see what lies ahead, to trust Him *as* the adventure unfolds?

In anticipation of this unprecedented coming year, expecting grand experiences, encounters and excursions, I have purchased an elegant, resplendent journal to chronicle every unmerited fear, challenging risk, travel escapade, superfluous frustration, serving gesture, unsolicited disappointment, exciting revelation, every saved soul.

Let's go for it!

DECEMBER 30

> Psalm
> 107:8, 9
> *Let them give
> thanks to the
> LORD for His
> lovingkindness,
> and for His
> wonders to the
> sons of men! For
> He has satisfied
> the thirsty soul,
> and the hungry
> soul He has
> filled with what
> is good.*

Who am I Lord that You would send me? Who am I that You would want me?

Doubt. Insecurity. Imperfect. Unlovely.
I cannot get it right.
Failure appears at every turn.

Who am I that You would love me?
Prideful—Insignificant
Sincere—Flippant
Loyal—Running Away
Thankful—Whining
Friendly—Recluse
Hopeful—Fearing

Knowing—Ignorant
Giving—Unreceptive
Carefree—Uncertain
Doubting—Released
Imperfect—Transformed

Fun-loving—Expectations
Rich—Pauper
Broken—Made Whole
Insecure—Redeemed
Unlovely—Beloved Bride

I am wholly Yours Abba
Surrendered to You Jesus
Moving through Your power Holy Spirit

Here am I. Send me.

ACKNOWLEDGEMENTS

Ecclesiastes 5:3
For the dream comes through much effort and the voice of a fool through many words.

That verse has been my mantra for over sixteen years. For many of those years I was excited about writing, even took some classes. But in reality I was the fool who talked about accomplishing the dream with very little to show for it.

Unless our dream is encased in that of Jesus' there is no kingdom value whatsoever. Loving and hungering for *The Three* takes precedence over any and all life visions or dreams. From that semi-fulfilled {for it is never completely fulfilled in this life} hunger flows the true nature and motive of the dream. This I am learning.

This devotional did indeed take much effort. Without the many hours of tireless labor, designing, formatting, typing and reeling this author in when she went off the deep end, by Kristi VanDuker, you would most certainly not be holding this book in your hand. Why would she volunteer for such a daunting project having never done anything like it before? Her deep love for God. Thank you does not express the immense gratitude for your excellent work, Kristi.

Thank you to my dear friend Janis Rubus, for offering her exquisite photo taken in the wee hours of a foggy Aberdour, Scotland morning.

My gratitude to Dave Sheets and Carrie Thompson from BelieversPress Publishing. Helpful, supportive, integrity.

To my prayer team who has prayed me through many projects and continue to faithfully cover me to this day. Abundant thanks.

To my many family members, friends, and readers {if I start naming names I will no doubt leave someone out and that is unacceptable} who encouraged me during the ten years of writing the email devotion, you know who you are. I would have never taken it to this level if it weren't for your heartfelt communication, encouraging words and love. Thank you from the deep recesses of my heart.

Most important, incalculable thanksgiving to *The Three* for inspiring every word. For carrying me during the difficult times. Laughing with me when life took a funny turn. For loving me unconditionally.

INDEX BY SUBJECT